SPANISH QUEER CINEMA

SPANISH QUEER CINEMA

Chris Perriam

EDINBURGH
University Press

For John

Edinburgh University Press Ltd
22 George Square, Edinburgh EH8 9LF

www.euppublishing.com

Typeset in 10/12.5 pt Sabon
by Servis Filmsetting Ltd, Stockport, Cheshire,
and printed and bound in the United States of America

A CIP record for this book is available from the British Library

ISBN 978 0 7486 6586 0 (hardback)
ISBN 978 0 7486 6587 7 (webready PDF)
ISBN 978 0 7486 6588 4 (epub)
ISBN 978 0 7486 6589 1 (Amazon ebook)

CONTENTS

Acknowledgements   vii

Introduction   1

1. Queer   9
   Queer Reconfigurations of LGBT Cultures in Spain   9
   Short-Film Production   15
   'Nos Casamos' (We're Getting Married)   21
   Queer Ethics/Positive Images   32

2. Legacies   37
   Spanish Critical Precedents: Representing Spanish Queer on Screen 39
   Comedy   42
   Moving Towards Visibility   45
   Coming Out and Self-Discovery   48
   Almodóvar   50
   Aftershocks   53
   Representing Older Lesbians and Gay Men   58

3. Icons   64
   Actors (I): Eusebio Poncela, Victoria Abril, Jordi Mollà, Rosa María
      Sardà   66
   Directors: Ventura Pons and Pedro Almodóvar   76
   Actors (II): Newer Names   81
   Popular Film-Makers   85

4. Audiences   91
   The Bookshop Image   92
   The Glamorous Lesbian Image   95
   Film, Cultural Activism, Videoart   101
   Festivals   112

5. Writers   123
  Off-the-Shelf Middlebrow Lesbian and Gay Imaginaries   123
  Screenwriters: Lucía Etxebarria, Elvira Lindo, Ángeles González-
    Sinde   129
  A-List Novelists: Eduardo Mendicutti and Vicente Molina Foix   135
  Writers' Lives on Screen: Federico García Lorca and Jaime Gil de
    Biedma   141

  Conclusion   148

  Filmography   150
  References   156
  Index   184

ACKNOWLEDGEMENTS

My thanks for help of various kinds are due as follows. In Spain: to all those independent film-makers and producers, especially Juanma Carrillo, Mariel Maciá, Rut Suso and María Pavón and others credited in the list of illustrations, who gave up time to discuss their work and share images with me; to Gerardo José Pérez Meliá (Director of LesGaiCineMad) and his team at the Fundación Triángulo; to Mili Hernández, for conversations, inside information and insights on LGBT culture and politics; to Margarita Lobo and Trinidad del Río at the Filmoteca Española, as knowledgable and patient as ever. In Manchester: at the Instituto Cervantes, Manchester, to Iñaki Abad Leguina and Kepa González López (Director and Cultural Director), to Yolanda Soler Onís (previously Director) and, especially, Francisco Duch Martínez (librarian) and Manuel Lafuente Ángel (previously assistant librarian), all of whose long-standing, collective commitment to building a major LGBT archival resource and to showcasing LGBT film from Spain and Latin America has changed the face of Hispanic Manchester and created a major regional resource.

The final phase of the preparation of this book was financed by the Arts and Humanities Research Council through a grant for the project Queer Cinema from Spain and France: The Translation of Desire and the Formation of Transnational Queer Identities (Grant Ref: AH/I026618/1). The project – undertaken by Chris Perriam, Darren Waldron and Ros Murray – carries forward, in part, some of the lines of enquiry opened up in this book. The larger part of the time and resources for the research and writing was provided by the University of Manchester through two semesters of leave, the collections and e-subscriptions of the John Rylands University Library and the selfless support of many colleagues at times of sudden administrative or assessment-related stress. Encarnación Gutiérrez Rodríguez, Ros Murray, Hilary Owen, Núria Triana Toribio and John Whyard read and commented on chapters in draft, and for their comments, encouragement and improvements I am enormously grateful, as also to the readers of the original proposal for their perceptive guiding comments.

INTRODUCTION

CONTENTS

This book is an analysis of the development of Lesbian Gay Bisexual Trans and Queer (LGBTQ) culture and film-making and film-watching in Spain from the end of the 1990s onwards. There are two reasons for the chosen period of coverage. Firstly, the 1990s were years of rising recognition for lesbian and gay, and New Queer, cinema worldwide, and Spain by the end of the decade had joined in; furthermore, 1998 was the year in which the Catalan government passed the first of a series of regional government laws in Spain on civil union, marking a substantial increase in the intensity and visibility of discourses – verbal and visual or performed – around LGBTQ identities. Changes to the Spanish Civil Code were, famously, passed into law in July 2005, providing 'access for same-sex married couples to rights of inheritance, residence, adoption of the other spouse's children, tax benefits, and to divorce rights' (Platero Méndez 2007b: 335). This sequence of surface events, with profound social and personal implications, created a ripple effect in the politics of the everyday and in the cultural expression and production of LGBTQ Spain: unsurprisingly, the effect is felt and amplified in some films, or tellingly ignored or simplified in others. Chapter 1 links its discussion of 'queer' to this phenomenon of liberalisation in terms of rights, and takes into account the clashes and exchanges between 'gay', 'queer' and 'lesbian' cultures, and how these inform the notion of a Spanish queer cinema. Chapter 1, then, is concerned with post-identity politics modes of being as well as of post-gay lifestyle ways of behaving in community. It indicates where these developments manifest themselves in, and are themselves inspired by, films of many kinds. Chapter 2 looks back through the lens of some key film historical studies and cultural analyses on legacies beneficial and detrimental alike; it then turns about and looks at traces of both sorts of legacy in the 2000s and beyond. The emergence in my chosen period of filmic representations of trans lives – few, but very new – counterbalances earlier exploitative accounts and, in the context of a new Ley de Identidad de Género (2007) (Gender Identity Law) brings vital images of resistance to the cautious and still semi-pathologising social discourses around the legislation (Platero 2011).

Secondly, as, again, Chapter 2 will show in detail, and as many who are enthusiasts of Spanish cinema will know, lesbian and gay film of the 1970s to 1990s has had fairly wide critical coverage already and, being in the main feature-film based, has often been seen and, even, re-released. I do not go back much over that ground, although there are some retrospective micro-rereadings here and there in the pages that follow. Instead I take advantage of the growing diversity in modes of distribution of more recent years to consider feature films and documentaries whose primary launch pad has been the niche festival, the short films which saw their own mini-boom in this period (some two hundred were viewed in preparation for the writing of this book; many others escaped me), and, newer, straight-to-website video productions of various kinds. This shift in modes and sources of viewing is to a certain degree paralleled by a move into the BTQ (or, in Spanish and Catalan usage, TBQ) end of the portmanteau acronym condensed down, for the purposes of this book, into 'queer' (on which risky move I have more to say below and in Chapter 1).

On the strength of these broad changes, a number of iconic figures emerged: actors on cinema and television screens and increasingly in the pages of networked social media, and directors themselves. Chapter 3 examines some of these figures in their creative contribution to queer culture in Spain, and for their not so queer interventions in performance, in scripting and directorial decisions, in press and online comments. By the end of the decade regular LGBT film festivals were established in Barcelona and Madrid and cultural centres and bookshops had started taking root in several urban and resort centres; a modest archive of marketable popular fiction written in Catalan or Castilian (mainly) was steadily growing; and the country's spectacular take-up of social networking in the period had its strong echoes in LGBTQ users. This new cultural formation is the subject matter of Chapter 4.

At certain points I follow a number of leads out of image into text and back. I deal, conventionally enough, with textual responses in print and online to the films and tendencies discussed, but I also consider the way that, for Spanish queer audiences, watching moving images is only one part of a wider cultural and creative participation in the construction of queer experience and identity (in particular, the way light popular fiction and magazines rub shoulders with DVDs in sales media and venues points to an obvious line of enquiry). Taking up the discussion of these wider cultural circumstances from Chapter 4, Chapter 5 is concerned with the interconnectedness of viewing, consuming, reading, surfing, zapping, cinema- and festival-going, borrowing and downloading. Many scriptwriters have a parallel activity as producers of popular fiction and journalistic essays, or they are novelists with a queer following in their own right. One, significantly, became Minister of Culture (Ángeles González-Sinde). Popular lesbian and gay literature has scriptwriter or actor protagonists and substantial plot references to films and film-going. Some novelists are also directors, and writer-directors are numerous. This is the broad material; I will now turn to the terms of this book's title and the framing of the issues and images involved.

COMING TO TERMS

The application of the term 'queer' to a segment of Spanish film culture was always going to be both acceptably or provisionally meaningful and unfortunately slippery. The films I am discussing here resonate in the imaginations, and make a difference to the lives, of viewers and audiences alert and averse to the heteronormativity and the processes of exclusion all around them in Spain. A good number of these products and their creative teams address the serious matter of being queer in post-1990s Spain with careful dramatisation, elaborate structuring or tactful research and insight. Some of them, though, take shortcuts by way of caricature, or seem to want to show the same old stories of same-sex romance with its associated tragedies. Their political awareness is dimmed down. They might entertain (sometimes), but they will also prompt irritated questions about, say, how the 'lesbian' in lesbian film in Spain has become so delimited and about why the 'gay' has come to be so self-satisfied, so very unchanged. In both these senses – the resonant and the irritant – they mean a lot. The combination of making a difference affirmatively and of making the identifications lesbian and gay, and bisexual and transgender (LGBT), themselves differential, in process, is queer. When we imagine these films as a corpus, and their makers as a loose or virtual collective, they could be said to 'multiply our pleasures and our personalities' – where 'we' are participants somewhere in the continuum of culture which amalgamates the L, G, B, T and Q – 'and to interrogate more radically [our] critical presumptions' (Hanson 1999b: 12). Enjoying them, and criticising them, can be part both of a 'nuanced analysis of queer desire and spectatorship' (12) and of being queer in Spain. This queer, nuanced process means that those involved might 'fundar un clan, alzar una partida, formar una banda . . . [ser] un punto de ternura ajeno a la economía heterosexual . . . conjurar machos y hembras' (Carrascosa 2005: 179) ('establish a clan, raise a combat unit, band together . . . [and be] a tender meeting point set far off from the heterosexual economy . . . convoking male and female alike'); or, more sociologically, they might take part in 'un ejercicio de contestación' ('exercise in contesting'): both normalisation from within the lesbian and gay movement and the invisibility and silence imposed by the dominant culture are contested (Trujillo Barbadillo 2005: 30).

That term 'radical', though, takes us with paradoxical directness to a consideration of the slipperiness of 'queer' in certain combinations. As is obvious in an everyday sense, the commercial enterprises advertised in QueerBCN.com, for example, are mostly very unlikely to be contestatory or radical; and it is questionable, at least, that Madrid's Chueca district is – except sometimes, and out-of-doors – a properly queer territory (*pace* Gras-Velázquez 2011), despite its apparent inclusiveness of different bodies and different generations, and given its overall lesbian-unfriendliness (Robbins 2011). As with these examples of queer shopping, queer nightlife and queer spaces in Spain, so too can 'queer Spanish cinema' seem to be a formulation which occupies itself with little in the way of the political practices and cultural representations which respond to the urgent social and intellectual claims of those 'disidencias sexuales' (manifestations of sexual dissidence) which gather together, for Trujillo Barbadillo (among others) (2005), under the umbrella *queer* ('paraguas' – her word: 30). Very few of the films I shall be discussing come out as radical in the senses used by the commentators just quoted, and thus they are not, in the main, politically 'queer'. Their advertising internationally in the Big Queer Film Festival List (<http://www.queerfilmfestivals.org/> [last accessed 30 October 2011]) aligns them more with a product than a politics. Overwhelmingly the festivals themselves favour variations on L, G, T and B for their names or their sections, or bring together several types of film made in Spain under one oddly national label split by traditional gender divisions (as in the case of the major LesGaiCineMad festival in Madrid coordinated by the Fundación Triángulo).

Excursions into post-porn – where much lesbian/queer radical creativity and thinking take place – have been infrequent.[1] Post-porn materials and interventions, indeed, are positioned outside the customary circuits and are principally, and empoweringly, web- and ephemeral performance-based phenomena. While this book does not engage with post-porn, or with commercial pornography (whose overlap with Spanish queer practice and thought is not necessarily extensive, and which belongs in different distribution circuits to those I focus on), the post-porn phenomenon in the Spanish context has prompted complex and wide-ranging analyses and creative interventions (Gimeno 2008; Llopis 2010; Preciado 2008; Sáez and Carrascosa 2011; Salanova 2012; Vidarte 2007b); it is part of the remit of the project Queer Cinema from Spain and France (see <http://www.llc.manchester.ac.uk/research/grants/queer_cinema_ahrc/>) to explore these. Films, or episodes in films, that represent the stories, politics and feelings of people living with HIV and affected by AIDS are included; factual and educational films about HIV infection, well-being, treatment regimes, public health and social attitudes to HIV and AIDS are, on the whole, not. The dividing lines here, as elsewhere, are problematic for a book such as this. For example, the medium short *Invulnerable* (Álvaro Pastor and Antonio Naharro, 2005) on an HIV-positive biology teacher Elías (with a very strong performance from Antonio Naharro) who bravely uses his own story in the classroom, while clearly being exemplary fiction, could almost be a re-enactment film; and, as we shall be seeing, several of the films embed an HIV/AIDS narrative in their plots.

None of this is to mention discussions of whether the anglicism 'queer' functions appropriately in Spanish cultural contexts beyond the academic (Fouz-Hernández 2004 and 2011; Martínez-Expósito 2004: 31–53; Pérez-Sánchez 2007: 6–8; Trujillo Barbadillo 2008b) and of the academy's and the activist community's complex struggles with it as one of a range of would-be equivalent terms vying for linguistic applicability – *marica/bollo*, *rarita* or *torcida* (when applied to the theory) (Córdoba et al. 2005; Llamas 1998; Martínez-Expósito 2004: 52). Why, then use it? These films in their contexts of production and reception make a difference and they form a distinctive cultural space – an imaginary – of inclusion. Though relatively small, this body of work and responses to it display a plurality of concerns. In some cases, there are images, sounds, performances and texts which make a mark aesthetically and ideologically because they push away from the ties of lesbian and gay cultural expression and the politics of the now conventional LGBT/LGTB constellation of concepts. They make visible and put into new social and locally collective contexts images of non-heteronormative lives and loves. As I have already mentioned, the period covered in this book corresponds to that in which Spain, at the socio-political and juridical level, has moved from institutionalising same-sex civil unions regionally (from 1998) to legal recognition of same-sex marriage (in 2005). Moving images and the debates and conversations around them have made a stand against homophobia and exclusion, responded to health and welfare crises, questioned or affirmed the value of same-sex marriage, and constructed new forms of intimacy and community. In the working sense that 'la principal característica para definir el cine *queer* siempre fue el compromiso con la causa y la crítica de situaciones discriminatorias e injustas' (García Rodríguez 2008: 456) ('the main characteristic of queer cinema has always been commitment to the cause and a critique of discrimination and injustice'), these films, film-makers and audiences have built a new Spanish queer imagination in parallel to the work of activists. They represent one specific and important point of engagement between the discourses of non-Spanish queer thought and action and, as Pérez-Sánchez puts it, 'the pluralised queer body of the [post-1975 Spanish] democracy . . . a body politic that, like queer theory, rejects simplistic binarisms and the imposition of "regimes of the normal"' (2007: 7, quoting Warner 1994: xxvi).

In this way there has been a move away from the usual understanding, among a wider public in Spain, of the notion of 'cine gay' as, precisely, a form of cinema which – while appearing to give visibility and kudos – obscures and closes off the routes to commitment and alternative cultural development, and is, in that sense, anti-queer. It is what Agustín Almodóvar and Esther García, the heads of production at El Deseo (the company behind Pedro Almodóvar's films), are reported as having identified as the cause of:

> una 'involución' en la manera en que el cine se acerca a la homosexuali-
> dad, ya que se priman 'proyectos comerciales' en los que los gays reciben
> 'un tratamiento banal y, a veces, paródico'. (Agencia EFE 2011)
> (a turning in on itself by cinema in the ways it approaches homosexual-
> ity, with 'commercially viable' projects being favoured, where gay men
> [*sic*] are afforded 'banal and parodic treatment'.)

Such projects – some of which I review in Chapter 2 – bring forward into the 2000s an inheritance of heteronormativisation and homophobia at various levels, amplified by an unhelpful 'frivolity' (Esther García's term: Agencia EFE 2011) on the one hand, and, on the other, a constantly reactivated legacy of damaging, marginalising and reactionary images of typification, the persistence of 'discursos antiguos' ('old-style discourses') (Melero 2010: 125).

Similarly, lesbian film in Spain – though still struggling under a shocking double discrimination in terms of representation and access to resourcing and dissemination (InCinema 2011) – has found a vitality and a visibility in filmmakers such as Marta Balletbò-Coll (a long-established name), Laura Cancho, Chus Gutiérrez (most prominently), Mariel Maciá, Rut Suso and María Pavón, Inés París and Daniela Fejerman, and Blanca Salazar, which move it so far on from what it had been in Spain until the 1990s (Pelayo 2009) that at the very least it should be thought of as a New Lesbian Spanish Cinema. That its images and stories interact in certain audience segments' minds so closely with high-profile lesbian television characters in popular television series (see the brief discussion in Chapter 3), and with a short-lived but intensely viewed webcast series *Chica busca chica* (*Girl Seeks Girl*), make it all the more permeable and culturally fissiparous – aesthetically queer if not always unambiguously feminist. Oddly, films with male directors make a substantial contribution to titles pitched to a lesbian audience, mainly, as in the case of *Eloïse* (Jesús Garay, 2009), or at least in part, as in the case of Julio Medem's *Habitación en Roma/ Room in Rome* (2010) (see Chapter 4), and this too is worth queer scrutiny.

There have been some high-profile representations of bisexuality as a transition zone in young protagonists – for example in the feature film *Krámpack* (*Nico and Dani*) (Cesc Gay, 2000), discussed in Chapter 3, *Mentiras y gordas* (*Sex, Party and Lies* [or Lies and Damned Fat Lies]) (David Menkes and Alfonso Albacete, 2009). In *El dios de madera* (*The Wooden God*) (Vicente Molina Foix, 2010) and *Los novios búlgaros* (*Bulgarian Lovers*) (Eloy de la Iglesia, 2003) twenty-to-thirty something men manifest a kind of organic, laid-back bisexuality (see Chapters 5 and 2). In *Segunda piel* (*Second Skin*) (Gerardo Vera, 2001) and *En la ciudad* (*In The City*) (Cesc Gay, 2003) characters are seen to think they might have been bisexual, but once the film's narrative gets going they become conflictedly gay in the first case or lesbian all along in the second. Bisexuality in a classic and stabilised sense is rarely represented in this period of film-making in Spain and the double excursions of some characters around the contours of homo- and heterosexuality are so labile and so imbricated in local socio-political implications that queer seems to be the best way of denoting them.

Trans issues – including, crucially, the excluding violence done by transphobia (Casanova 2007) – have been the subject of a number of strong documentaries and short films working close up to real experience. *El camino de Moïses* (Moses's Way) (Cecilia Barriga, 2004) has been shown on RTVE (26 September 2006) and is still live in the Documentos-TV archive;[2] *Guerriller@s*

Figure 1 Coral (Maribel Luis) and her violently inclined client (Guillermo Toledo) in
¡¡Todas!! (José Martret, 2007). Reproduced from Fundación Triángulo archive with
kind permission of the director.

(Montse Pujantell, 2010) is now pressed to DVD after substantial festival
exposure. The based-on-real-life fiction *¡¡¡Todas!!!* (*All!* [or, *Over Here
Girls!*]) (José Martret, 2003) is dedicated 'a TODAS esas transexuales que en
algún momento de su vida estuvieron en peligro y tuvieron que usar ese grito'
('to ALL those transexuals who have at some time in their lives been in danger
and have had to use the call: Over here, girls!') (see Figure 1). These works
have something of the 'militancia diferente' ('different form of militancy') witnessed to by Sáez as properly queer (see also Platero 2011). Also, with a higher
profile, trans characters have been represented in a primary role in the musical
Veinte centímetros (*Twenty Centimetres*) (Ramón Salazar, 2005) (which also,
arguably, has a kind of male bisexual secondary role) and in the ambiguously
aligned persona of Antonia San Juan.

This book's subject matter, then, is Spanish LGBTQ cinema with a particular weight on the Q: a weight placed there in order to start moving away from
the gravitational pull of the still oddly predominant would-be mainstream,
alternative-lifestyle representation of young, urban, non-immigrant, white,
healthy men who have sex with men and are supposed to represent a buzzing
New Spain, in order also to recognise the strong, overarching bond back
across from the Queer to the Lesbian. This latter bond depends on Spanish
lesbian feminism's major contribution to thinking through the challenges to

those living in non-straight sexual cultures in the Spain of apparent civic and moral liberalisation of the 2000s, in order – after Doty (1993: xvi–xvii) – to articulate these terms, have them shuffle and blur, 'intersecting or combining' (xvi), especially where a film, a film-maker, a festival or compilation 'evokes complex, often uncategorizable . . . responses from spectators who claim all sorts of real-life sexual identities' (xvi).

The cover of this book, of course, says just 'Queer', but even those who are outraged by such a potentially assimilationist and exclusivist, universalising and institutionalised tactic (Schehr 2005: 10), or simply by such a dumb short-cut, will know what lies behind it. If they can forgive it, they may read on.

Finally, a note on coverage and on the presentation of contextual data. My filmography is of material I have been able to view and is not intended as an exhaustive list of LGBTQ film production in the period. Some feature films I have viewed but decided not to discuss, simply because – whatever their merits – they presented images, arguments or narratives already found elsewhere in Spanish contexts. In the case of short films, there have been some twenty titles of potential significance to the argument which, in the end, I was unable to access for reasons of logistics or of intellectual property rights and permissions. For feature films that have no theatrical release or festival-based circulation, this fact is noted in the text; otherwise, the assumption is that of exposure to modest-sized, niche audiences. For short films and documentaries, the assumption is of at least one festival selection and/or a viewing count online in excess of two hundred (that is, twice the average LGBT festival audience attendance). Again, exceptions are noted where appropriate, and prizes awarded are mentioned where particularly significant (whether financially – which is uncommon – or in terms of audience response). Translated English titles are given in italics where this is the recognised international title or where a film has had distribution or festival exhibition with full English subtitling; otherwise, translated titles appear in normal type.

NOTES

1. The documentary *Mi sexualidad es una creación artística* (Lucía Egaña, 2011: 46 mins) is a useful entry point. It won the prize for best documentary at the Bilbao Zinegoak festival, 2012 and was programmed, along with a live performance piece and discussion, at the FRINGE! Film Festival, London (April 2012). It sets out to be '[una] cartografía ilustrada con videos postporno do it yourself, documentación de performances e intervenciones en el espacio público' ('an illustrated mapping with do-it-yourself postporn videos, documentation of performances and interventions in public space'). It features interviews with those involved on the Barcelona post-porno scene (Trans-Block 2011). Also of relevance is the feminist pro-sex, pro-dissident sexualities and pro-subversive forms of maternity website <http://girlswholikeporno.com/> [last accessed 12 May 2012]. See especially the category links Postporno and Queer/Transmarikabollo.
2. Available at <http://www.rtve.es/alacarta/videos/documentos-tv/documentos-tv-camino-moises/896649/> [last accessed 6 April 2012].

1. QUEER

In order to start drawing together the three parts of the title of this book, and of this section, and to elaborate on the issues alluded to in the Introduction, I begin by turning to precedents in discussions of British and French queer cinemas for placing the terms. Engaging in the now conventional struggle with introducing the word queer into a '"slippery" ménage[s] à trois' such as British Queer Cinema, Robin Griffiths constructs the category as containing directors, actors [and films] 'that . . . either directly address and/or seek to represent "lesbian", "gay", "bisexual" or "transgender" themes . . . or in some sense or another lend themselves to – or even openly solicit – queer modes of interpretation' (Griffiths 2006a: 33). On the thematic front, to take that possible category first, Spanish queer cinema (as a catch-all term) might be said to be highly conventional, including as it does positive images (on which more later), cautionary tales of damage and pain as well as morale-boosting reconciliations, and frequent returns to the generally entertaining and instructive task of simply showing or dramatising the circumstances of LGBT experience. The very preference for the term 'de temática' ('-themed') by festival programmers or by retailers and distributors tagging their products ('. . . gai'; '. . . lésbica', '. . . trans' – but rarely '. . . queer/bollo/marica') suggests a pragmatic, content-driven strategy, a make-do approach to the tricky style and implications of the images in question. As to the opening up of queer modes of interpretation (Griffith's second characteristic), I hope to show that online responses, fans and amateur critics construct between them a less conventional corpus of queer Spanish cinema than might be indicated by the thematic classification. Published professional film criticism and history, although it has tended to omit some of the more obvious sources of the unconventional (short films, videoart and a certain form of documentary project), has laid the ground for identifying the effects on audiences of a specifically queer Spanish cinema. Mira (2008) has pointed the way to a number of readings against the grain of popular world cinema from Spanish perspectives, and

I will be engaging (in Chapter 2) with the substantial work already done on lesbian- and gay-'themed' film of the mid-to-late-twentieth century in Spain – work which frequently evokes a resistant, contemporary audience of sorts, or takes a post-lesbian-and-gay perspective on narrative and subtext. Queerings of classic Spanish cinema include Gutiérrez-Albill (2008) on Buñuel, Perriam (2007b) on the work of Sara Montiel (hardly in need of such queering, it might be said) and, with a broader cultural and generic range, Pérez-Sánchez (2007) and Vilaseca (2010) – all, again, evoke a particular configuration of audience response at a slant to the norm in terms of cultural control, market expectation or, indeed, popular taste and selectivity. Focusing on the period 1998 to the early 2010s, my own interest, indeed, is in the potential for rethinking at least some of the directly LGBT-themed production in terms of a particular, queer, mode of interpretation (Griffith's term), formed around an odd, heterogeneous and anti-heteronormative, structurally imperfect and inconclusive experience of viewing.

French Queer Cinema, for Nick Rees-Roberts, is film and video production which can be seen from the critical perspectives alert to intersectionality – 'cultural contestation', 'vectors of power' in relation, for example, to race and ethnicity and gender, 'socio-political context' and 'local instances of sexual dissidence' (2008: 5) – and to differences and dissonances (see especially 129–49). With a few notable exceptions, the films that I am going to be discussing here do not map well onto such a contestatory space – except, perhaps, in the ways that audiences and varying commercial presentations recontextualise them. One or two of the films of Pedro Almodóvar and, in a much smaller market, those of Ventura Pons, are alert to these issues in other ways, in that they evince the 'tactical queerness' which Moore (2006: 168) associates in the British context with a film like *The Crying Game* (Neil Jordan, 1992), 'success-fully impressing itself on mainstream culture' and targeted on 'the very main-stream audience with most to learn from its queerness' (168). In the Spanish case, however, when the mainstream audience is targeted with queer images it is more often to get a laugh than to impart a lesson in experience and empathy. Queer Spanish Cinema both is and is not like those other queer cinemas with which in its festivals and distribution and sales outlets it has dealings and affinities.[1] At the core of this variable difference there may lie a particular evasiveness within queer which comes of a much discussed problem of cultural and linguistic translation.

The difficulties of transfer and translation of the term 'queer' to Spanish contexts has been a recurrent concern (Córdoba et al. 2005; Guasch and Viñuales 2003; Trujillo Barbadillo 2008b; Vosburg and Collins 2011a) and is due, in part, to the productive and problematic undecidability at the core of queer when considered, as it conventionally is, as 'a sort of vague and inde-finable set of practices and (political) positions that has the potential to chal-lenge normative knowledges and identities' (Sullivan 2003: 43–4). If the term is deliberately unfixed, and if what it can signify is diffuse and shifting, then it is understandable that its 'adoption . . . or [that of] the Spanish equivalent "bollo/marica" has been problematic', as Vosburg and Collins suggest (2011b: 11), adding that the 'limited number of groups' using one of these labels is itself a demonstration of the scope of the problem. As Schehr (2005) observes in a discussion of the presence and function of queer theory in Francophone areas, queer theory is '*made in the* USA' (10) but some of its foundational ideas are Italian (Mario Mieli) and French (Guy Hocquenhem) while queer theory is eminently redirectable into an engagement with local discourses, histories and practices (11). This potential for redirection into engagement is clear enough too in the Spanish case, especially in its elaboration in proximity to lesbian thought around community, biopolitics and culture (Hernández, C. 2007; López Penedo 2008; Platero Méndez 2008; Preciado 2011; Simonis 2007; Soley-Beltran 2010), and where queer theories and practices intersect (Colectivo Q8 2008; Grupo de Trabajo Queer 2005; Vidarte 2007a).

A number of the studies referenced in the paragraph above, as well as Llamas's (1998) earlier essay proposing a *teoría torcida* (bent or twisted theory, or theory on the slant), draw substantially on English-language queer theory, and an important introductory text for Catalan readers (Fernàndez 2000b) devotes space to important translations from the English and French of core theoretical texts and extracts. I myself began with Britain and France to orientate the discussion; however, queer is not so foreign as to be strange to Spain. Approximations to it in discourses visual and verbal, fictional and analytical, are perfectly visible and resonant in the languages and cultures of Spain. In cinema and its audiences, as also in theoretical writings and sociological accounts, there is a plurality of Spanish versions of living in that 'posición desde la que responder políticamente a las normatividades múltiple-mente impuestas' (Grupo de Trabajo Queer 2005: 26) ('position from which to respond politically to the many forms of enforced normativity'). There are emphatically post lesbian-and-gay citizens, actions, characters and storylines expressing their anti-heteronormativity in relative abundance in the films to be discussed, and they are seen from several positions within the different languages and cultures of the Spanish state and in different points in history. There are, it can be said, Spanish forms of queer on film.

That these can be perceived, imagined and screened is in part due to the work done in Spanish lesbian feminism to put sexuality on the frontline of politics (Osborne 2008: 85–6; Pineda 2008: 321–3) and to mark out the lines of resistance to a more conservative, hegemonic 'gay' male thinking (Osborne 2008: 95–6). In part it comes through work by radicalised men such as those contributing to the essays in Córdoba et al. (2005) and (with some overlap) the contributions to the volume by the Grupo de Trabajo Queer (2005) among others. To these social scientific and philosophical constructions of a new sexual politics can be added the work of those predecessors who had deline-ated homosexual and gay liberation politics for the Spanish contexts – as reviewed by Martínez-Expósito (2004: 31–54), Fuentes (2007: 381–91) and

Fouz-Hernández (2011), for example – and the cognate response in cultural criticism in and on Spain since 2000. This response has come in a context of belatedness, as Martínez-Expósito has remarked of literary studies, where sexuality '[seguía] siendo la gran asignatura pendiente . . . en España' (2004:31) ('[was] still a subject waiting to be broached . . . in Spain').

In the period under study in this book, the dialogue with queer writing in English and French in particular has grown louder and louder, to the extent that the casual user of a Spanish lesbian and gay book and film shop browsing the shelves or the web pages will be familiar, if not necessarily comfortable, with the juxtaposition of heavily identity-based same-sex romance on page or disk and Judith Butler, or the rigour of new S/M theory side by side with the belly laughs of mildly complacent self-recognition in stereotypical comedies. Madrid-based bookshop Berkana's April 2011 showcasing of books on queer theory (Especial Teoría Queer: circular mailing of 11 April) included eight titles by Spanish scholars and activists out of thirteen books profiled. Its physical in-shop displays have consistently given visibility to the growing body of work on queer theory, culture and politics in or translated into Castilian. Antinous, Barcelona, with a list of nearly five hundred titles in the 'essay' category shows a similar proportion of Catalan or Castilian titles to translated imports but with relatively few titles featuring the term 'queer' or its translations. Cómplices, in Barcelona, has approaching fifty titles under 'Teoría queer', the majority with Catalan or Castilian authors. The smaller lists of Liburudenda Librería (Bilbao) and alternative bookshops in other cities and parts of the web for Spain largely repeat these proportions. As the substantial dialogue with international debates on LGBTQ politics and cultures has developed in Spain (Vélez-Pellegrini 2011), arguments against the adoption of queer theory have been made (Fernàndez 2000c; Guasch and Viñuales 2003) and some influential scholars effectively leave the term ticking over in passive mode (Fouz-Hernández and Martínez-Expósito 2007; Mira 1999, 2004, 2008). The concept of queer has also been subject, as elsewhere, to a blurring at its edges which is sometimes beneficial to its protean, creative and anti-taxonomical dynamic but sometimes not.

Four years prior to the Berkana's Queer Theory Special, its sister publishing house, Egales, had already presented a compilation of autobiographical essays and accounts by those active in lesbian and gay politics in Spain, a book which felt able to subtitle itself 'La construcción de una cultura queer en España' (Herrero Brasas 2007) ('The construction of a queer culture in Spain'). Its understanding of the terms Spanish, queer and culture are worth dwelling on. Although all the pieces are written in Castilian and most hinge on a narrative of national change where nation equates to 'Spain', contributors bring to bear on the collection their experiences in institutionalised LGBT politics in Asturias, the Balearics, the Canaries, Catalunya, the Basque Country and the Community of Valencia. There is a strong sense of the interconnectedness of local action and political impacts on the state; the compilation structures its sense of the words 'activismo y ética' ('activism and ethics') – its second subtitle – in part around the flow from local to national, from organised grassroots to overarching organisation; it also has a strong sense, overall, of the duty to history and posterity, of how 'la memoria es la base de la ética' (Hernández, M. 2007: 212) ('memory is the basis of ethics'). 'Cultura', meanwhile, is conceived of largely in terms of a the process of political education of a community and its interlocutors. In his own work, Sáez (2007) has objected strongly and with clarity to the compilation's senses of culture, community and politics, seeing the book as assimilating 'los diversos activismos queer' past and present 'en el Estado español' ('the various forms of queer activism past and present in the Spanish State') under an 'umbrella' of gay and lesbian militancy, 'una tradición que tiene su sentido y su propia historia, pero que no tiene nada que ver con lo queer' ('a tradition with its own rationale and history but which has nothing to do with queer'). In what it excludes and in its focus on individuals, the book, for Sáez, is an attack on 'nuestra memoria colectiva' ('our collective memory') and elides the connected importance of 'proyectos políticos colectivos, asociativos y culturales', 'esos activismos maricas, bolleros y trans alternativos que llamos queer' ('collective, associative and cultural proyects', 'those forms of *marica*, *bollera* and alternative trans activism that we call queer'). Sáez's position is anticipated, and his anxiety to resist a hegemonic flattening out of history is shared, by a number of the contributors to the Herrero Brasas volume. Guasch (2007) makes it clear: that 'no me representan quienes lideran el movimiento gay hegemónico' (357) ('those who now lead the hegemonic gay movement don't represent me'); that he is post-gay (357–8) – post-homosexual, even (358); and that he is in flight from identity politics (358). Aliaga (2007) and Pineda (2007) are also writing unambiguous queer politics, Aliaga seeing the LGTB movement (his formulation) as needing to link back up with wider political initiatives and analyses (for example feminist and antiracist) (299), and Pineda turning readers' minds to the lesbian public kiss-in actions of the 1980s (319–20) to confront a prevailing 'amnesia colectiva' (322) ('collective amnesia').

Trujillo Barbadillo (2008b) ends her own discussion of the problematic transfer of queer (110–12) also by looking to the legacy of lesbian thought and activism in Spain, tellingly alighting on the non-queer named collectives Non Grata – as 'lesbianas que cambian al nombrarse' ('lesbians who change once named') – and the ingeniously mock-labelled LSD, whose activities ceased just as my period of study here began, around 1998. LSD is a designation which both collapses and expands into a proliferation of names, among them Lesbianas Sin Destino, Lesbianas Sin Duda and, ludically, Lesbianas Sospechosas de Delirio (Lesbians Without Direction, Lesbians Without Doubt, Lesbians Thought To Be Dizzy). This grouping's organisation of itself horizontally and organically as a 'suma de individualidades' ('sum of different individualities') rather than as a bloc-collective (Trujillo Barbadillo 2008b: 109) has a clear analogy in the formation of queer Spanish cinema as a sum of different images whose organisation, moreover, is prompted by context, by ephemeral event and by shifting responses, as I hope to show. Like LSD (and cognate groupings), independent feature films such as *Spinnin'* (discussed below), shorts like those of Juanma Carrillo (also, below) and LGBTQ-focalised plot lines or characters in otherwise non-LGBTQ targeted materials screen the in-between and map the usually unmarked, unremarked, everyday aspects of interconnected individual lives within a politics of playful, pleasurable occupation of the marginal, as Trujillo Barbadillo has it (109). Others make more angry or poignant claims on their audiences' and viewers' awareness, such as *Eloïse* (addressing lesbophobia), *Amic/Amat* (*Beloved, Friend*) (Ventura Pons, 1998) (age and loss), *El sueño de Ibiza* (Ibiza Dream) (Igor Fioravanti, 2002) (HIV/AIDS and the loss of illusion) and *Ander* (Roberto Castón, 2009) (rural isolation).

These dialogues and arguments and lost conversations – as well as others in meetings and radical gatherings such as Queeruption Barcelona in 2008, documented in *Gender Terrorists* (Anty Productions, 2008) or the FeminismoPornoPunk workshop at the Arteleku, San Sebastián in the same year – have sharpened up the sense of queer. However, in relation to cinema, the term 'queer' has tended to be used loosely by the most readily available sources, or even tacitly set aside or occasionally brought in alongside lesbian and gay, as I have already suggested. Critics such as Mira (2008) nonetheless usefully manipulate the category of 'cine gay' to make as open a discursive space as possible (opposing ghettoisation or niche-making) and Mira himself uses a trio of useful standards for filtering the films: the presence on screen of LGBT characters or narrative motivation; the involvement of known LGBT actors or film-makers; appropriation or supposition by way of affinity or identification. I borrow some of those filters in the chapters that follow, but try to open out the space by looking at the traffic between films and their ambient cultures as well as drawing my readers' attention to the lesbian and trans, as well as the 'gay' film-maker and viewer.

In a further example of the exclusion or reduction of queer in relation to Spanish film, of those loosely applying the queer term, Palencia's handbook on thirty-three 'queer' films from North America and Europe (2011) includes just one of the films I will be discussing – *Amic/Amat* – along with *El diputado* (*The Deputy/The Congressman*) (Eloy de la Iglesia, 1978) and *La ley del deseo* (*Law of Desire*) (Pedro Almodóvar. 1986), both from what might be thought of as the 'heritage' period – see Chapter 2). These three films, he implies reasonably enough, fall into a general and standard working definition of how queer culture might function – they are positioned counter to the normative and normalising, geared to marginalised cultural practices and sexualities beyond the LGB (and even T), and operate in – or make – a flexible space for the deployment of counter-heterosexist, non-straight and anti-mainstream thought, images and action (following, that is, Spargo 1999; Doty 1993; and other early queer theorists) (16). Palencia's listing in an appendix (199–206) of a further twenty-nine Spanish films and some actors and 'gay icons' slides towards the vaguely conflationary: it brings together the fairly obviously 'gay' *Las cosas del querer* (*The Things of Love*) (Jaime Chávarri, 1989) and *Alegre ma non troppo* (Fernando Colomo, 1994), the more or less lesbian *A mi madre le gustan las mujeres* (*My Mother Likes Women*) (Inés París and Daniela Fejerman, 2002) and the far more demanding and problematising *Tras el cristal* (*In a Glass Cage*) (Agustí Villaronga, 1986) and *20 Centímetros* (*20 Centimetres*) (Ramón Salazar, 2005).

Of course, 'una obra es . . . queer para una audiencia queer en tanto en cuanto subvierte la posición del sujeto gay o lésbico dentro de la identidad gay o lésbica' (López Penedo 2008: 209) ('a work is . . . queer for a queer audience in as far as it subverts the position of the gay or lesbian subject within gay or lesbian identities'). In such a context of 'subversive' (and anti-mainstream, anti-hegemonic) potential, the kind of combination that is found in Palencia's appendix, intentionally or not, can turn the 'sort of vague and indefinable' in queer very much in the direction of 'challeng[ing] normative knowledges and identities' (Sullivan 2003: 43–4). Taken as a collectivity of 'individual' crea-tions, testimonies, images or documents, the very wide-ranging body of films and responses I am going to be concerned with here – however it is packaged commercially, by agencies, festivals, blog and web spaces, or in casual home storage and conversations – has, I would argue, an overall or cumulative effect of queer. This is especially so in the sporadic, partial and even arbitrary viewing which is typical of the festival circuit where short film production is concerned (see Chapter 4). Moreover, given that the range across films and scenes is also wide in terms of production values, quality of script, conception and performance, there is a productive undecidability generated by juxtaposi-tion, by the jumbling of disparate films into event categories, catalogues, web showcases, 'L' or 'G' or 'T' (less often 'B') slots, shelves and chapters in film histories.

SHORT-FILM PRODUCTION

As well as being engaged with the ethics and aesthetics of the disparate, queer Spanish cinema also responds to a definition of queer as 'el compromiso con la causa y la crítica de situaciones discriminatorias e injustas' (García Rodríguez 2008: 456) ('commitment to the cause and a critique of discrimination and injustice where they occur') and is concerned with making a difference. This is particularly prominent in the short film. Early on in the period I am cover-ing, one critic-reporter was already noting that 'el formato corto sigue siendo la principal fuente de relatos gays' (Retamar 2000b) ('the short film is still the main source of gay storytelling') and, in a longer piece, had looked specifically at a 'proliferation' in Spain of short film exhibition both at festivals and with the backing of television (Canal + and RTVE 2) (Retamar 2000a: 66). This critic might have added that the same applies, but more acutely, to lesbian 'storytelling': in the wider viewing list worked through in preparation for this book some fifty titles would count more or less as lesbian short films, but I found only fifteen full-length features since 1998 that would count as at least mainly for or about lesbians, though – strikingly – only two were directed by women. Lesbian film-makers continue to find themselves doubly disadvantaged in a context where, according to director-producer Mariel Maciá, only 8 per cent of films produced in Spain are by women directors and only 20 per cent of screenplays have women writers, and where, plainly still, 'hay . . . una falta de referentes enorme en la temática lésbica española' (InCinema 2011) ('there is a substantial lack of examples of lesbian-themed [film-making]'). There are a number of ways in which the short film can be read as particularly queer, not least in its potential for adventurousness, for the 'type of fresh, edgy film- and video-making' and even 'punkish aggression' associated with the hard core of queer cinema in the moment of the early 1990s (MacKinnon 2006: 121), or simply for 'unusualness' in a refusal – as in the case of *My Beautiful Laundrette* (Stephen Frears, 1986) discussed by MacKinnon here – 'to foreground the categories of homo-hetero' any more than those of race and ethnicity (122) – notably, however, race and ethnicity are categories rarely registered in Spanish queer cinema's representations. More simply too, the legacy of the New Queer Cinema allows new film-makers with precarious resources to 'hablar de sí mismos y de las subculturas eróticas y comunidades de disidencia a las que pertenecen . . . sin complejos y con voz propia' (Nabal 2005: 237) ('speak about themselves and about the sexual subcultures and dissident communities to which they belong . . . openly and distinctively').

This is the case in *Fuckbuddies* (Juanma Carrillo, 2011). Its circle of distribution grew rapidly in the year following its premiere and, having been shortlisted in March 2012 for the Televisión Española-sponsored competition, the Concurso de Cortos Versión Española, it was shown as part of the prestigious film programme Versión Española on TV2 on the night of 18 April. An elegant and comical arc is stylishly and scandalously traced from sexual urgency to polymorphous banality. The opening seconds of the film show a rapid succession of images of close-up segments of the bodies of two men in frantic preparation for protected sex on the backseat of a car; by the end of the film, they have subsided into the low-key intimacy of a wind-down conversation about their lives with their girlfriend and wife, respectively, and mortgage rates and repayment periods. Wry images, gestures and dialogue punctuate the action: the car is prim and gleaming, barely quivering in response to what is going on inside and shot at a respectable distance with a nice panorama beyond it; the fuckee's darting eye movements, within, show comical uncertainty rather than the awe and eager surprise they might be expected to render in a more ordinary pornographic context of quick, casual sex (see Figure 2). His beautifully delivered, tentative and embarrassed 'no . . . es que, no . . .' ('um . . . it's not, it's not really . . .') quickly translates lust into fumbling. His friend, a clumsy and squeamish apprentice in the practicalities of foreplay, has to be

Figure 2 Two friends (Richard García Vázquez and Domingo Fernández) in the car in *Fuckbuddies* (Juanma Carrillo, 2011). Image provided by Juanma Carrillo; reproduced with kind permission.

coaxed like a child being taught how to mix paints or swim to the end of the pool ('go on, just a bit more') and when asked to spit, for lubrication, he spits in the wrong place (the other, unfortunate man's face). His excuse, that this is not like doing it with his wife, prompts the conventional disclaimer from him, 'no soy maricón' ('I'm not gay'), and the riposte is an enjoyable take on the solemnities of queer discourse: 'yo tampoco: soy funcionario' ('me neither, I'm a civil servant'). The close-quarters exploration of the filmic conventions of the Sequence-in-a-Car-Interior and the Odd-Couple allows a range of formal effects from the comic and parodic to the concomitantly dramatic and realist: as the two men chat, having failed to bond carnally, a bitter-sweet closeness is constructed around them based on the very lack of adventurousness and the banality of their everyday lives stretching out beyond the parked car. When the talk peters out and the film fades to black, the sound of the clumsy whirring of the electric motors of the side windows winding down bookmarks the small tragedy of disappointment, but it also points up the way in which fresh air has blown in upon it. This, then, is a memorable package of sounds and images for a viewer and an audience to take away and rethink with.

In *Pasajero* (Miguel Gabaldón Orcoyen, 2009) two young men, Manuel (Pablo de la Chica) and Arturo (Aitor Lizarribar), attempt a belated reconciliation against a classily lit, nocturnal Madrid background (see Figure 3). Wet pavements and distracting lights amplify the inevitability of the failures of their stop-start re-encounter with a love that, as the close-up expressions imply, Manuel has shoddily abandoned in favour of an easier life with a new, steady boyfriend. Two takes of Arturo's finally walking past Manuel – stationary and intense – sharply give form to indecision, to what might have been and

Figure 3 Arturo (Aitor Lizarribar) and Manuel (Pablo de la Chica) in their brief non-encounter in *Pasajero* (Miguel Gabaldón Orcoyen, 2009). Image provided by Ismael Martín for the Escuela de Cinematografía y del Audiovisual de la Comunidad de Madrid (ECAM); reproduced with kind permission.

to the impermanence of personality where once it seemed to centre love. *K* (Juan Simons, 2005) sketches the feelings of the eponymous anti-hero (Miguel Ángel Jiménez), a marginal, young hustler living precariously in a rundown neighbourhood, in love with his straight-identified neighbour Nelson (Álex Quiroga). The film constructs a harsh and emotionally arresting criss-crossing of looks and intentions, shades of intimacy and moments missed in a context of social exclusion.

In some cases the very fragmentary, oblique or fleeting form of presentation is what gives productive undecidability to the subjects briefly unfolding on screen. The micro-short *Pablo¿has puesto la lavadora?* (Pablo: Have You Put the Washing On?) (Javier Haba, 2005) is a low-key depiction through fragments of the domestic everyday of a twenty-something male couple. A lack of dialogue is matched by a deliberate lack of narrative motivation (indeed, of specific story at all), and the pivotal moment of intimacy – a kiss in front of the quivering, eponymous washing machine – is itself fragmented, the kiss out of frame. The film seems to deconstruct the love nest, gently, humorously, as a place of non-encounter; if seen, say, or recalled, in juxtaposition to *Aliteración* (Alliteration) (Roberto Menéndez, 2005), a grimmer and longer (at 8 minutes) exploration of the grip of heteronormativity on relationships, it gathers poignancy. Another micro-short, *Dreams Are the Matter We Are Made Of* (J. F. Blanco, 2007), gradually obliterates the mid-field screen image of a young male who is quickly framed as a casually dressed artist's model. A patchwork screen is laid close across the camera lens, in rapid stop motion, and constructed of partial shots of the model. The dynamics of looking and being looked at, between two men, and of the fragmentation and repositioning of the image of the younger man, shifts in and out of being homoerotic, in and out of being about the gaze, psychosexually, or more technically and aesthetically. It shifts between being an LGBTQ festival piece, and being a gallery piece. Some of the videoart pieces by Juanma Carrillo (see above) have a similar undecidability, as also do those by Rut Suso (both discussed in Chapter 4).

A number of short films, crossing over into the docu-fictional or biographical and testimonial, address the plainly political matter of queer in Spain in relation to global sexual and intersectional politics. In *Imagina* (Sagrario Villalba, 2005) two women walking together in their neighbourhood confront grotesque, everyday machismo and coarse jokes about same-sex marriage as their affection for one another grows; *Almas perdidas* (Lost Souls) (Julio de la Fuente, 2008) addresses small-town homophobia as a solitary, older man returns from a long fishing expedition off the northern coast of Spain to find that his lover has died but nobody on shore – least of all his family – will offer sympathy. Music over by Lluís Llach – the politically committed Catalan singer-songwriter who came to fame in the 1970s – further codes the film, over and above its unmistakable, remote Asturian sea- and landscapes, with specific forms of Spanish loss, grieving and melancholia associated with the years of Francoist repression of liberties (the years of the man's life).

Tiras de mi piel (You Tug At My Skin) (Ayo Cabrera and Enrique Poveda, 2009) is an activist-confessional documentary that talks of the effects on the 'skin' – the body and life experience – of an early HIV diagnosis and of 'los estragos causados por otra infección mucho peor, la de la sidafobia' (COGAM 2012) ('the damage caused by an even worse infection – AIDS-phobia') (see Figure 4). Kike Poveda's testimony in voice-over commentary is of being in, and then thrown out of, a homophobic communist party in the 1970s, of his work as an activist (then and again now since the early 1990s) and of his radical pleasures – serious drug use in the past, a decidedly un-vanilla sex life, smoking and being fucked, which he pointedly notes is itself a stigma, even in 'el mundo gay' ('the gay world'). The camera roams his body, showing glamorous and raunchy tatoos and piercings, the scars of infections, the marks of his first suicide attempt (at twenty-one) and stretch marks from fluid on the abdomen associated with hepatitis C. Until the final moments of the film the camera does not catch the speaker's whole face. His body is shown, in fragments, or sitting naked in the bar of a sauna complex, and there are partial profiles or the odd framing of an eye or the lips. At the end Kike, however, turns suddenly to offer a full close-up to camera, explaining (though still in voice-over) 'de ahí este ejercicio de visibilidad . . . Te cuento todo esto porque al contarlo me siento vivo. Mi vida está llena de huellas, de estigmas, de vida . . . Los estigmas se perciben cuando tiras de tu piel' ('that is the point of this exercise in visibility . . . I'm telling you this because telling it makes me feel alive. My life is covered in traces, stigmas, full of life itself . . . You notice the stigmas when you tug at your own skin'). Direct testimony and a discourse that has internalised (or has shared roots with) more abstract notions of the body as text or site of the inscription and reinscription of power – and specifically the queer body as such (in the tradition of Judith Butler or, in Hispanic contexts, of Pedro Lemebel) (López García 2008) – make this documentary a particularly pointed intervention in the debate on identity, risk, community and well-being (Villamil 2004: 41–66, 115–26). Back where the social stigmatisation and emotional turmoil might begin, *Sirenito* (Little Boy Mermaid) (María Crespo, 2004) and *Vestido nuevo* (A New Dress) (Sergi Pérez, 2007) (with 10,644 plays on the dalealplay website as at 12 December 2011) both dramatise the politics of parenting and the odd, simple complexities of the constructedness of gender through tales of young children dressing up 'wrong'. *Sirenito* deploys isolating long shots and framings which highlight the hugeness of adults or the vastness of school corridors to emphasise the bewildered shame of its young, cross-dressing protagonist who has been pulled out of his class activity as well as that of the scolding, concerned father who has come to fetch him. *Vestido nuevo* reprises many of these techniques and scenarios, adding to the audience's sense of horrible familiarity with the shamefulness of stigmatisation and a sense, yet, of redemptive indomitability in the young. These are sharp micro-dramas of the formation of queer personhood caught up in the moment of event, in the impulses of physical becoming and in the networks of other people's power.

Chapter 4 will offer a more extended analysis of the role of the short film in the conformation of LGBTQ audiences in Spain, but it will be useful for the reader to have in mind through the intervening pages – which deal as much with conventional film-making as with more radical projects – something of a sense of how queer Spanish film resides in the particular rhythms, sharp narrative arcs and cumulative (and randomly assembled) effects of festival viewings and browsing on YouTube, Vimeo or Vodpod. The brief foregoing review has rehearsed just such a viewing experience. In the next section, I focus on feature films and on one, core issue for a new queer Spain (and in some views, against it): marriage.

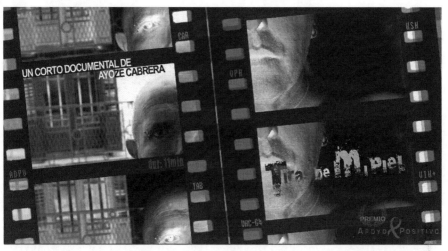

Figure 4 Section of publicity poster for *Tiras de mi piel* (Ayo Cabrera and Enrique Poveda, 2009). Image provided by Ayo Cabrera; reproduced with kind permission.

'Nos Casamos' ('We're Getting Married')

Following a long period of campaigning in Spain for partnership rights and same-sex marriage starting in the early 1990s (Calvo Borobiá 2005; Herrero Brasas 2001: 137–42; Platero Méndez 2007b: 333), and a succession of interventions from the Left and social movements on citizenship (331–2), changes to the Civil Code were passed into law in July 2005, providing 'access for same-sex married couples to rights of inheritance, residence, adoption of the other spouse's children, tax benefits, and to divorce rights' (335). During the long period of promises, proposals across the range of models from civil partnership to same-sex marriage, and the preparation of legislation after the electoral victory of the left-wing PSOE in 2004, the conservative Partido Popular (PP) and its parliamentary allies adopted a series of stances ranging from the minimally supportive of arguments on equal rights (short of marriage) to more clear-cut opposition to changes to the law. In their caution, they were working counter to public opinion in Spain (and parts of Europe) (Calvo Borobiá 2005: 38–46). For Pedro Zerolo, a prominent PSOE party member, the PP demonstrated at the time plain hostility and homophobia (Zerolo 2007: 45), aspects of which re-emerged in the run-up to and campaigning for the general elections of November 2011, with a core objection, to the adoption of children by same-sex couples, coming back into particular prominence ('Flick' 2011).

The passing of the amendment to the law was seen by Beatriz Gimeno, the then president of the Federación Estatal de Lesbianas, Gays y Transexuales (FELGT; subsequently FELGTB), as of exemplary importance – geopolitically for Europe, Latin America and North Africa, and historically for social movements advocating change as well as, specifically, pivotal for Spanish lesbian and gay politics (Gimeno 2007b: 33–4). Gimeno is unambiguous in her assessment of the organisation's role as politically efficacious and representative. Shaping up into being a key player in the negotiations with government, it moved the social and political debate away from civil partnership (Parejas de Hecho) to marriage and adoption and parenting rights, and (implicitly) shifted the focus away from sub-national activism and local practices (town hall registers and their management by mayors and councils) to 'un frente unido que hablaba con una sola voz' ('a united front speaking with one voice') (37). This story of expediency, of course, involves putting the lid on a considerable number of alternatives which might otherwise have sprung up: not the least of these are the sort of multi-levelled, non-centralised strategies for opening up space for collective action, for the networked, horizontal arrangements favoured, for example, by Catalan organisations, including the Coordinadora Gai-Lesbiana (Paternotte 2008: 940–7).

While recognising internal differences but putting them 'en suspenso' ('on hold'), the FELGT had felt it necessary to separate out '[la] cuestión puramente académica' (the 'purely academic' question) of whether or not the Federation was pursuing a variant of identity politics (Gimeno 2007b: 38), which was, of course, precisely to acknowledge the centrality to the marriage debate of live concerns for queer theory and activism. A very real discursive trace of identity politics inheres in the assumption of a more or less fixed mapping of sexual sub-jectivities to civic imperatives and social norms; marriage undeniably appeals to lifestyle issues for certain class segments (those mainly represented in the films discussed below) and to debates on rights – radicalised when coupled to questions of parenting or of gender reassignment, but nonetheless founded on older debates on equality. Being herself less distanced from 'academic' ques-tions than the organisation she had once represented, Gimeno aligns herself (39–40) with the lesbian feminist theorisation of marriage and same-sex mar-riage by Rosemary Hennessy (2000). Few would underestimate 'the state's jealous protection of heterosexual marriage, heteronormative family, and het-erosexual identity' (Hennessy 2000: 21) as a context for the debate on and the subsequent fact of legislative change. However, as Platero Méndez observed at the time (2005: 108–9), the debates of the early 2000s largely omitted any aspects of the international feminist critique of marriage (Young and Boyd 2007: 264–9, 271–4) and 'marriage-like dyads' (264), with the voices of queer and feminist collectives having their impact minimised by the discourse of una-nimity being deployed by the self-styled LGBT 'collective' (109). Little, too, has since been heard of arguments that might urge circumspection with regard to same-sex marriage's potential to provide equal citizenship unequivocally (Josephson 2005: 275–7), of the scope and persistence of lesbophobia working against such easy provision, or of the fact that 'las mujeres lesbianas estamos situadas diferencialmente frente a los varones – homosexuales o no' ('lesbian women are situated differentially vis-à-vis men – homosexual or otherwise') (Platero Méndez 2005: 112; also, in more detail, 2007a: 99). From a male perspective, Guasch (2007) has suggested that same-sex marriage is simply one of many pyrrhic victories by established lesbian and gay counter-politics (359):

> El Estado español es pionero en la lucha contra la discriminación y las agresiones; si bien la homofobia ambiental y la violencia simbólica que la comporta se mantienen casi inalterables. (260)
> (The Spanish State is a pioneer in the battle against discrimination and incidences of violence [relating to gender and sexuality], although under-lying homophobia and the symbolic violence that it brings with it remain unchanged.)

Same-sex marriage is radically disruptive of heteropatriarchal systems of power, and it makes clear the priority of civil institutions over religious ones (Gimeno 2007b: 40). Similarly, on the one hand:

> Simbólicamente, supone un gran paso el poder legitimar la existencia lesbiana como una ciudadanía situada de los márgenes de la normalidad, a estar situada dentro de una de las instituciones más conservadoras y tradicionales. (Platero Méndez 2005: 113)
> (Symbolically, it is a huge step for living as lesbian to be legitimated and placed not now as citizenship at the margins but as on the inside of one of the most conservative and traditional of institutions.)

But in reality, on the other hand, lesbians within marriage, argues Platero Méndez, move from exemplifying forms of sexuality which are disruptive of the gendered and socio-economic norm to fitting into established social roles 'que relegan a las mujeres a un espacio secundario' ('which relegate women to a secondary space') and which correspond to 'representaciones [que] desexualizan las relaciones lésbicas' ('representations which desexualise lesbian relations') (115).

A study of the complex links between versions of marriage and notions of citizenship in the USA in the mid-2000s crisply presents the source of a central dilemma which is present in the Spanish case too – how to be disruptive of heteronormative understandings of citizenship in a cautious and gradual pursuit of 'achievable political goals' (Josephson 2005: 277). While lack of access to marriage is a powerful sign of discrimination (273), it is, as 'a public institution' formed out of political choices over a long period, 'also a fundamentally conservative institution [which] posits a specific desirable form for intimacy and family life . . . and reinforces that form through legal, economic, political, and social privileges' (271). Thus, in the USA, 'many of the most prominent advocates of same-sex marriage are conservative gay men' (although 'some lesbian feminists also argue that same-sex marriage is necessary to assure full citizenship') (272).

Wrapped around that first dilemma is also that of

> la doble representación de las lesbianas como sexualidades políticas disruptivas, y al mismo tiempo, una representación dominante de las lesbianas como madres y esposas que buscan un reconocimiento ante el Estado. (Platero Méndez 2007a: 104)
> (the double representation of lesbians as on the one hand politically disruptive through their sexuality and at the same time, in a more dominant representation, as wives and mothers seeking recognition from the State.)

These images of the lesbian may or may not be compatible, suggests Platero Méndez, and may or may not point to a gradual, 'limited', transformation of the dominant norms ('los patrones dominantes') (104).

As in the North American case studied by Josephson (2005), in Spain 'marriage [had] become "the holy grail of gay politics" [and] a centerpiece for both opponents and proponents of greater rights' (Josephson 2005: 269). It had become the dominant issue, triumphantly from the point of view of, for example, Gimeno (2007b) or Zerolo (2007). However, as we have been seeing, arguments abroad by queer opponents of same-sex marriage about the institution's reinforcement of the patriarchal family and ascriptive forms of citizenship, and its exclusions – of queer youth and 'non-normative LGBT individuals' (Josephson 2005: 273, 277) – are echoed in the Spanish debates (Platero Méndez 2005, 2007a: 98–9, 102–4, 2007b: 336–8; Vidarte 2007a: 11–13, 129–32, 156–7). Consideration of such urgent matters as these, and grounds for a 'discussion of heterosexual marriage and the family [as] relevant to a radical queer sexual politics' (Hennessy 2000: 67), are not evident at the surface of the films that deal with the marriage question. They have to be supplied (or, indeed, ignored) at the point of reception; or they emerge (as I hope they might as this chapter progresses) once a more composite viewing – a putting together of the pieces of images – is undertaken or hypothesised. Some of the films take a distinctly perverse angle on the seriousness of the issues; some persuasively celebrate same-sex marriage (if usually leaving aside the associated life issues of care, adoption and so on); a few offer a critique of marriage, but not of same-sex marriage.

The disruptive potential of lesbianism when set against (heterosexual) marriage is explored in light-hearted and thereby potentially naturalising mode – let us start there – in the commercially-oriented semi-musical comedy of urban coupledom *Los dos lados de la cama* (*The Two* [or *Both*] *Sides of the Bed*) (Emilio Martínez Lázaro, 2005), with 1,540,361 ticket sales at the Spanish box office (MECD 2012) and, more modestly, the winner of a prize for its promotion of the LGBT cause at the Barcelona Mostra Lambda festival (later known as FIRE!!) in 2006. This is one of the several films that I shall be discussing which present an LGTBQ sub-plot or parallel narrative as a crucial part of a more or less light-hearted engagement with the purportedly rapid liberalisation in Spain of cultural and media representations of socio-sexual mores. The affair in the film between Marta (Verónica Sánchez) and Raquel (Lucía Jiménez) which prevents the wedding of Marta and Javier (Ernesto Alterio) is deployed as a light foil to some obvious redundancies of hetero-sexual coupledom and in order to highlight some aspects of complacent lack of emotional know-how in men.[2] Javier and Pedro (Guillermo Toledo) exchange tittle-tattle about marriage while their fiancées make out enthusiastically in the women's toilets on their joint stag/hen night. Raquel's profession as a night-club singer adds texture and generic appeal and even allows a reclaiming of the 1960s heterosexually oriented classic '¿Porqué te vas . . .?' ('Why Are You Leaving?') in one of the numbers. However, the song is performed in the incongruous context of a male strip club for women, involving Raquel in an economy of the look which is borrowed from (and props up in carnivalesque mode) heteropatriarchal mores; the setting, too, makes lesbianism a sideshow by association. The two women's *L-Word* style accoutrements and looks both give and take away – like that series (Beirne 2006) – new, empowering and memorable imaginings of the lesbian dynamic. When Pedro and Javier's homosocial friendship is amplified into frank erotic closeness by way of a two-sex threesome and a kiss between the two men the moment is soon bluffly disavowed. The status quo wobbles back into view. Although the heterosexual marriage is postponed, its underpinnings are not contested; its problematics are just so much song and dance here.

In the previous year, *Reinas* (*Queens*) (Manuel Gómez Pereira, 2005) had identified in the unfolding debates and legal changes across Europe sufficient material in same-sex marriage for a commercially successful comedy of culture clash, with a cumulative audience of 418,763 in Spain (MECD 2012). The film anticipated (by three months, on its release) the change of the law in Spain by dramatising a marriage ceremony for twenty gay couples held on Spanish soil by a judge despatched from Brussels for the purpose, acting, as she says, by the authority vested in her by the Spanish state. The 'queens' in question are not, in fact, any of the six men getting married but, in a borderline-offensive set of caricatures, their variously forceful, kooky, conflicted or frustrated mothers. In different ways, none take the marriages with equanimity, and one – the judge, Helena (Mercedes Sampietro) – is explicitly and unreconstructedly homopho-bic until the very event itself (which, ironically, she ends up presiding over). One of the six grooms on which the narrative focuses is a politically driven, young MEP (Hugo: Paco León) who has devoted a career to gay marriage (while, to bitter-sweet comic purpose, also secretly sleeping around though engaged and having an affair with his mother's male analyst). The narrative arc is shaped around the wedding event itself, part of a mass event exploit-ing a new, niche market, sanitising and gentrifying a space that otherwise might have been queer (Fouz-Hernández 2010: 84, 97). The often farcical tensions as well as the lavish arrangements associated with the build-up high-light many of the questions at the core of the phenomenon. As a formulaic and romantic comedy of near errors and perennial themes (in the established style of the director) it subsumes the radical potential (in Hennessy's sense) of men formalising their active sexual attraction to one another across class and national cultures into the familiar generic patterns of the dominant cinematic and social narrative in question. The only sex scene between fiancés – Miguel (Unax Ugalde), a rich, fastidious, art-and-media, Northern-European looking gay, and Oscar (Daniel Hendler), an Argentine sports instructor and masseur – is interrupted at the half-naked stage by the intrusion of the egomaniac mother and mother-in-law Ofelia (Bettiana Blum). Homoeroticism, as in a series of normalising feature films, is veiled or curtailed (Ellis 2010: 77; Fouz-Hernández 2010: 98). Similarly truncated is a line of argument brought out during strike action by the unionised labour force in the luxury hotel owned by one of the mothers, Magda (Carmen Maura) – that the whole event and its presuppositions are elitist and exclusivist. In the kitchens, when the mothers of the twenty couples pitch in to cook the banquet (and negate the strike from their non-unionised position), Magda remarks with fond acquiescence '¿has visto como son los hombres?; da igual que sean gays; al final acabamos trabajando para ellos' ('you see what men are like? Gay or not we women always end up working for them), but the remark has no retroactive critical hold on the narrative. Similarly, little or nothing comes from a sub-plot involving a rich actor (Marisa Paredes) and her initially haughty and reactionary treatment of her gardener (Lluis Homar) or of the social gap-closing being assumed to have been done between their sons (the highly telegenic Hugo Silva as Jonás and Raúl Jiménez as Rafa). In summary, '[g]iven the film's political motivation, it's amazing how little it scrapes the surface of the class issues that cloud some of its gay relationships' (Gonzalez 2006). However, the film still counts, as one commentator in 2006 put it, as a 'documento' ('a document') – albeit a light one:

> de un momento concreto de nuestra historia (o Historia) . . . huella no oficial de aquellos cambios que vivimos, una vez, allá por aquel ya lejano 2005. (DosManzanas 2006)
> (of a particular moment in our history with a capital H . . . an unofficial trace of the changes we lived through once upon a time in the distant year of 2005.)

The line-up of extremely famous female stars (as has been seen, with also Verónica Forqué as Núria, completing a trio of 'Almodóvar girls') and of good-looking young male actors, allowed the film a certain impetus. Its last words, in melancholy but plucky mode, refer to the importance of moving on, emotionally and politically (as Núria, in a Prozac haze, looks back on the enormity of all that has happened, and converses with a recently bereaved gay stranger on a train). Politically, however, the effect is at best neutralising and (falsely) naturalising (Ellis 2010).

A stronger take on the politics of partnership is facilitated by the representation of the interconnectedness of the sexual political with social issues in *Spinnin'* (Eusebio Pastrana, 2007). The film is low-budget, with an almost community-based project feel, which out of necessity (according to the director) opts for an unconventional style (The Big Bean and The Human Bean Band 2011). Still listed and on shelves in, for example, the Corte Inglés department store during 2011, it has accumulated a lasting and proto-cult appeal (La Higuera 2011). The narrative is focalised through the more-queer-than-gay couple Omar (Olav Fernández) and Gárate (Alejandro Tous, well-known for his part in Tele5's *Yo Soy Bea*, 2006–9) and lesbians Jana (Arantxa Valdivia) and Luna (Carolina Touceda). It takes in same-sex parenthood, access rights to children, civil partnership (between the women) and same-sex marriage as 'un derecho por conquistar' ('a right yet to be won') (the script and filming predate the change in law), AIDS and HIV, queer-bashing, and neighbourly responsibility. Gárate is a winningly good Samaritan, an ethical queer (Vidarte 2007a) par excellence; Omar works as a legal adviser at the Fundación Triángulo, no less (anachronistically: the film is set in 1995, one year prior to the founding of the organisation). One of his clients is dealing with the double discrimination of the lesbian single parent in a custody battle in a further sub-plot opening out to crucial queer feminist critiques of masculinist and lesbophobic exclusion (Gimeno 2007a). The film's first extended treatment of same-sex civil partnership and the possibility of marriage comes only sixteen minutes in. Jana and Luna tell the men that 'nos casamos' ('we're getting married'), and they explain, didactically, that they mean that they are entering into a civil partnership and that there is a proper ceremony now to this end (in 1995 the Comunidad de Madrid became one of the early local authorities to set up registers). Omar is clear in his objections (his allergy, as he puts it) to marriage, countering Luna's forceful belief in the significance of the fight for the right to marry with a scepticism born of his own more free-floating sexual politics and instinct for radical (if gentle) alternative patterns of commitment. The sequence is given deftness and lift by darting hand-held camera moves, the smiling conviviality of the four friends, and by the inclusion of the several happy kisses of congratulation exchanged into the quirky meta-structural frame whereby every on-screen kiss is marked by the (usually somewhat irritating) appearance of technical crew or out-of-character actors bearing boards, cards and other items with the sequential number of the kiss. (These kisses, one hundred and one, are the kisses dreamed by Gárate as having been exchanged by his parents and form part, in fact, of his grieving for a mother who never knew love.) The film's celebratory and playful strand of solidarity marks out the space of personal and generational battles for equality of access to care, rights of caring, dignity and citizenship.

Spinnin' reconfigured for its audiences in fictionalised everyday terms something of the euphoria of the times leading towards the making visible and self-recognition of Spanish LGBTQs as 'ciudadanos de primera' (Zerolo 2007:

49) ('first-rank citizens'). A different response to the need to record the history of the difficult struggles – also noted by Zerolo (2007: 49) – to conjoin the personal with the civic in this process comes in the documentary *Campillo sí, quiero* (Campillo, Yes; I Do) (Andrés Rubio, 2007; re-edited 2008). This is a direct treatment of the issues around same-sex marriage, but from a celebratory and a liberally indignant perspective that includes testimonial accounts of prejudice and inequality. Its chosen style is an effectively naive-didactic one with significant elements of usefully emotive sound and image. The first pre-title sequence inter-title states, in silence, the historical fact of the passing of the law, the second refers to local authorities who boycotted carrying it out, and a third goes direct to the introduction of the mayor of the hamlet of Campillo de Ranas (province of Guadalajara), Francisco (Paco) Maroto who, the audience is told, 'levantó la mano y dijo: "Yo caso"' ('raised his hand on high and said: "I will, I'll marry people"'). Airy music and a simple, rustic animation – with a little bee flitting from title to title – follow on, leading from the fields and trees to the happy, colourful community. Animation and music give way to a striking full-screen image of a majestic tree in a field, and the soundtrack is that of a young lamb's bleating. The mayor appears, ready to feed the lambs, anticipating poetically the reading at one ceremony, later in the film, of Whitman's 'We Two – How Long We Were Fooled', in Spanish translation ('somos naturaleza . . . nosotros dos entre rebaños' – 'we are nature . . . we are two among wild herds').

Overlaying this somewhat ahistorical and appealingly simple symbolism is real, national, social history and a measured visual account of the everyday textures of life in this small rural community. Shots of the local media covering the opening of a school replace the tending of the lambs; the mayor points out that if there are now enough young people living in Campillo (at risk of depopulation like so many small communities in Spain since the 1950s) it is due, precisely, to the decision to open up the town hall to marrying same-sex partners. Campillo is made a public, national and international place of social change and, as one student at a Spanish class for immigrants notes cannily enough, the weddings are good because they bring in work.

The first wedding ceremony shown (of grooms) gives a strong sense of the egalitarian and sincere spirit of the occasion and of the place, with refreshingly low-budget arrangements; Paco reads out, as he habitually does for the ceremonies, a text based around the phrase 'sí, quiero' ('I do'), tagging together a series of claims to rights in social equality including, crucially, 'I wish to bring up children'. A day visit by COGAM (Colectivo de Lesbianas, Gays, Transexuales y Bisexuales de Madrid) allows this aspect of rights-related politics to be emphasised, as well as for a micro-history of the enterprise to be rehearsed by way of a welcoming speech. Later, Paco's own memories of his adolescence in an unenlightened and unsupportive Madrid give specific texture and testimonial depth to the history, as also does the culminating ceremony, in June 2008, between Paco and a tense and camera-shy partner Enrique (with footage and an inter-title added to the originally exhibited version of 2007). The one lesbian wedding, between Pilar and Malena, with their grown-up children and grandchildren in attendance, suggests a long and difficult journey made by the two towards this moment. Their tears of angrily reclaimed joy match those of Enrique, another of the subjects whom the film gently, in its attention to facial gestures and tones of voice, shows to be as much an exhausted survivor of history as a pioneer.

One contradiction is left interestingly hanging in the high blue air. The alternative, lay beliefs and practices supporting same-sex marriage clash with the strong Catholic traditions of the town. A procession is filmed, with a statue of the virgin, a mass attended by the mayor and a snippet of a sermon (which sticks cautiously, it appears, to themes of hospitality and good works). The reality of the Church's opposition to same-sex marriage and the crux of the dispute over what is and is not 'natural' is elided. Nor does one heterosexual couple who have tricked out their celebration with cod-medieval fancy-dress and tents and old-world games (all, as the bride explains, hired online) register any awareness of the strong associations of such folkloric goings on with the evasive *costumbrismo* propagated by Francoism. The worst effects of that prior era – as epitomised in the use of unmarked mass graves for the bodies of the vanquished of the Civil War and the following repression (Jerez-Farrán and Amago 2010) – are obliquely but inevitably suggested in the attentive filming and discussion of the digging up of an ancient ossuary in the churchyard which gives this documentary further topicality and its issues a gravitas beyond, even, their own.

The gentle comedy of homosocial errors, *Nacidas para sufrir* (*Born to Suffer*) (Miguel Albaladejo, 2009) also sets the questions about same-sex marriage in a rural space, but takes a quirky angle that of itself manages to out some equivocal elements in the socio-romantic phenomenon of material union. Flora (Petra Martínez), the over-sixties owner of a big house and smallholding in a sunlit, generically rural (but in fact Valencian) Spain decides to take advantage of recent changes in the law to marry her help Purita (Adriana Ozores) in order to offer Purita stability and herself security of care (and protection of her property from a grasping family). The patrician Flora is able to rebuff the local priest's objections that the arrangement goes against Catholic doctrine, and is for convenience only (as, she retorts, most marriages, then) – the film thus ludically highlights one of the most serious sources of opposition to same-sex marriage, satirises heterosexual marriage (in a time-honoured way), but also acknowledges a potential for complicity in that shared, lesbian and straight, option of convenience. However, Purita is frightened all along that her family will find out about 'lo nuestro' ('our secret/our arrangement'), and, under pressure from her own family, is unable to resist the force of heteronormativity in the guise of imposed family duty. She abandons Flora, annulling the marriage. Flora pines not just for lost security and independence but – which is what saves the film and gives it edge – for the physical presence of Pura, albeit in the next and not the same bed. The two women have a conflicted eroticised love based on caring which is seen to flourish not so much while they are married (although at the annual village fiesta they are feted as its first same-sex couple, to their consternation) but in between, in the crisis of separation prior to Flora's angry but passionate '¿De manera que has venido a pedirme a que te perdone y que me case otra vez contigo?' ('So you've come to ask me to forgive you and marry you again?').

Although one blog sees the film as laughing at small-town intolerance and the power of communal homophobia (prompted by its programming in an anti-homophobia mini-season) (LesPlanet 2011), the film shows the rural community to be split between self-affirming inclusiveness that is very much to do with sexuality (containing it, perhaps), on the one hand, and on the other, gossip and received ideas about duty that are more to do with gender, social structures, class and kinship. It explores, in fact, a range of causes of uneven justice and denial of feelings, among these (while fondly and picturesquely reimagining it) marriage. Another blogger notes that 'El tema de la película es el matrimonio de conveniencia, no el matrimonio lésbico' ('the film's subject is marriages of convenience not lesbian marriage') ('Juan' 2010), but the queer comic twist – and classic, Spanish, 1960s comedic take (Albaladejo 2011) – on the subject immediately springs the social and the lesbian question. It is not for nothing that the film continued on the shelves of Berkana bookshop at least until the end of 2011, or was flagged as of interest in the web magazine *EurOut* (European Lesbian News) (Joreen 2010).

As in *Ander* (Roberto Castón, 2009) (see Chapter 4) the freshness as well as the isolation of the rural setting offsets in imaginative ways the usually urban and modern connotations of the marriage debate and pushes to the sidelines the usual terms of lesbian-to-lesbian and gay-to-gay relationship-making. The lesbian question, having been sprung, is redirected through setting and generic framing towards something more off-centre. The many looks which the two women exchange (usually with Purita avoiding them at first) are queer looks – not sexualised at all, but warm with the almost erotic sufficiency of living in a space structured by 'una película con aire de cuento, intemporal, más cercana al falso costumbrismo inventado por Fellini para *Amarcord*' (Albaladejo 2011) ('a film with an air of storytelling to it, a timelessness, closer perhaps to the false local realism invented by Fellini for *Amarcord*'). After the wedding, in the fields, both Flora and Purita realise, and declare, that they are happy – a rarity for them – with Flora setting this in the context of their work in the fields together and the beauty of the land around them. A mid long shot from higher up the field, cued by an affection-charged look in medium close-up by Flora at Purita, places them in eyeline match with one another on the horizontal across the screen, with the sound of the wind blowing the alfalfa caught for a few seconds before Purita recommences scything the crop. The film is indeed one of indirectness, of 'amor latente entre dos mujeres' (Europa Press 2009) ('latent love between two women'). As Adriana Ozores

has suggested, it is 'una película que presenta otra manera de entender lo gay
. . . creo que es lo que se plantea' (Cascales 2010a) ('a film which presents a
different way of understanding gay experience . . . I believe that this is what is
intended').

In Juan Pinzás's Galician trilogy *Era outra vez* (*Once Upon Another Time*)
(2000), *Días de voda* (*Wedding Days*) (2002) and *El desenlace* (*The Ending*)
(2003) marriage is under bleaker scrutiny. The trilogy has as one of its main
threads the character of gay novelist Rosendo (Monti Castiñeiras in the first
two films), whose wedding to his publisher's daughter is at the narrative core
of the central film. The three films are made in accordance with the Dogme
95 tenets, and are certificated as such (Prout 2010: 70).[3] Prout sees Dogme's
'prising open [of] familial and societal vaults' by the production in filming
and performance of an 'authentically differentiated emotional plane' as here
shifted to homosexual and transgender experience and identity (2010: 71), the
trilogy being 'structured around the epistemology of the closet' (79), not only
sexual[y but also linguistically and culturally. The first film 'suggest[s] parity
between the visible assumption of a gay identity and the audibility in public
space of the Galician language' (84); the second links a challenge to heteronormativity to a challenge of traditional views of Galician culture (in a scene I
will return to) (83); and in the third, Rosendo (now played by Carlos Bardem,
and in Castilian) has accepted that he was living a lie in a heterosexual marriage and has – in his relationship with Fabio (Víctor Rueda), who is a young
transitioning male-to-female cabaret artist (Fabiola) – 'emerge[d] from the gay
closet but [been] thrown back into the bilingual one' (85). As Prout observes
of the shift out of Galician for this last film – an effect in part of problems with
the production schedule (85–6) but nonetheless remarkable – 'it seems that a
Galician speaking gay man cannot cross [the threshold of the closet] without
reverting to Castilian' (85). Similarly, in the reproduction in the story of the
relationship of Rosendo and Fabio in conventional terms of an erotic, cross-
generational partnership of protection and power inequality, it seems as if that
same gay man cannot help himself reverting into a form of inauthenticy when
all around there are more egalitarian models to follow than those epitomised
in letting the younger, prettier partner have the keys to the (swanky) car and in
letting, at least by omission, the younger man be propositioned and emotionally exploited by your mixed-up, bohemian, ostensibly straight male friend
(Fernando, played by Javier Gurruchaga).

This unequal relationship repeats, by inversion, that which sows the discord
of inauthenticity at the heart of the marriage in *Días de voda*. Rosendo brings
himself to marry his publisher's daughter, Sofia (Comba Campoy), not only to
further his career but also because she reminds him of her father, Alexandre
(Ernesto Chao), with whom he has had a passionate affair and whom he kisses
in semi-public view outside the wedding feast. Rosendo's closetry as well as his
cavalier dedication to forwarding his career have led him to neglect the grand-
parents who brought him up and not even to have invited them to the wedding.

In a Dogme-style improvisation (Prout 2010: 83–4), they accuse Rosendo of a lack of integrity. This also calls into question the credibility of the discourse of family unity and the sacredness of commitment which has been part of the ritual diet of the day. In a parodically folkloric sequence later, a possibly lesbian and certainly black-sheep aunt reads the Tarot cards for Sofia and sees signs of dark family secrets and ill omen. Rosendo's absence from the table (and preference for the gentlemen's toilet, Alexandre and the kiss outside) as well as the evidence of his being a bad scion, mean that the priest, representing a rival set of supernatural beliefs, is hard put upon to make count his exhortation at the feast that everything be forgotten and the wedding be remembered as 'una voda feliz' ('a happy wedding day').

For Sonia, the single most visible and disruptive sign of the wedding turning out badly is Rosendo's dancing of the traditional centrepiece *muiñeira* not with her, as he should have done, but with Beatriz (Pilar Saavedra), the loud and big-egoed close friend and gleeful sexual confidante of his gayness. The sound of the traditional bagpipe band and the steps of the dance are, as Prout observes, provocatively eroticised here (2010: 81). Because of the anthropological and ethnographic interconnectedness of the wedding ceremony, the festivities, family, music, tradition and national identity (80–3), the film 'gravitates towards marriage as a key element of the Galician heritage industry which is ripe for deconstruction' (83). In its interrogation of the truths and lies of kinship and erotic commitment, and through this gravitation towards marriage, the film also reminds queer audiences of the institution itself as a nexus of problematic discourses in need of unravelling before they unravel themselves and catch up LGBTQ subjects in webs of damage, inauthenticity and confusion.

QUEER ETHICS/POSITIVE IMAGES

The ethical texture of *Spinnin'*, to return to that film, is grounded in queer social concerns, and the film offers a series of critiques of naturalised and naturalising received ideas. The character of Gárate serves, for example, as a cypher for common attitudes to parenthood. Although he bonds strongly with Adriana (Alejandra P. Pastrana) whose lesbian mother is losing a custody battle against the biological father, initially he is both reluctant to join Omar in his enthusiasm to be a father and tells his own father (when the latter asks the standard straight question, 'when are you going to have a child?') 'Papá, los maricas no tienen niños' ('Dad, queers don't have kids'). Then he changes: when he and Omar decide, both, to 'marry' Raquel, a.k.a. Kela (Zoraida Kroley), who is living with HIV-AIDS and is pregnant with a child who may or may not sero-reconvert, they also commit to her unborn child, to the pre- and post-natal anxieties, and to being, in García's words outside the registry office, *familia*. The film is enriched by a concern with death, dying, and grieving: less than four minutes into the film Gárate is telling his best friend García (Agustín

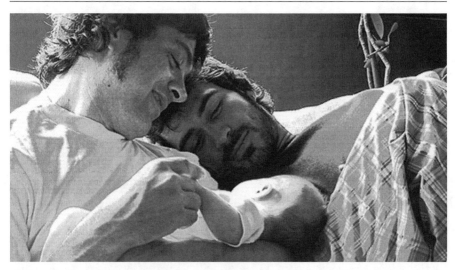

Figure 5 Omar (Olav Fernández) and Gárate (Alejandro Tous) adopting fatherhood in *Spinnin'* (Eusebio Pastrana, 2007). Screen grab reproduced with kind permission of The Big Bean, Productores.

Ruiz) of his intention to go to visit his mother's grave at the cemetery since it is the anniversary of her birthday. The second half is structured around Kela. Her eventual suicide leaves Gárate and Omar with the (healthy) baby – in perhaps another Almodovarian echo, alongside the cemetery scene, of *Todo sobre mi madre* (*All About My Mother*) (1999) – and leaves the film's viewers with a strong sentiment of sympathetic solidarity (as is summarised in the compendium of critical views on the film's Facebook website: Fans de Spinnin) (see Figure 5).

Such a seriously freighted narrative structure, though, is saved from clumsy exposition by adventurous editing which intersperses the story with the following: whimsical vignettes (several involving two municipal policemen gradually falling in love on patrol, watched over by a chubby fairy godfather figure); scenes of adulation of Atlético Madrid football team (Gárate is named after the legendary player of the 1970s, José Eulogio Gárate Ormaechea); the intermittent, dancing appearance of a middle-aged, shaven-headed tutu-wearing male; brief scenes (and one extended musical one, at the end) of whirling and spinning; and experiments, in the kissing countdown already mentioned, with the kind of numerical estrangement produced once before by Peter Greenaway's *Drowning by Numbers* (1988).

It proved hard for viewers to be anything but positive about this film – and something of its upbeat, inclusive style is also to be found in the (unusually for Spanish LGBTQ productions) race-aware short *Happy Day in Barcelona* (Johann Pérez Viera, 2009), where happiness depends absolutely on awareness and understanding of the other, and where Muslim co-protagonist Meriam's lesbianism makes no sense outside the frame of family, religious custom, self-knowledge and non-sexual commitment to others. However, some of the goodness of *Spinnin'* is based on far from complex or philosophical apprehensions such as are encapsulated in the (sincere enough) motif 'El amor tiene aristas, las heridas te mantienen vivo . . .' ('Love has sharp edges, its wounds keep you feeling alive'), frequently repeated verbatim, in the mouths of different characters. Similarly, a long soliloquy on grief and pain, spoken by two separate characters, threatens to tip tragedy into portentousness, but the rhetoric overwhelms the sentiment on any conventional reading and viewing of the scenes. Furthermore, despite its clear and successful politics of making visible the everyday experiences of those affected by discrimination or social exclusion, some of its modes of representation risk moving towards assimilation and normalisation, and the film is very white by comparison to independent films in other LGBTQ film traditions (and as *Happy Day in Barcelona* emphasises by contrast). A two-shot intervention to camera by Jana and Luna, speculating on the life of the baby girl about to be born to them, notes (astutely enough) that should she be lesbian then the world which awaits her is likely to to be one whose prejudices will still be based around the comforting doublet of the fashionability of gay men and the consequent invisibility of 'nosotras', we lesbians. So far, so political. However, in a dissonant echo of the commercial aesthetic whereby 'the lesbian imagination can easily be . . . exploited and recuperated by the homogenising dream-machine' (Cairns 2006: 5), the women are conventionally beautiful, long-haired, golden-skinned and lit from back right by sunlight through the white pillars of a portico, whereas elsewhere in the film they seem more ordinary. It is as if an ironic reference to Gárate's own, sporadic, profession as an advertising creative had backfired.

The film is an example of the unintentional queer aesthetic which the collective of films I am discussing pieces together; despite its easy popular and youth appeal, and the sense of a fairly simple if emotionally demanding set of story lines, *Spinnin'* is odd, bitty, sometimes edgy, juxtaposing a comfortable feel with formal disruption and coincidental parody of normative behaviours and attitudes. In her discussion of *Beautiful Thing* (Hettie Macdonald, 1996), Jennings (2006) adapts the notion of 'positive unoriginality' to the British context, situating it as a mode which combines 'typical strategies associated with positive images and traditional identity politics' with 'some uncertain forms of viewing identification' (193). This, she argues, is done to specifically queer effect, that is there is an effect on queer audiences which is complex and productive and observable (192). There are some similarities to Spanish productions. *Beautiful Thing*'s mélange of conventional coming-out tale framed by television-drama-style social realism with overt self-reflexivity with regard to genre (186) and its productively contradictory representations of secondary characters (189) matches up with a queer tendency in Spanish films to mismatch the highly conventional – in one or other formal category or in look – and the unexpected (and sometimes unintended) effect, outcome or emotion.

In a different register, and with a bigger draw at the Spanish box office

(76,432 tickets sold: MECD 2012) plus substantial availability on DVD, *Cachorro* (*Bear Cub*) (Miguel Albaladejo, 2004) essays a similar combination. Its setting – gay central Madrid, and particularly Chueca, as 'a universally recognisable queer space' (Fouz-Hernández 2010: 84) – was in many ways, by 2004, positively unoriginal, its narrative premise of a sex- and fun-loving lifestyle suddenly being interrupted by the need to care for a child, a traditional one (in the mode of *Trois hommes et un couffin* (*Three Men and a Cradle*) (Coline Serreau, 1985)). Its combination of narrative and representational elements is more thought-provoking and has an ethical edge. There is a serious and engaging representation of a sexually active and attractive 'bear'-type male protagonist Pedro (José Luis García Pérez) – an anti-normative representation in terms of image (Fouz-Hernández 2010: 92–3), at the time at least – living proudly as part of a supportive older male community and living with HIV-AIDS. There is the narrative treatment of surrogate parental care (by Pedro of his nephew) and a key questioning of the hegemonic, ideological 'split between domesticity and sex' (Fouz-Hernández 2010: 88), although the parallel satire of heteronormative family control is less convincing as a radical strategy. The sense of '"alternative family" formation' (96) is, for much of the film, truly alternative, precisely because it is sexualised from the start (98) (Fouz-Hernández and Martínez-Expósito 2007: 192); the domestic space of Pedro's flat is also intersected powerfully by community concerns. It shares with *Reinas* (see above) and *Chuecatown* (*Boystown*) (Juan Flahn, 2007) (see Chapter 2), a 'redeeming factor [that] may be their general disregard for "gayness" as a problem', suggests Fouz-Hernández (2010: 95), adding that '[t]his might be problematic in itself' (95). It might be: the process of normalisation is fraught with exclusion, and to make a representational point about being LGTB being no different, and to do so in entertaining mode, is often to redeploy old stereotypes, old standbys, a preterite mode. In the next chapter I review a number of studies of filmic representation of lesbian and gay subjects from the Spanish past; I move forward in time a little to consider some overlaps of positive images, identity politics and a nascent queer, radically original mode; and I build a sense of heritage, good and bad.

NOTES

1. One of the many omissions of this book is a close study, however, of the affinities of Spanish with certain Latin, Central and Spanish-speaking North America queer cinemas. The Fundación Triángulo/LesGaiCine's projects in relation to these cinemas makes the connection in practical terms (see <http://www.lesgaicinemad.com/Archivo/Lesgai11/introduccion.htm> [last accessed 21 May 2012]). On relevant aspects of Latin American queer cinema (in Spanish-speaking territories), and an extensive review of existing studies, see Subero (forthcoming).
2. Part of this discussion appears in a longer piece on comedy and musicals in Labanyi and Pavlović (2012: 193–223).
3. The certificates are reproduced at <http://www.atlanticofilms.com/AF_Dogma.asp [last accessed 21 October 2011], with that for *El desenlace* dated 2 July 2002, just

as the closure of the Dogme 'Secretariat' and the end of certification was announced (see statement in the appendix in Stevenson 2003: 291–2). Pinzás appears to have made his promise about its mode of production to Dogme far in advance of the shooting (in 2004: see <http://www.atlanticofilms.com/AF_noticia_01_04.asp> [last accessed 21 October 2011]) and of the final shaping for release in 2005.

2. LEGACIES

This chapter looks back through the earlier 1990s in Spain and the mini-boom of gay-themed films alluded to in the Introduction and Chapter 1, and beyond that into the past representations of lesbianism and male homosexuality on the Spanish screen. It does so in order to explore how film and cultural scholars have helped shape the question: what are the roots of Spanish queer cinema? A review of these studies and films will help establish which are the most significant precursors in Spain for a new period of queer film-making. I am also concerned to see to what extent this newer set of practices is embedded in compromises with the past (especially in commercial production) and to what extent pastness informs the production of new films and ideas as they, in turn, draw on the short history of Spanish queer film-making.

Pastness I understand to imply the use of heritage images, inherited ideas, a continuity of pride and indignation, an aesthetic and testimonial tradition, and a 'correspondence with [and] disposition towards the past' (Sargeant 2002: 203, 206). In the context of the pivotal, and monumental, documentation of LGTBQ cultures in Spain, Alberto Mira's *Para entendernos. Diccionario de cultura homosexual, gay y lésbica* (1999), the entry on Activism had made the polemical suggestion that nothing had yet been done to 'apropriar la tradición cultural hispana para la causa gay' ('to appropriate Hispanic cultural tradition for the gay cause') and to build a specifically Spanish agenda 'basada en nuestra propia historia y en nuestra propia problemática' (Mira and Vila 1999) ('based on our own history and our own set of problems'). In the twenty or so years since the formulation of that statement the range of academic and critical discussion has widened considerably. This expansion has been prompted in part by the early 1990s mini-boom (in a transnational context of market consolidation of LGBT cinema), in part by the effects of those socio-political moments and imperatives, as outlined in Chapter 1, and in part by a renewal of interest in the undercurrents of the periods immediately surrounding the death of Francisco Franco in 1975 and that of the transition out of the Franco years, into the 1980s (Feenstra 2006; Martin-Márquez 1999: 141–277; Pavlović 2003; Vilarós 1998).[1] It has included: scientifically historicised analysis of literary chronicles of male homosexual subcultures (Vázquez García and Cleminson 2011: 217–64); critical evaluations of cultural, literary and auto-biographical constructions of gay and lesbian subjectivities and identities (Castrejón 2008; Martínez-Expósito 1998, 2004; Norandi 2009; Rodríguez González 2007; Simonis 2007a; Vilaseca 2003; Vosburg and Collins 2011a); and a book-length analysis of the ways in which LGBT cultures contributed to the 'processes of democratic transition in Spain' and how 'queer culture took the lead in the lively debates about modernism and postmodernism [and] dramatised both an avowal and disavowal of the intermingling of high and low culture' (Pérez-Sánchez 2007: 187).

The first part of this chapter, then, reviews some of the work done to establish a distinctive tradition of queer Spanish cinema in the thirty or so years which precede my starting date of 1998; Melero's study of the period 1973–81, *Placeres ocultos* (Hidden Pleasures) (2010), is my point of departure. That part of his book which studies commercially exploitative images of homosexuality in Spain for mainly heterosexual audiences is exhaustive, while Mira (2008) supplies a range of comparative materials in international context (65–99). Melero locates many of those points where reactionary roots tangle and choke a nascent tradition of progressive representations, which is his book's other concern. The consideration, here, of the construction of lesbian 'personajes' ('characters': often, however, mere cyphers) within the Spanish horror genre, in sexploitation films and in location-defined dramas (prison, convent, school) is of particular interest and sensitises the viewer of later films to those older resonances. These are sometimes picked up on parodically as in *Entre tinieblas* (*Dark Habits*) (Pedro Almodóvar, 1983), or used with intended hilarity as in the short *Lesbos Invaders From Outer Space* (Víctor Conde, 2008), or dealt with face-on as in the harrowing, true-story melodrama *Electroshock* (Juan Carlos Claver, 2006). Melero's work can be productively set alongside Pelayo García's important doctoral work (2009) on lesbian characters in Spanish cinema from 1972 to 2005, to which I return. The second part of my chapter looks first at films which, though made and seen after as well as before 1998, are tellingly anachronistic in their assumptions, characterisation and structures. Many of these are comedies (the mainstay of the 1990s mini-boom). However, as basic Foucauldian theory might predict, these comedies can produce discourses that are as much constituted around countering and dismantling structures and processes of control and prohibition as they are around causing their persistence and amplification. I then move on to test how a nascent lesbian cinema in Spain might or might not move towards producing resistant viewings and meanings by being, precisely, entertaining. Here I link the politically significant notion of visibility to some of the methodological categories used by Spanish scholars of lesbian and gay cinema's histories in a discussion of examples of a popular film *Todo me pasa a mí* (*Everything Happens To Me*) (Miguel García Borda, 2001), an entertaining director, Marta Balletbò-Coll, and a well-known actor, Victoria Abril.

Two sections explore, respectively, a generic legacy – that of the coming-out film and its continuity through into the twenty-first century – and an auteurial one, in the shape of Pedro Almodóvar. In the final section of the chapter, I turn to feature films where the queer past, or past socio-political issues impinging on the queer present, are the subject matter (as, to some extent, they are in mid-period Almodóvar too). Discussed here are five films in different modes: Agustí Villaronga's *El mar* (*The Sea*) (2000), set in the 1940s; the made-for-television *Electroshock*, whose narrative present is 1998 with extended flashback narration of a period running roughly from 1972 to 1976; Antonio Hernández's *En la ciudad sin límites* (*In the City Without Limits*) (2002), set in around 2000 but structured around memories of the 1940s; Roberto Castón's *Ander* (2009), set in 1999 and exploring the persistence of homophobically produced historic inhibitions and prohibitions; and Jon Garaño and José María Goenaga's *80 egunean* (*For 80 Days*) (2010), exploring similar material through one character, but through another affirming the power of affection and of adolescent memory to span stretches of the lesbian continuum. Discussion of some more obviously Spanish Queer Heritage Movies in the more usual cinematic sense of 'heritage' will be postponed until Chapters 4 and 5 so that they can be considered in the contexts of performance and celebrity or of their connections to literary traditions – for example, *Los novios búlgaros* (*Bulgarian Lovers*) (Eloy de la Iglesia, 2003) and *El consul de Sodoma* (*The Consul of Sodom*) (Sigrid Monleón, 2009).

SPANISH CRITICAL PRECEDENTS: REPRESENTING SPANISH QUEER ON SCREEN

In his book, Melero (2010) works with the reasonable enough traditional assumption of cinema being an agent for change and as a mirror on the Spain of its time, albeit an unfaithful one (12). Asserting the importance of the films of the Transition to Democracy to an understanding of 'los discursos cinematográficos actuales' ('present-day film-making practice and theory') (268), he establishes a line of inheritance which can serve as a reminder of the political and personal struggles of a generation (268), and in particular of lesbians and gays. Some of the bitter-sweet pleasures to be found in rewatching the films and reviewing the cultural history of this period are, the book implies, liberating in a sexual political sense. The issue-based films, or sub-plots of films, to be discussed in the coming chapters bear witness strongly to this legacy of political awareness, some, like *Spinnin'* (see Chapter 1), matching a lightly radical aesthetic to their problem-packed plots and storylines, others aspiring to be neat and well-made films of a traditional cut but with a dissident import to one degree or another. Some examples of newer films that end up foregrounding a certain pastness while also making images of urgency and immediacy are: *Krámpack* (*Nico and Dani*) (Cesc Gay, 2000) which addresses teenage sexuality with potential disruptive intensity and good humour but which is also restricted by being a vintage coming-of-age drama; *Eloïse* (Jesús

Garay, 2009) which highlights urgent and radical concerns with lesbophobia, internalised and social, and dangerous mother–daughter dynamics, but which parks its proto-lesbian protagonist in a conventional side-drama of flashback narration from the comatose, and easily scripted, point of view of a hospital bed; or *El dios de madera* (The Wooden God) (Vicente Molina Foix, 2010) which considers immigration from Africa, the sexuality of older women, online virtual transsexualism and the sensibility of the younger gay man adrift but is essentially a human-interest narrative in three acts. In the short films too (and in at least one documentary already discussed – *Campillo sí, quiero*) there is frequently a mix of conventional structuring (including the structuring of concepts) with anti-normative actions, motivations or declarations and dialogue. Examples are: *A oscuras* (In the Dark) (Eli Navarro, 2009) which uses the double convention of the power cut and confined spaces to spring secrets and confessions; and *Yo sólo miro* (I Only Watch) (Gorka Cornejo, 2008) which like many short films relies on a late-reveal twist, switching from a brutal focus on deception by a closeted husband in a heterosexual marriage (in a way a staple tale) to an unusual exploration of vicariousness, substitution and desolation as elements in his wife's sexuality.

However, the short films also attest to an active legacy of politicised image- and story-making which can often escape the twin demands of commercial viability and generic conformity. In them we can trace some of the ways in which certain tendencies or directors in the cinema of the Transition (Melero's key case is Eloy de la Iglesia – 2010: 222–62) took up the early gay and lesbian movement's insistence on 'la educación y el didacticismo, la búsqueda de un espacio político y la representación positiva de las minorías sexuales' (220) ('education and didactic content – the search for a new political space and for positive representation of sexual minorities').

For Melero, de la Iglesia's films are not only a break with the past of cinematic practice (at least in terms of narrative) but an unfolding manifesto of resistance and refusal. He draws attention to the new narrative and imagistic practices of the times, and to the militant, resistant or progressively didactic import of certain modes of film-making. These films are pioneering in showing the (fictionalised) lives of sexual minorities in completely different ways than had been possible up to that time in Spain and by constituting a new sexual politics through film narrative (262). Similar ideas had also been explored by Smith (1992: 129–62), Tropiano (1997) and Ballesteros (2001: 92–110), and they chime with Mira's subsequent extension (2008) to Spanish audiences of the notion of the *mirada insumisa* (the dissident gaze, or the look that will not be outstared). Esteban (1999a) notes that the films of the Transition might appear outdated to current Spanish audiences but from an outside perspective (in this case, from the Thirteenth Tokyo International Gay Film Festival's Spanish retrospective) may be recognised as examples of 'cine aperturista, arriesgado y transgresor' (70) ('opening up new debates, daring and transgressive'). By moving outside the commercial sphere too, the more experimental film-makers such as Juanma Carrillo and Rut Suso (see Chapter 4) exhibit this mix of qualities, as do those deploying uncompromising narratives to make visible (rather than to normalise) aspects of LGBTQ experience, such as Antonio Hens or Blanca H. Salazar in the satirical *Bañophobia* (Fear of the Ladies) (2009).

Complementing and expanding upon work already done by Alfeo Álvarez (1999, 2001, 2003 [1997]), Melero (2010) explores the ways in which the sudden easing up of control over the cinematic image in the context of an 'explosión de liberaciones' (12) ('a surge of liberalisation') inflected the politics of representation and the sexual politics of Spanish cinema. His study focuses on the oddly overlooked fact of the high visibility – saturation, indeed, in certain sub-genres – of 'personajes gays y lesbianas' (84) ('gay and lesbian characters') in the popular cinema of the time. These are the (not so) hidden pleasures of a proto-queer, marginal and marginalised tradition.

Over these films and their audiences, however, sits the shadow of reactionary practices, attitudes and modes of representation. Melero sees it cast across the screen well into the late 1970s and early 1980s (2010: 125, 146–54, 267); there are strong connections to the formalised censorship of pre-Transition Spain (Mira 2008: 55–62) and to habits of self-censorship and market-led expectations of veiled, discreet presentations of homosexuality (63–94). Melero, then, traces the persistence through the Transition of institutional and popular notions of homosexuality as more or less mildly grotesque and as inferior, and of gay characters presented according to type and stereotype (as comic figure, as sad, as lonely, as strange and other – particularly in the films of Mariano Ozores (Melero 2010: 127–80). Spain's contribution to mid-twentieth-century World Cinema's 'representación de la homosexualidad como drama terrible' (182) ('representation of homosexuality as something terrible and dramatic') is linked both to the wider industry's pre-1970s traditions (cf. Mira 2008: 65–83) and to the legal and medical discourses of later the later Franco years, Melero argues.

Dealing with lesbianism on film, in research developed more or less in chronological parallel to Melero's, Pelayo (2009) works with the same historical context for part of her study. Her thesis looks at the representation of lesbianism through the lens of character presentation in twenty-two feature films, four of them in the period under discussion here. (A complementary listing, including co-productions involving Spain, is given in González 2011: 226.) Pelayo adapts Alfeo Álvarez's scheme of modalities of representation: hidden (replaced for Pelayo's purposes by 'erotic' and designed for the heterosexual male gaze), committed, incidental and integrated (Alfeo Álvarez 1999, 2001, 2003). She suggests that there is a consistent pattern or sensibility (2009: 29–148) among those making these films (men in all but four cases). She identifies certain constants in a specifically Spanish filmic representation of lesbianism during the period: lesbian protagonists tend to be single and between nineteen and thirty years old; they look and act conventionally femme (to the exclusion of other stereotypical representations or classifications); they have only loosely identifiable family ties; and their lesbianism has little resonance beyond the personal and is defined by individual or interpersonal actions rather than in relation to the social milieu or by a particular look. There is little sense of any process of identity construction; coming out produces conflict in public but acceptance in private in all but two of the films; the context of lesbian experience tends to be domestic or indoors; and relationships tend to be long-lasting and tied to the everyday (297–310). Unsurprisingly, there are two discernible phases in which at first, up to 1986, lesbian protagonists are vulnerable and misunderstood victims but are subsequently more empowered, albeit within restricted parameters. Whereas the four modes of hidden, committed, incidental and integrated representation correspond roughly, and in sequence, to a historical chronology running from late Francoism to 1986, in the lesbian case the modes (with the first replaced by the erotic) are achronological and may overlap (although the erotic mode is focused particularly on the period 1977–82, the boom years of *destape* or tops-off cinema). Indeed, in at least one case, the short *Sombras en el viento* (*Shadows in the Wind*) (Julia Guillén Creach, 2009), the equation of lesbianism, glamour, the literary past and slow and swooning death carefully cross-stitches several of the more restrictive modes and phases.

COMEDY

For Melero, in this strand of queer film history in Spain, there is not so much overlap as an undertow of continuity. Output such as that of Ignacio F. Iquino's 'es un eslabón más en la cadena de discursos antiguos' (2010: 125) ('is one more link in the chain of old-style discourses') and highlights more generally 'los contenidos reaccionarios de la ola erótica de los setenta' (109) ('the reactionary content of the rising tide of erotic films of the 1970s'). His discussion of the *comedia de mariquitas* (comedies with gay characters as the source or target of humour) (127–80) includes an analysis of the box-office hit *No desearás al vecino del quinto* (Thou Shalt Not Covet Thy Fifth-Floor Neighbour) (Ramón Fernández, 1970) which adapts the old burlesque of the man who pretends to be a woman to get his girl to a newer one of the man who pretend to be gay to the same end. As Melero notes (129), the film was only shifted from its position as the most viewed Spanish film in 1998, and the persistence of the motif is such that Jorge Sanz – see Chapter 3 – is able to give the cliché one more twist and pretend to be lesbian to get his girl in the Spanish-Argentine co-production *Almejas y mejillones* (Mussels and Cockles) (Marcos Carnevale) in a film released in 2000. Melero's analysis includes the necessary reminder that the laughter in cases such as these was expected, precisely, of a non-gay audience (160) and poses the interesting question of whether, if the comedy is based on the well-known distancing effect (to laugh and to stand back from the humorous event or personage are concomitant) (157–60), then how might it work for an audience or spectator which, precisely because they were gay, could not or cannot stand back (160)?

Playing – whether intentionally or not – with 'contenidos reaccionarios' (109) ('reactionary content') and a dependency on old modes of comic effect, several of the commercially oriented gay- and, less often, lesbian-themed feature films that continue to be popular into the twenty-first century bring this question to the fore once more. As Drake (2003) reminds us, in relation to 1990s Hollywood retro, 'the styles of the past provide a powerful means' of branding and marketing (184). The gay man as effeminate or closeted, as a chaotic spectacle, as entertainingly promiscuous; secret or unexpected attraction between men or between women as a key element in semi-farcical comedy screen business; self-deprecating lesbians not taking themselves seriously to a wryly humorous extent; homophobic jokes presented as just jokes or amusing plays on words: these are surprisingly prominent motifs, giving these quite recent films a thematic and ideological pastness. The 'styles of the past' are also clearly intended, in LGBT contexts, to confer on a certain audience – one that cannot stand back, in Melero's terms – some sense of belonging, community or empathy at least. García Rodríguez's review (2008: 331–9) of the 1980s and 1990s carries forward one strand of Melero's work and places in the category of 'gayxploitation', in imitation of select North American and Western European box-office successes (331, 335), *Más que amor frenesí* (*More Than Love, Frenzy*) (Alfonso Albacete, David Menkes and Miguel Bardem, 1995), *Las cosas del querer II* (*The Things of Love II*) (Jaime Chavarri, 1994) and *Perdona bonita, pero Lucas me quería a mí* (Excuse Me Darling, But Lucas Was in Love With *Me!*) (Dunia Ayaso and Félix Sabroso, 1997).

The effect of these entertainments is not unequivocally pernicious (Fouz-Hernández and Perriam 2007) and they can make a serious contribution to visibility (while, however, not necessarily guiding the eye to any harder truths). However, *Reinas* (see Chapter 1), *A mi madre le gustan las mujeres* (*My Mother Likes Women*) (Inés París and Daniela Fejerman, 2002) and *Los dos lados de la cama* (*Both Sides of the Bed*) (Emilio Martínez Lázaro, 2005) (both discussed by Pelayo and also by González 2012; also see Chapters 3 and 4), *Chuecatown* (*Boystown*) (Juan Flahn, 2007) and *Los novios búlgaros* (see Chapters 3 and 5) all at some stage become caught up in a dependence on the simple humour of transgression. They may not look like retro films – and all but the last of those just cited would not wish to do so – but their sense of humour and their key scenarios '[mobilise] particular codes that have come to connote past sensibility', as Drake puts it (2003: 188), 'as it is selectively re-remembered in the present.' This mobilisation is matched or exacerbated, at the extra-filmic level, by a commercial aversion to risk and innovation. Although *A mi madre le gustan las mujeres* is in many ways affirmative and amusingly no-nonsense, and despite the politically attuned Mostra Lambda's 2005 award for *Los dos lados de la cama* with its almost complete 'flooding' of its prequel's plot with homosexuality, even these films lack edge (García Rodríguez 2008:

420). Neither the directness of narrative treatment (the making visible of the lesbian and gay, in other words), nor the pleasant surprise of the presence of actors with perfectly un-queer career associations, nor the destabilising effect of the better gags, can guarantee queer acuity. Just as manifest in the Spanish films as they are transnationally are the following features: the stock tactic of light normalisation whereby the dilemmas of the LGBT character are no more than amplifications or, indeed, ludicrously minor reflections of heterosexual experience; stereotypical linkages (homosexuality with sadness or badness or madness); and familiar takes on socialisation and identity formation.

There is also occasional transfer of this mode of humour and the accompanying social thematics across into short-film production, where it might be expected that the twin jokes of normalisation and knowing deprecation (as of the zany gay, trans as a manic state or the stern lesbian), or recourse to familiar tragicomic tropes, might well need a different spin. They do get this, but in varying degrees. So, *Mariquita con perro* (Queen with Dog) (Vicente Villanueva, 2007; web presence only, but with 22,895 YouTube viewings as at 15 February 2012) is a riff on the comic stereotype of the evil queen (as Bad Woman) but which is partially saved from lack of originality by a sharp ironic treatment. The oblivious narrator-protagonist falls from the bitchy grace of the well-paid fashionista, through career and emotional mayhem and a knifing, and on into the banality of days filled with chit-chat exchanged with dog walkers in the park. *Los requisitos de Nati* (Nati's Requirements) (Roberto Castón, 2007) is shot as a shaky online dating video by a bisexual woman in search of Madonna or Antonio Banderas look-alikes and in denial of a past full of emotional 'malos rollos' ('bad situations') including a boyfriend stolen from her by her brother (and the two now settling down with children). Here, a wild, throwaway manner with poor-taste clichés (for example, about queers and cunnilingus) chaotically spices up what is otherwise just comfortable, reactionary camp cliché (hingeing on the supposed sadness of the single woman – and the single bisexual). In *Luz* (Pablo Aragüés, 2011), the lesbian vampire gets a semi-comic comeback (see also Chapter 4 on this film) and the women are so stern and focused that they bite. In *Terapia de choque* (Shock Therapy) (Salva Cortés, 2010), winner of the audience prize at La Pecca, Seville, 2010, a mother, hell-bent on preventing the same-sex marriage of her son, locks him up in a hotel room and forces a (female) prostitute on him, having also signed him up for football training, cancelled his gym membership and arranged for a removals firm to get him out of his Chueca flat. She is concerned about 'esa gente tan rara que va y viene todo el rato por la calle' ('all these strange-looking people wandering up and down outside all the time'), and wonders '¿qué busca, qué hace esa gente? ¿a qué se dedica?' ('what are they after? what do they do for a living?'). Recourse to the caricatured strong, conservative mother and to the reflexive flagging of the characteristics of the metropolitan gay man – nearly always considered lightly amusing (as in *Will and Grace*, NBC, 1998–2006; and in Spain 2003–8, various channels) – is countered by a well-founded and professionally crafted satire on ultra-conservative thinking around sexuality as susceptible to conversion, and on the barely suppressed tide at the time of the making and festival release of the film of anti-same-sex marriage discourse from the right in Spain.

In the integrated mode of representation, according to the taxonomy favoured by Pelayo (after Alfeo Álvarez 1999, 2003) homosexuality is represented as an integral or amalgamated part of a polymorphic range of variations in human sexuality and the lesbian identity of the protagonist is neither differentiated from the identity formation of other characters nor carries with it any sense of blame or shame (Pelayo 2009: 50; also Alfeo Álvarez 2001: 144). Apparent non-differentiation of this sort, along with a kind of flagrant blameless-ness, is the mainstay of a series of films of the 1990s (Fouz-Hernández and Perriam 2007; Martínez-Expósito 2004: 241–7; Mira 2004: 593–6), including serious dramatic treatments in the Argentine-Spanish *Martín (Hache)* (Adolfo Aristarain, 1997), in the Catalan *Carícies (Caresses)* (Ventura Pons, 1998) and, in the character of Diego (only), *Segunda piel (Second Skin)* (Gerardo Vera, 1999), and in entertainments such as *Amor de hombre (The Love of a Man)* (Yolanda García Serrano and Juan Luis Iborra, 1997) and *Más que amor frenesí*. Three films with lesbian characters in this mode are listed by Pelayo, all of them of the post-1998 period: *En la ciudad/A la ciutat (In the City)* (Cesc Gay, 2003), *Los dos lados de la cama* (although in these two films, I would argue, 'integration' is incoherent and illusory, whereas differentiation is strongly marked) and *Todo me pasa a mí (Everything Happens to Me)* (Miguel García Borda, 2001), a would-be zany comedy whose interest in the lesbian Aina's (Cristina Brondo) discovery of heterosexuality might be queer were it not for the reinscription of her lesbianism as, basically, a temporary mistake or stop-gap.

In this film's first minutes (in its second sequence) Aina and her girlfriend Txell (Lola Dueñas) have already been regaled with corny straight advice in light comedy mode from the woman in the local fruit shop: no matter how liberal a woman you are, she assures them, you need a man. This textbook feisty and sympathetic folk-comic character's greeting of the two of them as 'pareja' is more as 'the twins' than as a couple and anticipates the scenario described by Pelayo whereby Aina and Txell are out at home and to friends but not in public (2009: 114). Interestingly, lesbian visibility – of which this film has plenty – runs counter to integration in Alfeo Álvarez's and Pelayo's sense. Aina and Txell soon shift from being emphatically visible to being merely incidental, in Pelayo's sense. In this mode, lesbianism is a minor plot element, or an inferred characteristic or somehow even just a lifestyle 'choice' (Pelayo 2009: 48). Not so visible – though far more obvious – are the contrasting, closeted feelings (115–16) of their friends and neighbours, Edu (a died-blonde

Jordi Collet) and Ángel (Javier Albalá, with a famous gay sex scene in *Más que amor frenesí* as precedent). Their anxious – and farcical – tiptoeing in the dark on the beach at night around not saying anything about their feelings for men (in Edu's case generally, although he denies it) or for one another (more exclusively in Ángel's case) immediately follows a colourful and brightly lit scene between Aina and Txell where they break up articulately and more or less honestly. The shame and conflictedness stays with the men, in their non-integrated homoeroticism; lesbianism has its moment of integration (paradoxically threatened by visibility) only when the lesbian relationship is terminated. Weighing down on these scenes of potentially open integration is the force of normalising reintegration into the heterosexist plot. In the end, it is questionable whether this mode of characterisation and of emplotting the lesbian speaks to the queerly attuned lesbian audience in terms other than those of reinscription, in cautionary tones, that is. Along with the more numerous representations of the integrated, but borderline incidental, gay male in the plots of Spanish films of the 1990s, these images prove to be an ambivalent recent legacy, one in which 'encontramos homosexuales ya hechos, dotados de una sexualidad casi sin fisuras, sin dudas, sin evolución, testigos de un mundo en el que al parecer existen acuerdos unánimes sobre qué es y cómo se es homosexual' (Martínez-Expósito 2004: 246) ('we find ready-made homosexuals whose sexuality is seamless, untroubled by doubts or outcomes, and who live in a world where there seems to be unanimous agreement as to what homosexuality is and in what ways one is or is not homosexual').

Some of the problems with the 'integrated mode', and with lesbian and gay visibility on screen when deployed as such and for its own sake, are the old, persistent problems of affirmation cinema (Dyer 1990: 274–86) – forgetful as it can be of real conflict within LBGT experience, and essentialist (274, 275) – and of positive images (Becker et al. 1981) (versions of which, as we shall see, continue to be ephemeral favourites at the festivals as well as with more commercial enterprises). Positive images, historically, have been forged as a set of tactics around identity politics 'stem[ming] from a political tradition of individualism, pluralism, and liberal democracy' and may be credited with mass appeal among lesbian and gay audiences (Waugh 2000: 183, 267). The riskily context-specific and relative status of the term 'positive' and its implication of a 'naive commitment to absolute value and essential identity' (Henderson 2008: 134), these haunt, but do not necessarily overwhelm, the continuing Spanish recourse to 'visibility'. These considerations of limitation may also apply to the committed or affirmative mode ('modalidad reivindicativa'), where lesbianism is central to plot, unequivocally visible and not for the male gaze, has reference to the construction of a collective lesbian identity, and (more questionably included in this mode) comes out of a failed heterosexual relationship (Pelayo 2009: 43–7). Two of the films placed by Pelayo in this mode fall into the post-1998 period: *A mi madre le gustan las mujeres* (see Chapter 3) and *Sévigné (Júlia Berkowitz)* (Marta Balletbò-Coll, 2004). The first of these certainly has widespread appeal and critical coverage (as will be seen later); the second is probably less seen – with a roughly indicative mere 7,600 tickets sold (MECD 2012), but still in DVD distribution in 2012 – but it has more to say about visibility.

Sévigné plots the interrelated development of a script for a play based on the letters of Marie de Rabutin-Chantal, Marquise de Sévigné, (1626–96) to her daughter, the Comtesse de Grignan, and the non-sexually erotic relationship that builds between the play's artistic director (Júlia Berkowitz, played by Anna Azcona) and Marina Ferrer (Marta Balletbò-Coll), whose brainchild the adaptation is and whose erratic but obsessive energies lead her to present the proposal. Júlia is primarily heterosexually identified (complete with overbearing, intellectual, weary *machista* husband and fresh, handsome young colleague-lover). Marta is, in an asexual and comically endearing manner, more or less lesbian. Of her one previous big affairs – to the now married and with children American Joanne (Leslie Charles) – she says 'I think I blew [it]'. Her crush on Júlia and their joint interest in the nature of the love underlying the Sévigné letters are patent; so too is her otherness in the eyes of her mother, who makes a tacit analogy between her lesbianism and the theatre during a conversation at home about womanliness and normal life: 'ès un mon fals; i . . . no ès per a nosaltres' ('it's a false world . . . : not for the likes of us'). It is, though, the theatrical project and the bringing into voiced drama of the intense seventeenth-century exchange between two women that gives a textured structure to the representation here of love between women as curative and cathartic (Pelayo 2009: 125–6). Although it is Júlia's husband, Gerardo (Josep Maria Pou), who has the outer frame of voice-over narration in a pompous critical account of the significance of theatre and this film's story, Marta's own variably eccentric, forceful, tentative and purposeful voice-over supplies the central tone and perspective. The audience is kept attuned to the unconventional by a disruptive editing style – almost certainly a happy side-effect of the compressed shooting schedule noted by Pelayo (2009: 124) – with jump cuts, asynchronous sound bridges and strange dissolves mixed with an overall hand-held, realist mode. The film has a queer look, an odd reflexive take on bonding between women, a smart way with the emotional configuration of undeclared regret, misdirection and also a kind of cheerful acceptance of otherness.

Balletbò-Coll's *Costa Brava (Family Album)* (1994), despite its initial recording in English, had already become a well-known milestone in the history of entertaining lesbian cinema in Spain (Pelayo 2009: 108), 'lo más parecido al cine queer en España' (García Rodríguez 2008: 332) ('the closest one can get to queer cinema in Spain'). It was also one, as Fernàndez suggests (2000d), that cross-inscribed the stories of Catalan national identity and those of incipient lesbianism (395), presenting Catalan identity to an international audience through a lesbian point of view (404).The film was followed (and, in terms of distribution, overtaken) by *Gazon maudit (French Twist)* (1995), in which one of Spanish cinema's most prominent stars, Victoria Abril, plays a role where lesbianism is an unambiguous central plot motivator (Waldron 2001: 65). Balletbò-Coll directs the attention of her international queer audience towards the homophobic stereotyping of lesbianism (Hayward 1998: 133) and Abril's character and performance become the problematising meeting point of some destabilising questions around bisexuality, bilingualism and bilocationality (Waldron 2001: 68–9). She allows the film to play up, in a self-aware manner, stereotypical notions of Spanish culture's relative superiority in matters of passion and vitality (Perriam 2007a: 31–4). As an ambivalent embodiment of pastness and dissidence – to anticipate my discussion of her in Chapter 3 – she becomes a Trojan horse of anti-heteronormative disruption on Spanish screens.

Abril carries forward in her career a series of highly visible, sexualised, dramatic negotiations of the borderlines between the nostalgic-reactionary and proleptic-progressive. That pivotal moment of working with Balletbò-Coll, whose own work so much counters pervading assumptions of hiddenness, invisibility and lack of awareness of the lesbian (as summarised in Vosburg and Collins 2011a), is one case among several where actors' careers have seen them take on roles within different modes of representation of LGB experience in ways which map or condense the trajectories from exploitative typification and denigration to the creative construction of new spaces in which to represent and perform queerer identities and actions. Eusebio Poncela, through his work with Pedro Almodóvar and Ventura Pons, is another such case, and I shall also come back to him in the next chapter. Jordi Mollà too, with a career taking off some ten years later than Abril's and two decades on from Poncela, has traversed the modes, playing both liberated and repressed, both conventional, apolitical gay and queer (Perriam 2003a: 121–44; also Chapter 5). It as if the uncertainties and many directions of the 1970s and 1980s in Spain keep returning to the surface of these actors' bodies and keep returning to the texture of the narratives of the films of the later, politically less closed-in years.

COMING OUT AND SELF-DISCOVERY

In a discussion of *Los claros motivos del deseo* (The Clear Motives of Desire) (Miguel Picazo, 1977), Melero identifies the beginnings of 'lo que hoy es todo un subgénero del cine gay' ('what is today a fully fledged sub-genre in gay cinema'), the sexual self-discovery film (2010: 192), also the related and equally pervasive sub-genre the Coming Out Story. Both these have, of course, international inheritances to draw upon, and both have had their heydays of high-profile affirmation. Mira (2008) reminds his Spanish readers that gay films of the 1980s had been dominated by this theme (483) but that by the end of the 1990s 'había ya una cantidad sustancial de referentes que podían simplificar el proceso de autoaceptación' ('there were by then substantial points of reference to make the process of self-acceptance easier') (483). More inventive, often comic, modes of treating the topic were being turned to (484–6).[2] Alfeo Álvarez et al. (2011), with their focus on adolescence on screen, offer evidence of a diversity and complexity of characterisation, semiotic deployment and context which sets Spain apart from other (unspecified) traditions of filmic and televisual representation (10, 14). Their arguments lie substantially in the pre-1998 period, but their later examples are: *Pajarico* (Carlos Saura, 1998) which, they argue, shows a change in hegemonic views of homosexuality when its adolescent protagonist witnesses a primal scene of male same-sex sex involving his father as just another, if powerful, part of growing up (34); *Krámpack*; *Food of love* (Spanish title *Manjar de amor*) (Ventura Pons, 2002) and *Clandestinos* (*In Hiding*) (Antonio Hens, 2007) both of which, very differently, present teenagers who are at ease with their queer sexuality and able to negotiate power relations with older men; *El Calentito* (Chus Gutiérrez, 2005), where young lesbian love is unhindered by the need to justify itself (Alfeo Álvarez et al. 2011: 44); and *Mentiras y gordas* (*Sex, Party and Lies*) (Alfonso Albacete and David Menkes, 2009), which is less dense and coherent, and more melodramatic, in its treatment of the gay teenager than the other examples (46) but on the lesbian couple more articulate (46–7). However, the standard coming-out narreme persists in Spain as also does a concern to explore, as if anew, the intricacies and dilemmas of self-acceptance or denial. *Mentiras y gordas* – for all its apparent attention to the protean, 'fluid' qualities of teenage sexuality (Alfeo Álvarez et al. 2011: 51–2) – runs conventionally through the looking-for-identity and looking-for-love story in what is a sparky enough new homage to an old-established tradition. More famously, and with more agility, *Krámpack* works over similar ground, even though it eschews the drama of guilt and secrecy of earlier years and other cinematic traditions in favour of 'una representación natural y fresca de la adolescencia gay' (Alfeo Álvarez et al. 2011: 40) ('a fresh, natural representation of gay adolescence').

The coming out and the self-discovery stories are as perennial in Spanish LGBT festivals and as apparently popular (at least with selection juries) as elsewhere. The TVE-sponsored film-school (ECAM) exhibition short *Cara o cruz* (Heads or Tails) (Jacobo Echevarría, 2008) makes deft use of the image of a tossed coin to denote a kind of elated and yet fearful indecision (see Figure 6). While Jota stolidly thinks that the flips of the coin are to help Javi decide his future or to dare each other to go and chat up the girls in the park, Javi (who is certainly no good at the latter activity) has more invested in the moments of suspense between them. With 3,041 views on YouTube and 8,563 views on Dailymotion (as at 1 March 2012), this is a much watched, stylishly framed exploration of the half-spoken answer to the question 'y ¿tú y yo?' ('and what about you and me?'), with something of the look, feel and dramatic-didactic intentions in miniature of *Beautiful Thing* (Hettie Macdonald, 1996). A smart, no-nonsense lesbian version of this set-up is *Lo que nunca te dije* (What I Never Told You) (Carlos Gómez Baker, 2010) in which Pache, having rehearsed all the preparatory discursive moves (over less than four minutes),

Figure 6 Javi (Adrián Marín) and Jota (Alejandro Parra) in *Cara o cruz* (Jacobo Echeverría, 2008). Screen grab reproduced with kind permission of Ismael Martín for the Escuela de Cinematografía y del Audiovisual de la Comunidad de Madrid (ECAM).

saves her best friend Andrea the discomfort of her revelation with a comically but poignantly flat observation (of the view over the river basin from San Juan de Aznalfarache, Seville) that 'es un sitio bonito, ¿no?' ('it's a nice spot, isn't it?'). Another short, *A los que gritan* (*Sara's Shout* [or, To Those Who Shout Insults]) (Juanan Martínez, 2010) brings coming out to the family table, propelled by the necessity provoked by public lesbophobia (see Chapter 4). *Todo me pasa a mí* takes the story into twenty- and thirty-something territory, as does, for lesbian coming out in a side-plot, *El sueño de Ibiza* (Igor Fioravanti 2001). Cesc Gay's *En la ciudad* and the films of Ventura Pons (see Chapter 3) explore intensively the identity-based problems of older generations. Finally, this same narrative inheritance is still depended upon, albeit subversively, in the much-circulated short *En malas compañías* (*Doors Cut Down* [or, Keeping Bad Company]) (Antonio Hens, 2000).

ALMODÓVAR

So far I have looked at the concept of legacy in the following ways: from the perspectives of critical categories (modalities and frameworks of representation); through the crossing paths of one woman actor and one woman director and, briefly, in the mixed trajectories of a handful of men on screen; and through the reiteration of the revelation-and-discovery narreme as a piece of handed-down content. A more conventional, but problematically linear and hierarchising, way of mapping the legacy of the last thirty or so years of the twentieth century in Spanish culture would have been to look more for land-mark films and directors. To the pioneering sexual politics of Eloy de la Iglesia or to Jaime Chavarri's look into an even older heritage in his exploration of the problem of queer bad faith in *A un dios desconocido* (*To An Unknown God*) (1977) could be added a number of aesthetic or thematic precursors to the post-1998 queer cinema. These would include Ventura Pons's *Ocaña, retrat intermitent* (*Ocaña, An Intermittent Portrait*) (1978), Iván Zulueta's *Arrebato* (*Rapture*) (1980),[3] Agustí Villaronga's *Tras el cristal* (*In a Glass Cage*) (1987) and, not least in terms of fame, the early films of Pedro Almodóvar, on whom I will, indeed, now pause (and also return to in Chapter 3).

Mira (2008: 320–2) sets his discussion of Almodóvar and the question of a gay aesthetic in the familiar context of the director's connections to the Madrid *movida*, the alternative, cultural aggregation of interventions (rather than a movement) which is associated with the early 1980s phase of the Transition (see also Aguado 2009; Allinson 2001; Pérez-Sánchez 2007: 143–86; Smith 2000a: 13–20, 33–4). His strategic use, in these early years, of camp and parody (Mira 2008: 416–17), his appeal to 'the queer-coded registers of kitsch and camp' (Smith 2000a: 2) and his frequently eroticised visual and narrative shock tactics place him alongside (or on the other side of the coin of) de la Iglesia in contributing to the timely, and revolutionary, revelation of 'the unaccustomed power of sex and politics – of sex in politics – in a young democracy' (Smith 2011: 37). The pioneering qualities of *La ley del deseo* (*Law of Desire*) (1987) as marking 'un punto y aparte en lo que a homosexu-alidad y cine en España se refiere' (Esteban 1999b: 70) ('the turning of a new page as far as homosexuality and cinema in Spain are concerned') are well documented (as summarised in Fouz-Hernández and Perriam 2007: 63–5). A recent semi-popularising, though theoretically aware, guide recapitulates the case by conjoining the film's unusual openness in depicting gay experience – or its 'explicitud y sinceridad' (García Rodríguez 2008: 259) ('explicitness and sincerity') – with its rejection of rigid notions of identity (Palencia 2011: 137), and drawing attention to the tension between 'lo *queer*' and 'lo no-*queer*' (136) and to the theatrical trying out of identities (138).

The semi-self-reflexive gesture in *La ley del deseo* of having a film director protagonist (Pablo, played by Eusebio Poncela) as the focus of a queer obses-sion (emanating from Antonio, played by Antonio Banderas) and as a member of a queer alternative family – with 'a glamorous transsexual sister, Tina (Carmen Maura), whose name mimics that of Almodóvar's own . . . brother and business partner' (Smith 2000a: 79) – amplifies the possibilities of iden-tification with boldly drawn characters in an exacerbated process of finding themselves (no less).

Almodóvar, as one blog (in its twenty-eight comments) emphasises, is to be recognised, thanked (Madrid 2009) and admired ('Crasamet' 2009), not only for the emotional richness of the films but also for the sheer number of differ-ent characters 'en que nos hemos mirado y reconocido' ('in whom we have seen and recognised ourselves'), and for the fact that any heterosexual audience member assuming such characters to be made up is soon disabused when the lights go up and they look around (Madrid 2009). He is noted, by these commentators, for his contribution to the making visible of LGBT people and for their integration into his narratives (their 'normalización social') ('Nazareno' 2009), although 'lol' (2009) and 'iure' (2009), at least, beg to differ. That recognition of verisimilitude and inclusion is odd, since Almodóvar is, at most, realist in patches and only renowned for shaking off labels, including that of gay film director. As if strategically wary of the problems of affirmation and positive images, Almodóvar's long cinematic project of constructing empathy for the non-normative sexual subject and the socially marginalised figure has been famously both oblique (taking some odd angles on social and personal difficulties) and extreme (variously melodramatic or hilarious, intermittently attentive to people and issues habitually ignored in Spanish mid to high culture and yet star-struck). Overall, the result is plainly contradictory. In *Entre tinieblas* (*Dark Habits*) (1983) old habits of representation of lesbianism as seen through the male gaze and associated with blame or shame and the sensationalist pretext for the screen drama are set aside in favour of a new form of presentation (Pelayo 2009: 89). On the other hand, in a passing moment in *La ley del deseo*, just after Antonio (Antonio Banderas) has seen Pablo's (Eusebio Poncela) film, two lesbians – already, knowingly, positioned on a lower level in a bar full of men – are brushed off by Pablo, never to be seen again, and lesbianism was to wait six years in Almodóvar's filmography to surface again, in *Kika* (1993), stereotypically, and another six years, in *Todo sobre mi madre* (*All About My Mother*) (1999), movingly and dramatically, but scarcely representatively. Moreover, Almodóvar has only once returned to a more or less direct representation of the drama of male homosexuality, and that in terms both more ingeniously convoluted and yet also more textbook compliant than *La ley del deseo*.

In that film, *La mala educación* (*Bad Education*) (2004), a gay film-maker is at the centre of things, and again his conflicted feelings are mediated by a script. Enrique (Fele Martínez) is presented as somehow blank and directionless – too smooth, too successful: like Pablo – until Juan (pretending to be one Ignacio) (Gael García Bernal), brings him an idea for a script which references their schooldays and in which he wishes to play cross-dressed as Zahara, the trans performer, that the Ignacio within the script becomes. Hedged about by the film's gloriously obvious images of splitting – of identity, history and character's stories, as D'Lugo has pointed out (2006: 119–26) – and by the confusion of imposture (Juan's), Enrique is far from being an ordinary Spanish gay man or, even, an ordinary mixed-up indie or art-house director.

The film is freighted with national history in various ways. Its long gestation (Pingree 2004: 5) and a sensitivity to confessional remembering (and to the issues surrounding sexual abuse by priests) fit the cultural and political mood of the years immediately following its release, in the build-up to the 2007 Law of

Historical Memory.[4] In one way it is 'a prosopography – a collective biography for [a] country . . . asking questions about its identity' (Pingree 2004: 7), who it includes and what it means (8). Its powerful reconstructions of late childhood sentimental education in the early 1960s gives it a popular cultural seductiveness and cinephile appeal, both based on nostalgia (D'Lugo 2006: 115, 121). Moreover, the film may be read as 'a political allegory of the susceptibility [to] false nostalgia' that reveals new demons raised by the 'pervasive [reactionary] cultural processes' (and the specific political moment) of the time of its release (128; also D'Lugo 2009: 362–4, 382) – less a collective biography, more a forensic examination of a hypothetical collective confession. Its homage to, or use of, Sara Montiel, in particular, 'channels the complex dynamics of nostalgia' as well as inducing the audience to 'engage . . . in a critical interrogation of personal and collective manipulations of history and memory' (D'Lugo 2009: 361) and to rethink 'its own place in the flow of contemporary Spanish culture' (362). Such a rethink entails a queer history of seeing significance in Montiel (371–3). Her 'condition of "pastness"', through the 'privileging of anachronism as camp', becomes a cipher for the film's 'historicising project' (373). The impostor Juan, as Ignacio/Zahara, is an access point to the film's most arresting images of queerness. Both in drag and in shorts as the defrocked priest's straight-acting but seductive Lolito in the last part of the film, his presence is layered with the emotional back story. It is coherent, involving and disruptive – effects which are not due alone to García Bernal's piercing eyes and gleaming body (at one stage swimming, in the last reel doing press-ups) but to the ways in which Ignacio's (fictionalised) quest for truth and reconciliation (or revenge) and the strangely enabling authenticity of Juan's performance of Ignacio intertwine. The delicate, if melodramatic, complexity of this simultaneous re-enactment and falsification of a story of coming, painfully, to queerness (and love) is threatened by contrast with the flailing and only superficially motivated characterisation of Paca, Zahara's drag-queen accomplice, played by Javier Cámara. Cámara is also encouraged to have recourse to anachronistic stereotyping, 'channel[ing] Benny Hill' (Klemm 2009) later, in *Fuera de carta* (*Chef's Special*) (Nacho G. Velilla, 2008). His Paca is yet another in the lengthening line of comic-theatrical but smaller-than-life trans characters on the Spanish screen; whether it was Enrique or Juan or Almodóvar himself who sent his performance in such a direction, it constitutes one of those links in the chain to the repressive past that Melero identifies.

AFTERSHOCKS

In Almodóvar's film, resonances of repression in the 1960s and rebellion in the 1970s disturb and inform the repositioned queer image of the present, one in which painfully the grand ideas of transformation are all thwarted, even as they are exalted. Marín-Dòmine (2006) emphasises how two films saturated with pastness, *El mar* (*The Sea*) (Agustí Villaronga, 2000) and *En la ciudad sin límites* (*In the City Without Limits*) Antonio Hernández, 2002), deal obliquely with the 'incorporación o cristalización' ('incorporation or crystallisation') of the effects and events of the Spanish Civil War in later generations through the representation of the suffering body (paras 19 and 22). Specifically, she suggests (para. 28) that repressed homosexuality between men is, or represents itself as, an effect of the past on the body of protagonists in the narrative present. The aftershocks of conflict inform the queer present, and inflect the queer image on screen, in significant ways in these two films.

In *El mar*, Manuel Tur's (Bruno Bergonzini) erotic fixation on Andreu Ramallo (Roger Casamajor) and their eventual and fatal homosexual consummation are a consequence 'de la fascinación ejercida por [una] escena original traumática' (para. 38) ('of the fascination produced by an originary traumatic scene'), that of a brutal wartime assassination. In *En la ciudad sin límites*, Max (Fernando Fernán-Gómez) is dying of an illness whose mental effects, at least, create an analogue of the state of a once actively acknowledged homosexuality that has been subdued by family priorities for decades. In *El mar*, languishing in a tuberculosis hospital sited on Mallorca in 1946, Manuel and Andreu punish themselves, the former through extreme religious obedience and self-mortification, the latter through his disgusted and long-established acceptance of the role imposed on him by a powerful black-marketeer, that is 'a robar i esser la seva puta' ('to steal and to be your whore'). Andreu – in better shape than Manuel, markedly handsome and ostensibly straight – also tortures Manuel by teasing flirtations which he knows will be amplified by Manuel's obsessions with sin and the body. These moments he spices up and intersperses with dangerous flare-ups of contained homophobic sentiment. The drama takes place against the tonalities of white walls, sheets, faces and upper bodies – all, nonetheless, frequently spattered with blood in one of the film's most obvious visual markings of the body of the present with the ever-returning violence of the past – and against a predominant thematic of horror, death, dying and dead bodies (Marín-Dòmine 2006: paras 35–43).[5] In a wild, breathtakingly serious and affecting parody of horror scenarios combining religious mania, Satanism and pre-emptive necrophiliac fantasy, Manuel, with Ramiro having run away, *in extremis* tears down Christ on a crucifix on the wall to replace it with spreadeagled overalls impregnated with the smell of Ramiro. He rubs himself off against them salaciously but justifies the whole psychodramatic procedure in terms of having punished Satan by crucifixion. There is indeed, as Mira (2008: 496–7) notes, no wholesome, conventional self-discovery, no learning to come out and no crossing of clear lines between homosexual and heterosexual desires here. Taking to a further extreme the aesthetic of explicit sexual ecstasy in abjection of *Querelle* (Rainer Werner Fassbinder, 1982) or, later, the Argentine *Un año sin amor* (*A Year Without Love*) (Anahí Berneri, 2005), in this strand of the film Villaronga engages with 'una forma de sexualidad particularmente desestabilizante, subversiva, y, en definitiva, queer' (Martínez Pulet 2005: 214) ('a form of sexuality that is particularly destabilising, subversive and, in the end, queer'). S&M is deployed 'como metáfora política y sexual' (Martínez Pulet's subtitle) ('as political and sexual metaphor'), in a classic use of what Dyer (1990) dubs the 'Genet iconography' (99) which returns constantly to the 'trouble [predicated on] the way the whole of society has constructed sexuality' as proximate to unacceptability and bestiality (99). Ramiro murders first a cat, then his exploiter-lover, then his own inadmissible love for a younger, and even prettier, patient (who also expires). Manuel, while being violated – semi-volitionally – by Ramiro, stabs him to death, slits his own wrists and bleeds to death in the bathtub which is the sardonic false analogue for the waters of the sea that in Ramiro's own fantasy life are redemptive. There is, then, no lack of dramatic closure here. What is certainly not exhausted, though, once the film comes to a close, is the bloody flow out from and back into the violent and emotionally stunting past.

In *En la ciudad sin límites*, which on one surface reading seems to be a 'melodrama' about 'the unhealed wounds of the Civil War' (del Amo 2002: 12), the violence is more tacit and more structural, although the body still bears the marks and rehearses the pain of the past, as Marín-Dòmine argues (2006: paras 30–43). Victor (Leonardo Sbaraglia) has come to Paris from Argentina to see his father Max, who is seriously ill and part delusional – for Marín-Dòmine, wracked by the emotional work of moving beyond repressed memory (2006: paras 30–2). Max, now the head of a bourgeois family firm, has had an intense affair as a young man, sharing a modest Parisian left-bank apartment with a radical, out-gay communist exile, Rancel – now Joaquín (Alfredo Alcón) – who had taken part in resistance assignments within Franco's Spain. Max is now convinced in his sickness that he betrayed Rancel and failed to warn him against boarding a train which led to his capture; the fact is that Víctor's mother, Marie (Geraldine Chaplin), has all along been fired by jealous rage against Rancel, whom she supplanted, and the memory and mention of whom she has long been able to suppress. As I have explored at greater length elsewhere (Perriam forthcoming), Chaplin's presence heightens the storyline's thematic associations with representations on screen of the Spanish past that had used family bonds and conflicts to signal social, national and political ones and her co-star Fernando Fernán Gómez's status as an icon of Spanish cinema is a memorial in itself, recapitulating a film-cultural history of repression. Rancel's silent appearance at the graveside in the film's last moments and his gothically envisaged emergence from the dark riverside street on the night of his meeting with Víctor, as well as Geraldine Chaplin's spectral presentation of Marie, are as much a manifestation of the effects of alienation and marginalisation incurred through homophobic action as of the effects of the grief, pain and separation incurred in the political violence which is Rancel and Max's backstory. However, if Marie and the family's surveillance act as a 'repressive force' (Saenz 2009), as the persistence of heteronormativity and emotional dysfunction, Rancel/Joaquín is not only clear about his desires but is something of a forerunner of the radical queer politics of the 1980s. He confronts the family and all it represents. His life has combined uncompromising visibility (interpreted homophobically by Marie as arrogantly confrontational) with a rigorous political commitment.

A graveside reading, in Fernán Gómez's voice-over, of the text of the letter acknowledging his love that he had always meant to get to Rancel evokes an alternative image of Max's family – the children watching over the two men, naked and embracing – which at one and the same time acknowledges but exorcises the preventative power of heteronormativity. It also connects this story and this particular mode of queer communication with the generic cultural past. In the postscript to his study of epistolary fiction and queer desire, Garlinger (2005) notes how:

> The genre's formal and historical constraints enable queer desire by allowing for the intimate expression between correspondents who might not otherwise share such thoughts, but they also constrict that expression: queer mail, associated with confession and confidentiality, struggles to articulate a concept of homosexual desire not stained by stigma, shame, and guilt. (186)

Something of that stain clings to Max's unanswerable letter, but Rancel's dignified resistance to Marie goes some way towards dispelling it. As a staging of a confession the film produces and enables a discourse which can 'expose the social homophobia and psychic ambivalences around sexuality and identity that were foundational in the emergence of homosexuality as a category and with which gays and lesbians still struggle' (xv). Its expression of historicised queer desire escapes the constriction Garlinger describes; the metaphorical limitlessness of the title of the film ceases to be a cause of oppression and confusion and begins to be liberation.

Stigma, shame and guilt, as well as the violent interventions of family, state and pseudo-medical control are at the core of the story recalled for her psychiatrist by Elvira (Susi Sánchez) from her bed in hospital following her failed part in a suicide pact with her disturbed lover Pilar (Carmen Elias) in *Electroshock*. Flagged as based on real events (brought to light in a trial in Valencia in 2001: Gara 2007), this made-for-television film recounts first, with nicely observed period detail, the beginnings of their affair in 1972. Pilar, at this stage alive with sexual confidence, gently but firmly brings Elvira into intimate companionship with her. On a sunny afternoon, in a park near the school where they both teach, Pilar gives her a beautiful locket in a scene overshadowed – but as yet not overwhelmed – by the censorious gaze of old Spain surviving into the 1970s, part of a regime of vigilance explored in detail in the film's uses of space (González 2011: 240). A middle-aged, obviously married heterosexual couple peer over the hedge at the two women (as also, in the same scene, does their son, a pupil at the school) (see Figure 7). By way of a simple device of tragic

Figure 7 Elvira (Susi Sánchez) and Pilar (Carmen Elias) caught in the heterosexual gaze in *Electroshock* (Juan Carlos Claver, 2006). Screen grab reproduced with kind permission of DACSA Producciones.

inevitability, the scene of giving and acceptance explodes into a narrative of injustice and extreme lesbophobia. The head of the family who sees the shocking idyll on the grass – a military man – exerts pressure at the school. Elvira has to move on, but far worse, through the intervention of a fanatical mother (Julieta Serrano, somewhat typically cast), Pilar is taken away for corrective psychiatric treatment and internment. She is subjected to a regime of aversion therapy through the application of electric shocks through electrodes to her skull – 'no se preocupe, señorita', warns the caricatured but frightening doctor, 'le curaremos de todas sus aberraciones' ('don't worry, young lady, we will cure you of all your aberrations'). The sound of building electrical charges and discharges, and of a woman's screams, opens the film, giving it a melodramatic directness, heightening its denunciatory politics with horror and, in its first expository scene, with blood – on Elvira's hands, but obviously by redirection on Spain's and on patriarchy's hands. The neurological and psychological damage done to Pilar leads to severe depression as, once she is released, and the country has moved on into the post-Franco era, the two remake a life together; the past recursively swamps their present, however. In 1998 – with a video suicide note to her mother, but more widely urging that no such suffering be allowed again – Pilar throws herself on a knife that she has thrust into Elvira's hands.

Representing Older Lesbians and Gay Men

Representations of older LGBT subjects in Spanish (as in most) cinema are scarce, but not always as harrowing in their stories of growing older as in *Electroshock*. Pelayo's tabulation of characters' ages in her 1972–2005 range of films counts only two in the age range 51 and above (2009: 325); Alfeo Álvarez's researches on the representation of the male homosexual in films released 1961–95 show only 4.17 per cent of characters in the same range ([1997] 2003: 138). More recently, the older, or older-looking, men in the otherwise strenuously modern corpus of films by Ventura Pons are constructed (perhaps because of the dramatic and literary sources from which they are drawn) as in extreme middle-age and middle-class crisis. In this mould are the well-heeled, rent boy-using Santi in *Barcelona, un mapa* (*Barcelona – A Map*) (Ventura Pons, 2007), or Jaume in *Amic-Amat* (*Beloved-Friend*) (see Chapter 3). In the bitter-sweet *Nacidas para sufrir* (see Chapter 1), Flora (Petra Martínez) thinks she is making a wily (same-sex) marriage of convenience but gets entrammeled not only by her own denial of her feelings but by a fear of village hearsay and by old-fashioned biological family cupidity. The documentary *El muro rosa* (The Pink Wall) (Enrique del Pozo and Julián Lara, 2011) collects together the testimonies on living under Francoism and through the Transition of older activists, ex-activists and cultural figures (including Mili Hernández and Eduardo Mendicutti) (see Chapters 1 and 5), with some echoes of the thematics of *Electroshock*. The short *Almas perdidas* (see Chapter 1) encapsulates in music and flashback the quandaries and loneliness of the older gay male (and, indeed, his younger self) in a small community, and at the end of *Tú eliges* (It's Your Choice) (Antonia San Juan, 2009) Rosa (Antonia San Juan) is left melodramatically isolated by age (and the script). Such images are never too far removed from that 'herencia de congoja y pesimismo' ('inheritance of sharp anxiety and pessimism') that Melero (2010: 204) sees in Jaime Chavarri's *A un dios desconocido* (1977), which is, indeed, one of the gloomiest, though most thoughtful, representations in Spanish cinema of the loneliness caused by the generational gap between lovers or between the enunciating queer voice and its audiences.

Reporting on the showing of the Basque film *Ander* (Roberto Castón, 2009) at the 2009 Berlinale (the event's first Basque dialogue work, indeed), Müller (2009) opens his piece with a telling understatement that it 'trata del tema homosexual en el inusual escenario del caserío vasco' ('deals with the homosexual question in the unusual setting of a Basque farmhouse'). This sense of the unusual is shared by Belinchón (2010) and repeated as an easy journalistic hook in several comments on the film. Though set far from the coastal, urban, bourgeois setting of *La muerte de Mikel* (*The Death of Mikel*) (Imanol Uribe, 1984) – Basque cinema's other notable treatment of the 'homosexual question', of closetry and family – the spaces through which the eponymous Ander (Joxean Bengoetxea) carries his personal drama are emphatically recognisable for those in tune with Spanish cinematic, literary and theatre history. The film opens and closes with the extended static shot of a farmhouse silent in the dark, the rain shining on its sturdy stone walls (a striking image of the building is on the front of the press pack) (Ander 2009). Inside, for the half of the film in which she still survives her heart disease, a stern mother jealously controls her adult son and the stifling, meagre rituals of the kitchen table are dramatically deployed. In part as a correlative to the bright, shy smile of the handsome, young, Peruvian-immigrant farmhand Jose (Christian Esquivel) – taken on after Ander breaks his ankle, much to the xenophobic dismay of the mother – the hill farm landscapes of deep vistas, lush pasture, cows and their tinkling bells, sunshine and scudding clouds all lift the film while grounding it in its own pictorial tradition. There are echoes of the look and conflicted family stories of Julio Medem's *Vacas* (*Cows*) (1992), Jose Luis Borau's *Furtivos* (*Poachers*) (1975) (set, though not entirely filmed, in the Navarra woodlands) and of the writers Pío Baroja (1872–1956) and Bernardo Atxaga (b. 1951). More distantly echoed too are Saura's *Cría cuervos* (*Raise Ravens*) (1976) and even Federico García Lorca's use of imposed domestic silence in the face of village gossip and illicit passion in the play *La casa de Bernarda Alba* (*The House of Bernarda Alba*) (1936), several times adapted for the screen. Nor is there much unusual, as far as gay dramas are concerned, in the contrastive juxtaposition of the pivotal – and only – moment of same-sex lovemaking between Ander and Jose at a heterosexual wedding, complete with toasts not only to the bride and groom but to grandchildren to come. (The tactic of a montage of gay erotic encounter on another part of the set used to stage a heterosexual wedding had been used to similar effect in *Día de Vodas* – see Chapter 1.) What is unusual, however, is the low-key intensity with which the difficult recognition of same-sex desire is played out, and which makes new use of those classic features of rural isolation, the force of tradition and family control. It is suggested that not only is Ander's problem an external one, of reactionary social values, but just as much – and, of course, in an interconnected manner – it is one inherent in masculinity and personality. Commonly enough, for a gay drama (were this to be one), Ander and Jose have sex in a toilet (at the wedding), but there is no sense of fun, excitement, transgression or knowingness to the event. Jose, who has helped the still crutch-using Ander to get to the urinal, finds his holding of Ander round the waist turning imperceptibly into squeezing him, discovers (as Esquivel's acting conveys) that this feels right, even that Ander smells right (he sniffs at his upper back and the nape of his neck with animalistic simplicity and abandon). The act is wordless; at the end, Ander's muffled cries as he is fucked (counter to age-related convention) turn to tears, tears which inaugurate for a third of the film a new regime of silence and denial which survives the death of the mother who had seemed up until now to be the main source of repression. Ander's gruffness, shocked now into intensification by the stolen pleasure given to him by Jose, refines the legacy of family absences (a difficult, distant and dead father; now the dead mother) into the specific lack of a sentimental education. Social isolation has compounded this with an absence of supportive knowledge. Ander has aged beyond his years under the effects of lack of social and intellectual resource, and Jose only seems to make him older (even when they finally are living together). The Castilian-speaking Reme (Mamen Rivera), whose lack of luck with the wayward father of her toddler has forced her into sex work and (in a further highly customary trope of such dramas) enhanced worldly wisdom, declares 'Dios, ¡qué miedo tenéis los hombres a vosotros mismos' ('God, how frightened you men are of each other') in response to Ander's crisis and silence. Ander seems to have nowhere to look in order to teach himself the way out of this.

Müller is let down by his newspaper, which heads his piece 'La española *Ander* presenta una historia sobre el mundo gay rural' (2009) ('The Spanish film *Ander* presents a story of the rural gay world'): the film's point is, in fact, the absence in this community of such of a supporting world. As Reme asks Ander, in a crucial doorstep conversation: does he think he will ever get another opportunity like this (that is, to ask Jose to stay with him)? Does he want to live alone? The unspoken words are 'here', and 'look around you'. Indeed, from where they are placed – she in the doorway, he on a seat outside – the valleys fall away, the sky is vast and the mountains rear up, green and empty. Below, unseen, there is also the rest of the hamlet, the source of another pressing anxiety, as expressed in the same spot by Evaristo (Pedro Oteagi), chastely in love all his life with the now dead mother of Ander: what will people say? One thing that the bragging and bluff, macho womaniser Peio (Pako Revueltas) does say of the set-up in the farmhouse – angrily but not in full cognisance – is that Ander and Jose are a couple of queers (for not wanting to party, that is to share Reme's body with him one afternoon). The question is freighted, too, with her need to move in (since Peio has withdrawn his support of her) and Ander subsequently, quietly and in a roundabout way, at the very kitchen table which once was the site of prohibition, lets it be known that Reme and her child should consider themselves from now on to be living in the house, not with him alone, but 'con nosotros' ('with us').

The film, shown originally at the seventh Festival de Cine y Derechos Humanos (Festival of Film and Human Rights) at San Sebastián in 2009, was supported by BerdinDu!, the Basque Government Community and Social Affairs department's LGBT support agency (though not without controversy) and has a clear socio-political remit in line with Berdindu's declared aims (as adjusted for the purposes of the promotion of the film) of: increasing the participation, integration and self-esteem of Basque LGBT citizens, promoting values of respect and dignity, and, using a specifically Basque cultural base to enhance the social usefulness of cinema by the inclusion in Basque cinema of LGBT films (Ander 2009).[6] Although not on theatrical or DVD release, the film was made available for viewing (free) on the Festival de Cine Online site April–May 2011, won the Valladolid CinHomo jury prize for best feature (2009) and was shown as part of the Instituto Cervantes' multi-site season of

Spanish gay films (Manchester, February–March 2011; Sydney, June 2011). It was also shown at the alternative Pride events coordinated by the indignados protesters on 18 June 2011, drawing attention for its combination of issues of sexuality and migration (Orgullo Indignado 2011). Director Castañón's experience as the director of Zinegoak, Bilbao from 2003 may well have contributed to the social sensibilities and reach of the film.

Better known than *Ander* is the Basque love story between two women in their seventies, *80 egunean* (*For 80 Days*) (Jon Garaño and Jose Maria Goenaga, 2010). Like *Ander*, it juxtaposes traditional heteronormativity (a dull, married, village life for one of its characters) with a conflictedly recognised same-sex attraction. It won the 2010 Sebastiane prize, unofficially linked to the San Sebastián Film Festival; it has a DVD release listed by the main LGBT retail outlets discussed in Chapter 4, but a modest 21,974 sales at the box office (MECD 2012); it is available for pay-to-view streaming at filmin. es; it has substantial Facebook and Twitter trails (pages named after the film in both cases); and it had wide exposure in North America by way of the 3rd Annual Festival of New Spanish Cinema (in 2011).

Axun (Itziar Aizpuru) and Maite (Mariasun Pagoaga) – once close friends, for one intense year in childhood – are unexpectedly reunited around the hospital bed of the former's ex son-in-law, in a coma, as is Maite's brother. Maite is an out lesbian with vivid mementos of a previous relationship in her home, and she confides to her friend and music teacher colleague, Julian (Zorion Eguileor), that she thinks she might have had a crush on Axun as a girl. She gently tries to tease out from Axun something of the warmth of their earlier friendship as well as to help free her from the conventional and oppressive routines of her married life with Juan Mari (José Ramón Argoitia) over the course of their bedside conversations. While heteronormative domestic life for Axun centres, as in *Ander*, around the rural home, vegetable patch, valley views and mute kitchen-table meals dominated by a television set, Maite brings into the hospital room laughter, vitality, exuberant earrings hand-crafted by her, and a CD of *pasodobles* for the two of them to dance to. The latter links them back to their past, and the dancing recalls for Axun their first, and so far only, kiss, as girls, dancing to a gramophone. Otherwise, Maite, and, through her, lesbianism itself, indicates escape, rediscovery, the persistence of youthful energy in the present: a way of making the eponymous eighty days count. Axun's clumsiness when she first dares to kiss Maite, during a mishap-ridden day trip to the Santa Clara island off San Sebastián (see cover image), points starkly to the muting effect on emotional intelligence of conventional heterosexual partnership gone stale. It is also a powerful vignette of the personal-political differences that may lie between non-out object of affection when she is emboldened to flirt with the committed, and emotionally attuned, lesbian.

Although the (male) directors point up, for pragmatic purposes no doubt, the universality of the story, placing emphasis on the film as 'una historia sobre dos personas que se enfrentan al miedo de materializar un deseo' (Garaño and

Goenaga, 2012) ('a story about two people who confront their fear of making a desire come true'), the poignant and muted lesbian feminist politics of it, and the seriousness with which it treats its subject and its characters, is unmistakably sensitised to a far more robust and partially intersectional strand in queer politics, a strand that links brute desire with considerations of class, locality, age, educational trajectory and, not least, social needs and demands framed by the geo-politics and linguistic specifics of the autonomous region (as reflected in the disappeared declarations of Berdindu, as cited above). The tone is low-key, 'sin el dramatismo con el que se suelen tratar las historias de homosexualidad' ('without the over-dramatic approach that is usual when dealing with homosexuality'), in Goenaga's words (reported in Brito 2010). However, the romantic pairing of two older women not only stands out in terms of cinematic convention (Brito 2010) but is given strong disruptive force by the Basque settings, as Brito implies (2010) and reporters J. O. (2010) and Belinchón (2010) make explicit in their evocations of the conservative mindset and purportedly famed sexlessness of rural Euskadi. The film has impressed lesbian commentators for its realism and sincerity and for Aizpuru and Pagoaga's ability to transmit a sense of restrained emotion ('Rogue' 2010); for the way that moral self-affirmation and a break with familiar routine is played out (partly) in the convincing rural setting and around the physical closeness of these two older women, 'en la piel de dos mujeres maduras' ('Ex-usuaria' 2010) (literally, 'on the surface of their skin'). Maite and Axun, and Ander and Jose, in their way, present a kind of exemplary resistance to a reactionary past. They offer low-key alternatives to the more prominent representatives of resistance – in this case more to a dull or repressive present – who are the subject of my next chapter.

Notes

1. Also the work collected in the Seminario Internacional La Transición Democrática en España. Aspectos Cinematográficos y Televisivos (March 2009) as part of the project Cultura, Sociedad y Televisión en España (1956–2006) directed by Manual Palacio (Grupo de Investigación 'Televisión: memoria, representación e industria') and the Área de Comunicación Audiovisual del Departamento de Periodismo y Comunicación Audiovisual de la Universidad Carlos III de Madrid.
2. Amazon's list of Gay Coming Out Movies (list no. 8) offers a sample: <http://www.amazon.com/Gay-coming-out-movies-List/lm/R1AX7ANAYW69C2> [last accessed 7 June 2011].
3. See Smith (2011: 37) on the film in the context of the June 2011 London BFI season Good Morning Freedom – Spanish Cinema After Franco.
4. In its full title, 'LEY 52/2007, de 26 de diciembre, por la que se reconocen y amplían derechos y se establecen medidas en favor de quienes padecieron persecución o violencia durante la guerra civil y la dictadura'. Text available at <http://www.boe.es/boe/dias/2007/12/27/pdfs/A53410-53416.pdf> [last accessed 1 March 2012].
5. In Villaronga's *Pa negre* (*Black Bread* [or, Rye Bread]) 2010) tuberculosis again forms part of a cluster of metaphors indicating tacit homoeroticism and violent homophobia – in this case collective.

6. A claim that Berdindu!'s management organisation, Aukeratu, misappropriated public funds in financing the film was presented by the Basque Government to the Supreme Court in March 2011 (Barriuso 2011; Martínez 2011). The organisation's aims have subsequently been simplified and reduced to social welfare issues only, and those cited in the text above have been removed from all official sites. The site <http://www.berdindu.es> has been removed and the site <http://www.ander.com.es> has been infected with malware (attempted access February, April and December 2011 and 5 January 2012).

3. ICONS

This chapter examines some of the film-making personalities with whom queer viewers in Spain might be said to bond imaginatively and, at times, be influenced by in their real or their fantasy lives. In looking at some established, near-canonical actors and directors – Eusebio Poncela, Victoria Abril, Jordi Mollà, Rosa Maria Sardà, Ventura Pons and Pedro Almodóvar – the suggestion will be that they respond to what López Penedo in her discussion of queer cultural representations and the imaginative production of queer common space (2008: 209–26) calls 'figuras de culto' (226) ('cult figures'). I also explore some newer and, in many cases, intellectually or histrionically lighter, figures – such as Pablo Puyol, Pepón Nieto and Carlos Fuentes as well as the 1990s heritage comedy directors Alfonso Albacete and David Menkes, who use both cult figures (Jorge Sanz and Veronica Forqué) and new (Mario Casas and Ana María Polvorosa). These younger figures may or may not become cult, but they are, at the time of writing, visible, much watched and commented upon. In as much as the images, stories and performances embodied by these artists represent opposition to a sexually politicised norm, all evoke 'una respuesta de afecto, identificación y admiración por parte de una devota audiencia queer' (226) ('a response on the part of a dedicated queer audience which is affective, identificatory or admiring').

Published surveys and guides to LGBT cinema in Spain as well as the labelling of Internet discussions and sites all establish relatively fixed and conventional points of reference. On the one hand, anthologised and reiterated names of films and film-makers – with the paraphernalia of bios, plot summaries and micro-filmographies – appear earnestly to consolidate a common culture, fixing identities in past histories. They carry forward, in Spanish contexts, the important work done in relation to other cultures of pulling together a counter-canon or queering of film studies (Hamer and Budge 1994; Hanson 1999a; Stacey and Street 2007), of opening up the canon for a queerer view (Russo 1987; Bad Object Choices 1991; Mira 2008), of mapping queer film to specific nations or regions (Jackson and Tapp 1997; Foster 2003; Griffiths 2008; Rees-Roberts 2008). On the other hand, despite new names displacing old, or marriage tales replacing coming out stories, the sense of culture as process is sidelined in these Spanish surveys and the range of the moving image's impact on Spanish queer culture is progressively reduced to the mainly gay and the mainly feature-length fictional. García Rodríguez (2008), for example, is an exception on the latter front, with coverage of documentaries and short films, but on the former point is able to discuss only one feature film by women, *A mi madre le gustan las mujeres* (*My Mother Likes Women*) (Inés París and Daniela Fejerman, 2002), one about women, *Electroshock* (Juan Carlos Claver, 2005) and a handful of mentions of treatments of trans-gender subjects and issues (416–27). His proposal for a 'new canon' includes as its only two Spanish films (out of thirty) *Cambio de sexo* (*Sex Change*) (Vicente Aranda, 1975) and *La ley del deseo* (*The Law of Desire*) (Pedro Almodóvar, 1987).

Facebook and other social networking sites associated with LGBTQ organisations and events provide a supplementary thread of names, titles and events in context.[1] More dynamically still, periodical and web-based publications and web and blog sites balance the received 'new' canons, the slow build of tagged names and the iteration of slightly old news with the calculated urgency of the press release and its sub-products. Interview and photoset appearances brokered by agents or festival promotion teams (for example Promofest) join snappily editorialised lists of who is 'in' and on the up, thus countering fossilisation (for example in the 'Sala XY' in 7Pekados.com, or the section 'Iconos y mitos' in the now expired blog Cultura Lesbiana). The more familiar lists compete with the ever-changing names and titles alternately exalted or dismissed by fans (mainly, of course, in relation to television but with significant activity on various sites in relation to the web series *Chica busca chica* (*Girl Seeks Girl*) (Sonia Sebastián, Terra TV 2008–9) and to *Mentiras y gordas* (*Sex, Party and Lies* [or, Lies and Big Fat Lies]) (Alfonso Albacete and David Menkes, 2009) (discussed below)). *Zero* magazine's section De Zero a 100 was, while the publication was extant (1998–2008), reliably attuned to the tides of celebrity and trends (for example, Esteban (1999c) on key names and the future of 'homosexuality in our films' and features on Antonia San Juan and Eusebio Poncela, discussed below). Taking up where *Zero* left off, *Oh My God* (from 2009) supplies gay (mainly) men with a regular shortlist (usually of one quickly browsable page) of who in the film world is culturally hot. *Shangay* magazine, with a web as well as a free hard-copy presence, as well as its supplement Shangay Style, is as liable to look back into queer cultural history – connecting Concha Velasco's early career representations of lesbians on screen to her role in *Chuecatown* (discussed below) (Shangay Express 2008) – as it is to highlight from time to time new careers. On example is Israel Rodríguez, who is co-star with Pablo Puyol in the well-known gay short *En malas compañías* (*Doors Cut Down* [or, In Bad Company]) (2000) and has the lead role of Xabi in the queer thriller-feature *Clandestinos* (2007) (where Puyol has a minor role as a fellow rent boy), both by Antonio Hens; he also plays Borja in Antena 3's television series *Física o química* (Physics or Chemistry)

(2010) (Giraldo 2011b). The websites of CineLGBT, lesbianlips, the primary festivals and linked event spaces build a formidably accumulated but easily searchable sets of lists and links.[2] As Mariel Maciá, speaking as a maker and, at the time, a marketer of Spanish LGBTQ films, puts it, the audience is a very specific but also a demanding one: 'genera sus propias estrellas, sus propios autores y su propio mapa de eventos' (Maciá 2010) ('it generates its own stars, its own auteurs and its own map of relevant events'). Those 'estrellas' – more 'actors and celebrities' than stars, in reality – and 'autores' are the focus of this chapter; the 'map of events' I shall be looking at in Chapter 4 on audiences.

Actors (I): Eusebio Poncela, Victoria Abril, Jordi Mollà, Rosa María Sardà

Elsewhere (Perriam 2003a) I have looked at gay roles played by Antonio Banderas, Imanol Arias, Javier Bardem and Eduardo Noriega – all major figures in recent LGBTQ screen history whose careers have nevertheless not included further such roles. They are names out of the heritage era I have delineated in Chapter 2, although Bardem, of course, is still a vivid presence for mainstream audiences in Spain and in Spanish-speaking (as well as English-speaking) roles, and Noriega has a growing transnational presence (Perriam 2011). Starring with (or above) Banderas in Almodóvar's *La ley del deseo* and in *Matador* (1986) but with his being noticed for queer roles petering out in the early part of the period under consideration in this book is Eusebio Poncela, with whom I start the section. Also of that era or category, and in rough order of frequency of return into involvement with queer roles or projects, are Jordi Mollà, Jorge Sanz, Victoria Abril and notably Rosa María Sardà, in Catalan and Castilian roles working for, among others, Ventura Pons, Almodóvar (in *Todo sobre mi madre* (*All About My Mother*)) and the *Chuecatown* phenomenon but also in *A mi madre le gustan las mujeres*. Of these actors, only Eusebio Poncela is out, despite a cultivated air of ambiguity and enigma (García Rodríguez 2008: 266; and visible in the front-page portrait of him in *Zero* magazine, February 2000). This air is nearly always transferred direct to the characters he has played, going back to the brilliantly strange *Arrebato* (*Rapture*) (Iván Zulueta, 1980) (see Smith 2011: 37), which was revived in 2008, at the eleventh Málaga Film Festival, with a two-disc DVD re-release by Ediciones Coleccionista. Like Almodóvar – and unhelpfully for straightfor-wardly minded LGBTQ activists – Poncela refuses to be drawn on the question of the relationship of his roles to issues in LGBT activism, and his view just before the release of *Sagitario* (Vicente Molina Foix, 2001) was 'no creo en los grupos, todo está en la actitud personal' ('I don't believe in groups, it all comes down to one's personal attitude') (Villora 2000). In Molina Foix's film, Poncela's character Jaime is somewhat hermetically looking for himself by way of abandoning a long-term relationship with an older man, the Argentine Darío (Héctor Alterio), in favour of falling for a rent boy he hires one night, while being in strenuous denial of the love obsessively shown for him by his close friend Rosa (Angela Molina). Rather like Diego (Javier Bardem) and Alberto (Jordi Mollà) in *Segunda piel* (*Second Skin*) (Gerardo Vera, 1999) Jaime navigates his confusion and desires with no guidance from the burgeoning queer culture he would have known in Buenos Aires with his ex, or that which must have surrounded the cabaret milieu in which he now (sporadically) works in Madrid. On the other hand, Poncela's association through his roles with such cool detachment from identification with the politics of identity, and his own standing back from conventional LGTB politics, has a strongly queer impulse to it, despite the absence of any politics of action. Mainly male-oriented bisexual Dante in *Martín* (*Hache*) had believed in falling in lust with people's minds; Jaime, in *Sagitario*, believes in fate. Poncela himself consistently presents as marginal, unconventional and (in a word overused by the press and generally in circulation subculturally) 'raro' (odd, queer) (Pita 2001; Villora 2000). He has, though, a strong and half-ironically self-assured sense of the cultural importance of his work. Awarded a prize at the 3rd Zinegoak Festival (Bilbao, 2006) in recognition of his contribution to LGBT cinema in Spain, in interview he draws attention to his early career roles as breaking with the heritage of caricature representation of gay men, suggesting that 'Fui el primer actor que hizo de gay normal y corriente y el primero en mostrar una parte de mí' (Gómez 2006) ('I was the first actor [in Spain] to play an ordinary gay man, and the first to show a part of myself in my role').

I move on now to consider the actor Victoria Abril.[3] Abril has a long-established dual-national acting career in Spain and France – especially since *Gazon maudit* of 1995 (see Chapter 2) – and is a star marked by her famously emphatic embodiments of intense, dissident or troubled sexuality. As in the case of Poncela, there is a traditional perception of her as a difficult or distant personality. Her career reveals a cross-mapping of issues of place and placelessness onto issues of sexuality in a sustained disruption of hegemonic paradigms of gender-related behaviours and experiences. In particular, the Spanishness which Abril is seen to represent is associated with 'the psychological intensity and sexual disinhibition of her performances' (Stone 2004: 165), with her representation of assertiveness (Evans 2002: 130–4) and (more straightforwardly) with her prominent involvement in some obviously 'Spanish' products. These include not only a string of popular movies, comedies and thrillers, exploring in a middlebrow way the erotic and lifestyle vicissitudes of modern Spanish urban living, but also in the mid-career films of Pedro Almodóvar – *Átame* (1990), *Tacones lejanos* (*High Heels*) (1991) and *Kika* (1993), all very tightly woven with threads of national concern. She has also been involved in edgy heritage films where Spanish historical events violently bear down on the construction of, and playing out, of female sexuality – Vicente Aranda's *Si te dicen que caí* (*If They Say I Fell*) (1989) and *Amantes* (*Lovers*) (1991), as well as the more contemporary exploration of gender-power relations in a socially and psychoanalytically deconstructed patriarchal Spain in Díaz Yanes's *Nadie hablará de nosotras cuando hayamos muerto* (*No-one Will Speak of Us Once We're Dead*) (1995) which is the basis of Stone's (2004) analysis of her.

Abril's representation of sexuality as both strangely fixed (by stereotyping) and wildly decentred (by aspects of her performance) has involved several versions of lesbianism – bi-ambiguous in *Padre nuestro* (Our Father) (Francisco Regueivo, 1985), emerging from the mess of a heterosexual marriage in *Gazon maudit*, and in the form of the rebel (but also rather folkloric-exotic) incomer in *101 Reykjavik* (Baltasar Kormakur, 2001). In Agustín Díaz Yanes's fantasy *Sin noticias de dios* (*Don't Tempt Me*) (2001) Abril is an agent from heaven, Lola, pitted against Hell's agent, Carmen (Penélope Cruz) whose migrated, male-gendered soul not only makes her very 'manly' (with Cruz playing the tomboy) but adds an erotic charge to the rivalry and eventual comradeship between Carmen and Lola. Abril manages to convey sharply in facial gesture and physical recoil and rapprochement her character's fear of her attraction to Carmen as (apparently) lesbian other.

In *101 Reykjavik* Abril's character Lola (again) has arrived in Reykjavik and set up a flamenco class. Although she has sex with the narrator anti-hero of the film, Hlynur Björn, she is fundamentally lesbian and takes up with Hlynur's mother but is pregnant by Hlynur. This leads to critiques of family dysfunction and to disturbing play with disruptive alternative relationships: 'what do I say?' asks Hlynur, when told about the two women's relationship, 'I've never cheated on my mother before', and, crucially, 'what sort of lesbian are you anyway?' This last question is a good one in relation to Abril's representation of this character and to lesbian feminist thinking after Wittig, too. The film uses the strange mix of far Northern angst, youth disenchantment and an Abril coded both as typically Spanish and typically lesbian to present a challenging narrative of two women, one man and a baby, and it invites a rethink of affectivity in a context of a critique of identity and of heterosexuality, participating, albeit in comic mode, in that wider queer project which at its more intense '[sería] una manera muy diferente de entender la cultura y la política, una forma de disidencia, una corriente abisal que centrifuga a la dominante' (Vila Nuñez 2005: 183) ('would provide a very different way of understanding culture and politics, a dissident way, a swirling, downward current which would send the dominant culture spinning centrifugally away').

Abril's career keeps asking what can be done with some of the emptier clichés of nationality and sexuality through often quirky representations of anti-heteronormativity disguised by typicality. When she appears in the short *Carne de neón* (Red Light Fodder) (Paco Cabezas, 2005) as the sex worker Pura returning home from jail to the early-Almodovaresque chaos of the lives of son Ricky (Óscar Jaenada) and male-to-female trans La Infantita (Dámaso Conde) – 'y la polla, usarla, no la uso' ('as for my cock, I don't really use it') – it is in cameo a recapitulation of her associative queerness.[4]

My next example of an established actor with a history of positionings in anti-heteronormative roles, or roles which critique masculinity by exaggerating its attributes and contradictions, is Jordi Mollà. Like Poncela, Jordi Mollà is an actor often commented on in terms of his apartness from his contemporaries in film acting in terms of technique and roles chosen, and as with Poncela, that epithet 'raro' has been applied to him for his seriousness and intellectualism in person and performance (Perriam 2003a: 126). His career in the 1990s, following on from his decidedly queer representation of the affectively ineffectual and socio-economically entrapped heterosexual male, José Luis, in *Jamón, jamón* (Juan José Bigas Luna, 1992), included high-profile roles as a closeted homosexual in his twenties in *Historias del Kronen* (*Stories of the Kronen*) (Montzo Armendáriz, 1995), as loudly out-gay in a rare comedy role as Toni in *Perdona, bonita, pero Lucas me quería a mí* (*Excuse me Darling, But Lucas Loved Me!*) (Dunia Ayaso and Félix Sabroso, 1997), and as a closeted homosexual in a straight marriage, queer enough to understand – and run a mile from – the difficult script of running his double life and queer enough to be enthralled by sex with the suave, toned, metrosexual-gay Diego (Javier Bardem) in *Segunda piel*. Within its melodramatic carapace of homoerotic passion, denial and nervous and marital breakdown, the film is problematically normalising (Mira 2004: 596–7), with Diego's gayness seemingly stuck in a comfortable and depoliticised past and Alberto's crisis open to diversion into its interpretation as universally human – a drama of coupledom in a film directed, it seems, at a heterosexual audience (598). As Fouz-Hernández and Martínez-Expósito rightly observe (2007: 126), it is suspiciously close to the stereotyping and ultimately homophobic 'negative elements of earlier gay-themed narratives', not least in its killing off of the failed queer and in a discourse associating homosexuality with sickness (126–7), although I have previously argued (Perriam 2003a: 125–6) that the film, through Mollà's character, cracks open some hard truths about homophobia, the closet and the stranglehold of social expectations. Mollà, then, found himself here working to a script whose didactic usefulness and emotional authenticity for an LGBTQ audience needed to be accessed – as very often with retro or retrograde material in this respect – by way of selective and differential identification using the wisdom of collective hindsight, or in the light of other film versions of similar disasters in the making – for example, Pinzás's *Días de voda* (see Chapter 1).

His role as the poet Jaime Gil de Biedma (1929–90) in *El cónsul de Sodoma* (*The Consul of Sodom*) (Sigrid Monleón, 2010) – winner of the 2010 Premio LesGai al Cine (LesGaiCineMad festival, Madrid) – is considered by the critics as having 'rasgos de hondura' ('touches of profundity'), a measured approach to the tricky task of embodying such a famous subject (Molina Foix 2010a; Batlle Caminal 2010) or, like the film itself (according to one blogger critic), 'emocionante en ocasiones, brillante cuando la cámara capta su mirada [el de Mollà] de soslayo y desproporcionada en otras cuando nadie pone coto a la desmesura del actor' (Tormo 2010) ('moving at times, brilliant when the camera catches Mollà's look at a slant but disproportionate when he has not been told to be less over the top'). Popular opinion has variously seen his performance as set in an unfortunate context of old clichés about gay men and promiscuity and lack of morality (Soria 2009) (this commentator also worries anachronistically about the representation of unsafe sex), as 'uneven' and implicitly contributing to the old-fashioned feel of the film ('eduardo' 2010) or as 'digno' (solid) ('George/tres tristes tigres' 2010) and as adding further weight to his claim to a Goya ('¡El Goya para Jordi Mollà!', Facebook page).

His careful representation in the opening sequence of the suave, dinner-jacketed homosexual roué making a pass at the waiter at a polite cocktail party is a not very demanding call upon an audience to recognise, if it cares to, some standard cross-class transgression. The subsequent slumming-it at a (straight) sex show and a night spent with a lad in his family's shack in the slums of Manila leads to a sex scene of a certain amount of straightforward innocence. A naked Mollà, deploying a subtle, tender look, playing the poet, tenderly caresses the back and buttocks of his one-night lover; again, there are the pleasures of familiarity here for a certain audience (perhaps one which might have both Fassbinder's *Querelle* (1982) and Gilbert's *Wilde* (1997) on their shelves), and an interesting sense of Mollà playing the privileged queer adventurer-explorer. The brave resistance that the poet puts up to the insinu-ating questioning about his literary connections, and his own apparently anti-establishment poetry when visited at the family home by agents of the Brigada Político-Social (the police intelligence service), is culminated, in Mollà's per-formance of the scene, by a chilling stare out of the window away from them, half turned from the camera, as they report to him that people say that he is 'un maricón, muy inteligente' ('a queer, a very clever one'). The narrative – that of the film and that of the poet's life – frames these gestures in the equivoca-tions of the man who sleeps with (younger) men but takes the advantages of heteronormativity where he can. The action takes place in a wealthy world of lavish *mise en scène*, travel and smoke- and gin-filled rooms with writers and business men. The actor's gestures sustain, nonetheless, a sting of the radical, a sense of queer dissident history and an out-of-the-ordinary mode of deflecting the normative and repressive. Here, for a queer audience, is a representation, through Mollà, of much a more decided bisexual than Alberto in *Segunda piel*, and – of course – a much more seriously deployed wildcard than Toni in *Perdona, bonita*. . . . In the 1970s phase of the story, Gil de Biedma establishes the twenty-something Toni (Isaac de los Reyes), a photographer just ending his military service, in what turns out to be rural, domestic servitude. This scenario presents good opportunities for Mollà to register in fleeting facial ges-tures the banal irony inherent in the older, wiser, richer man's having fallen for the impoverishing illusion that the kept younger man will stay or stay happy, that two cultures might fully cross – a lowering of the eyes at supper or during an elegant dinner out, a look of sad self-incrimination or a glimmer of anxiety that a gift from Toni might turn out to be tasteless. The break-up, appropri-ately, is political as much as it is affective. Toni's clear-sighted sense, at a house party on the night of the death of Franco, of the poet's circle of friends as themselves closet right-wingers (in the sense of their visibly successful pursuit of comfort and liberal lifestyle) meets with theatrical looks of mild sarcasm, well chosen from the given arsenal of gestures by Mollà. His character that night wants to play down all contradictions and simply frame Toni as his cheeky, sexy, rough little cadet. What is acted out, then, transects class, sexuality and politics (the power of the state over Toni, which previously has called him into service, has its match in the social power of commodification, denial and disempowerment). Close to death (from AIDS), watching a beautiful rent boy dance for him (with the Pet Shop Boys playing extradiegetically, but with the dance synched to it), the poet's regrets, memories and present pleasure in the erotic spectacle of the naked, youthful body in movement is registered by Mollà with lips twitching into and out of a smile, an eyelid spasming towards tears and a steady gaze, finally, into camera, into the space where the dancer's pelvis and perfect cock earlier had been passing. This dramatic moment, focused close up on the actor, elicits a response of pathos across a wide audience, it may be assumed. For a gay audience keyed into the values of Gil de Biedma's writing or with a sense of how the Barcelona so-called *gauche divine* intersected with nascent queer politics during the poet's life, or even simply taken by such stories of 'un maricón . . . muy inteligente', what is acted out is close and poignant. (I return to this film, and some of these literary questions, in Chapter 5.)

With a completely different audience in mind – although the alphabetical proximity of this title to the Monleón on the shelf or in the webpage list is not as banal a detail as might appear, taking consumer habits into account – *Chuecatown* (*Boystown*) (Juan Flahn, 2007) is one of the key popular successes of the period under discussion in this book. It was released in distribution by Filmax in early July 2007 to coincide with the immediate euphoric aftermath of the Europride celebrations in Madrid, on DVD in September, and it has a continuing and vigorous shelf life (and presence on download sites), despite being a far from quality product. As a comedy with the dubious premise for its main plot of a linkage between murder and the spread of gay identity, it potentially reactivates denigratory elements familiar from the films of the 'heritage' period (Melero 2010: 127–80) and is considered even by the Orange-hosted commercially oriented gay entertainment site chueca.com to be extremely light and conventional (Joric 2007). On the other hand, it makes the space of the traditional street neighbourhood a place of LGBT visibility, of national coming out. There is a cross-mapping to a well-known television moment in Antena 3's *Aquí no hay quien viva* (This Is No Place for Anyone To Live In) in which Adrià Collado – already with roles in LGBT-themed films *Sobreviviré* (*I Will Survive*) (Alfonso Albacete and David Menkes, 1999) and *El sueño de Ibiza* (Ibiza Dream) (Igor Fioravanti, 2002) – gained prominence for his character Fernando's public, street-balcony coming out and for his long, loving on-screen kissing of boyfriend Mauri played by Luis Merlo. The show registered a 49 per cent audience share in 2004 (Generelo 2004). To this extent, in Spain certain neighbourhoods are already queered spaces – and this is registered, in more matter-of-fact modes, by those interviewed on the street and at market stalls in the short documentary *Las esquinas del arco iris* (The Different Corners of the Rainbow) (Purificación Mora, 2006) who see the same-sex relationships and community cultural life happening around them as part of a wider socio-political dynamic of radical change (for the slightly better is the implication of the tones of voice and looks of wry resignation recorded).

As a lighthearted and no-nonsense treatment of the sort of life that a young and beefy plumber and a slightly older and even beefier driving instructor might live as a couple, it is one of those gay, post-heritage comedies which add to LGBTQ culture in Spain another lump of sugar, pleasantly and in a normalising mode. Neither the sugar nor the unwelcome droplet of retrograde sourness soaking in are much noticed for that part of the screen-time in which two greats of the Spanish screen – Rosa María Sardà and Concha Velasco – entertainingly coast through their matched roles as domineering, widowed mothers, embracing clichés only to swat them out of the way. Sardà, winner of the Academia de Cine's prestigious Gold Medal in 2010, and with a vast career in Castilian and Catalan-speaking theatre, television and cinema (Academia de Cine 2010), is also the holder of more modest prizes closer to the LGBT audience interests: the Homocine Gayo prize for her part and Elisca Sirova's as Best Lesbian Couple in *A mi madre le gustan las mujeres* in 2001 and the Zinegoak prize of distinction in 2007. She is commonly included in that loosely knit category of 'icono'. Velasco has an even longer acting career with some starring roles in classics of Spanish film of the 1960s and 1970s, and a high profile as a television presenter and drama series star in the 1980s and 1990s. For the LGBTQ media, Velasco signifies some sort of loose connection to the political cause and had joined with the FELGT and other prominent actors during the Pride celebrations of 2005 in support of the manifesto Orgullo Ciudadano against the then emerging objections to the inclusion in the package of legislation relating to same-sex marriage of full rights of parenthood and family building (Agencia EFE 2005). She posed with six other prominent pubic figures in issue 107 of *Zero* magazine (2008), dedicated to women's equality; for *Oh My God!* magazine, Nacha la Macha interviews her as 'la siempre grande y querida Concha Velasco' (ohmygodmagazine 2010) ('the forever great and forever beloved Concha Velasco') and she poses during the spot with a naked pin-up boy for Joan Crisol.[5] For an older generation there are memories of the flirtation of her character with Ana Belén's in *Jaque a la dama* (*Queen in Check*) (Francisco Rodríguez, 1978); a long-standing, camp fascination for her as one of a range of divas inspiring drag-act imitations is documented in Pierrot (2010). For newer audiences her cameo appearance in the, for lesbians, must-watch series *Hospital Central* (Tele 5; in two episodes, series 18, 2010) has further resonance. Although at least one mainstream critic deplores her performance, in the context of what he sees as 'tradicional costumbrismo' (Sánchez 2007) ('traditional folksy social realism'), she takes up with gusto the possibilities of a light (albeit heavy-handedly scripted) satire on Spanish comedy's own hyper-representations of the strong mother. With a certain grotesquery, she brings on the possibility, in this particular context, of a lightweight and rough-queer critique of the heteropatriarchy which has left her character fizzing with anger about her dead husband, dismissive of her three caring daughters and determined to control her son.

Sardà's character, Mina, is a satirical amalgam of strong woman detective inspector roles from popular screen culture. Velasco plays the chain-smoking and coarsely selfish Antonia, the mother of Rey, the plumber 'cub' (Carlos Fuentes) whom she is pleased is gay because at least that way no common Everygirl could take him away from her. During questioning by the detective inspector, Velasco is given a nicely self-reflexive line in cliché to volley back across to Sardà: having noted the very gay shirt on Mina's son and junior detective colleague, she observes that the two of them share the same cross in life – sons who have fallen prey to men who have turned them gay as soon as their mother's backs were turned. The performances of these two divas comically enhance and deflate at one and the same time the stereotypes and suppositions they are based on (most neatly, perhaps, in the gag that includes in Mina's complex range of hypochondriac symptoms an allergy to showing strong emotion). The script's successful way with easy parodies of heteronormative idiocy, strengthened by its own (tellingly paradoxical) satire of the normalisation of gay life in Madrid through the commercial 'modernisation' of Chueca, allows some shards of queer-affiliated social and sexual political comment to pierce the unyielding fabric of the thriller-cum-farce which is the main narrative. Sardà (to whose more serious side I shall return in the discussion of Ventura Pons in the second part of this chapter) has built a career on allowing her deadpan timing to deflect otherwise deadening effects in screenwriting or direction. When finally she tracks down the killer, Víctor (Pablo Puyol), who is a body-fascist criminal in the mould of Patrick Bateman as played by Christian Bale, and the property developer from hell – throttling elderly widows in flats around Chueca in order to clear them out – Mina is, as the script spells out, the saviour of lives, of gay couples and (less spelled out and less coherent) of Chueca's integrity. This all coalesces around the powerful and stoutly dressed figures of Sardà and Velasco, guns in hand, on the ramp of an underground car park, US crime drama-style, with the perspiring, naked body of Puyol first defiant, then prone (there has been a chase through a gay sauna, naturally). This interesting moment foils the soft pornographic voyeuristic instincts of one possible segment of the audience (which cannot fail to be drawn to the classic pseudo-fetishistic image of Puyol here: muscle on concrete) and insists on the superior spectacularity of the two women, infusing the film with the values of their own careers and of the audience identifications which have adhered to them.

Sardà plays an exemplary figure in a different register, and for a different audience, in *A mi madre le gustan las mujeres*. As Pelayo points out (2009:

117), the plot-line of the mother who discovers in middle age that she is lesbian has precedents in Spanish cinema but is here given primacy, though not physicality (119) (also Collins 2007: 157). Sardà's representation of Sofia is 'discreet' (Mira 2008: 67). Sofia passes as straight, and the classical music which wraps the tale around (Sofia teaches piano: Eliska – Eliska Sirova – for whom she falls, is a professional pianist) has a similar sanitising, highbrow effect as it does in Ventura Pons's *Food of Love* (2002). Web comments by lesbian rental viewers (on lesbianlips 2009) are on average lukewarm but appreciate the comedy, the presence of an older lesbian and the prominence given to family reactions to a coming out of this sort. Elsewhere online there is agreement that it is the family reaction which is important, but also the unusual fact of a happy ending (Collins 2007: 155; 'Sofia/Srta Russ' 2007). Sardà s performance is at the core of a lightly addressed ambivalence regarding what is being said – or what can be said – about lesbian mothers (Collins 2007: 151–2, 154–8). As Sofia dances at a celebration marking the bond between the two women and the beginning of the creation of one between their two families Sardà embodies either the lesbian mother who is, against all stereotyping, also the good mother or, conversely, the re-establishing of patriarchal and heteronormative control over the roles of woman, motherhood and family (Collins 2007: 156). This ambivalence is fostered by the stated intention of the directors to present the lesbian relationship as 'normal and natural' (Camí-Vela 2005: 369, quoted by Collins 2007: 158), an intention partially – and thankfully – sabotaged by Sardà's accumulated sardonic manner and eccentricity.

Sardà has a long association with the Catalan director Pons (discussed below) (Esteban 1999a: 97), whose films have been characterised as 'el millor exponent de l'articulació d'una subjectivitat gai dins la cinematografia catalana' (Martí-Olivella 2000: 373) ('the most important exponent of the articulation of a gay identity in Catalan cinema') and, as will be seen, of substantial international profile on the festival circuits. In the final episode of the omnibus film *Carícies* (*Caresses*) (1998) Sardà is an alienated mother transferring her tenderness from her unresponsive son to a near stranger – a young male neighbour, the victim of domestic violence. Her character stands at the centre of a release of tension (Faulkner 2004: 75) caused by the alienation and dislocation of the space of the modern city, explored by Faulkner in Lefebvre's terms (66–78). It issues in an 'idyll . . . of the city prior to its abstraction, a space which is both urban and "absolute"' (77). She also focuses one aspect of the 'bleak portrayal of contemporary family life' of the original Sergi Belbel play (George 2002: 92). Sardà sustains throughout the sequence with her son a look of embittered and sardonic loneliness. Blocking any possibility of her son's communicating with her at first (or of his breaking through what he tries to tell her is a feeling of blankness) the mother works through a litany of the day's small setbacks and Sardà's movements transmit tired resignation and domestic entrapment. The mother's anecdote about a phone call leads into spoken thoughts of aging and death, but slyly she helps herself to some cash from the son's wallet (suggesting an unconscious recognition of where he might be getting money from – the audience knows it is prostitution). What the son is finally able to articulate is that the two must know that they are both in a state of perpetual waiting, that they are both damaged by this. However, when the battered neighbour calls at the door and the mother brings him in to tend his wounds, Sardà has her character move back in time, away from the rigidity of fear and begrudging, to a more tender time of mothering. With a caress she prompts a caress, and a delicate recognition of attraction to the man; with a smile she allows Pons to establish a healing tableau of silent communication. In Pons's words, '[l]a cámara se serena y sale despacio por el balcón a contemplar la calle de forma relajada y tranquila porque, por fin, ha encontrado lo que buscaba: caricias' (Campo Vidal 2004a) ('the camera becomes calm and moves slowly out onto the balcony to look down on the street, tranquil and relaxed now because it has found what is was looking for: caresses').

In *Amic/Amat* (*Beloved/Friend*) (Ventura Pons, 1998), as Fanny – one of a group of characters struggling inheritors of the ideals of 1968 – Sardà, was thought to bring 'sublime' moments of great intensity and mastery to the role (according to Pons's account of the filming) (Campo Vidal 2004b). Her character (introduced along with that of her pregnant daughter Alba in the adaptation from Josep Maria Benet i Jornet's play *Testament*) provides 'a link between the private and the public, between the personal and the political' through her backstory as a leftist and as a woman who has chosen whether or not to carry her pregnancies to term (Fernàndez 2008: 228); she and Alba – and women as a whole – 'transmit a political and cultural memory' (228) within a drama of a 'sexual politics [that] is dependent on, and reveals the effects of, an ancient patriarchal legacy based on male domination, . . . express[ing] a crisis in its transmission' (218). Sardà's performance of a woman who knows that the men around her – men as a whole – have her caught up in a crisis of transmission of vibrant political ideals and in a repudiation of her own sexual-emotional needs is central in making those links. In response to Alba's confidence that she has been tempted to sleep with her attractive female flat-mate, Fanny declares 'yo seria la perfecta mare d'una lesbiana' ('I would be the perfect mother for a lesbian'). This is said in part recognition of having been left behind, with a sexual politics now far less polarised than in her youth, and it is said with a bitter-sweet, light but complex touch – the gestural prelude to a magnificently sustained soliloquy of despair (personal and sexual-political) addressed to Alba. This soliloquy takes place against the backdrop of manifold significations which is the church of Santa Maria del Mar and the skyline of downtown Barcelona – the 'cultural legacy' which is the counterpart to the biological legacy whose precariousness is also the film's concern (Fernàndez 2008: 223 and *passim*). Her reined-in look, the heavy-lidded eyes which trans-mit with equal ease ironic acceptance and helpless closeness to tears, and a way of delivering the bleakest of lines with a matter-of-factness which belies – by way of crafted contrast – Sardà's association with lighter film roles: all these techniques knit together around the female body the strands of a film that, while appearing to be mainly concerned with the bodies of the masculine gender of its title and to be closed in tight around the dyad of the principal two male characters (to whom I shall return in the next section), 'shows us that there is a legacy of subordination (national, social, sexual) that Catalan society needs to deal with' (Fernàndez 2008: 232). She, with Irene Montalà, performs just this warning: they point to a crisis being played out around a version of homosexuality which reaffirms while also disabling a system of transmission of power and reiteration of symbolic violence between men. The film's (and the play's) key question is, again in Pons's words:

> ¿Qué es lo que dejamos? La herencia heterosexual se focaliza siempre en función de la continuidad biológica de la especie. ¿Pero existe una herencia homosexual? (Campo Vidal 2004b)
> (What do we leave behind? Heterosexual inheritance is always seen from the point of view of the biological continuation of the species. But is there a homosexual inheritance?)

Sardà's position as a potent heritage figure across Catalan and Spanish cinema, her roles as unconventional or parodically excessive mother and the plot connections to queer and lesbian issues put her in a strong position to help an audience see their way into, and out of, Pons's important question.

DIRECTORS: VENTURA PONS AND PEDRO ALMODÓVAR

As one recent and substantial survey for the LGBTQ market in Spanish puts it, Pons 'no [es] de los más taquilleros ni de los más famosos, pero [con] un gran prestigio internacional' (García Rodríguez 2008: 339) ('is not the greatest of box office successes or the most famous but with substantial international prestige'). As an openly gay pioneer in the representation of homosexuality on film (Mira 2008: 547) from the late 1970s onwards and as a pragmatic and creatively flexible film-maker he has built a doubly national (Catalan and Castilian) reputation and an international profile for his work (Zatlin 2007: 434–5, 445). This can be associated in part with a turn to literary material (and a greater breadth of genre and theme) in the 1990s after a period as a maker of film comedies for a local, Catalan market, and in part also to his grounding as an established theatre director (Faulkner 2004: 72; George 2002: 90). A major part of Pons's strategy of provocation (Martí-Olivella 2000) is his use of actors with a strong presence on the theatre scene, like Sardà, as well as of Catalan-sourced adaptation in itself (Smith 2003: 129–37; Zatlin 2007: 439, 435).

A particularly successful retrospective and presentation of *Carícies* in London in January–February 1999 (Esteban 1999a: 97) was followed by a sequence of prestigious festival selections, retrospectives and homages (Campo Vidal 2004a; Pons 2011). He has been special guest and subject of retrospectives at the LGBT festivals FanCineGay 2006 (Extremadura), Entendiéndonos 2009 (Granada) and LesGaiCineMad 2009. His work is somewhat undecidable. Frequently an embodiment or a dramatisation of what for reasons of sexuality and desire will not fit conventional social or formal schemes, it deploys 'l'impostura' (Martí-Olivella 2000) ('imposture'). *Ocaña: retrat inrermitent* (*Ocaña: An Intermittent Portrait*) (1978) was radical, anti-hegemonic and countercultural (Martí-Olivella 2000: 381). Later, in *Amic/Amat* the camera

> pos[a] el nas /o l'ull . . . allà on no els ho demanen: dins l'armari fosc dels nostres sentiments, ès a dir, al bell mig de la nostra herència textual. (390)
> (pokes its nose in, or looks in, right where it's not invited: right into the dark closet of our feelings, into the very middle, that is, of our textual [or cultural] inheritance.)

In another way, however, Pons's interest in the material of a playwright like Sergi Belbel seems to move some distance away from a politics of sexuality which variously might place the ludic, the anti-normative or the sexually intense at its heart. Belbel is concerned with illustrating how 'sexual gratification is not necessarily – and is indeed rarely – part of a deeper communication between human beings' (George 2002: 93). Similarly, if *Amic/Amat* deploys 'a sexual discourse [that] does not grant much psychic depth to sexual choice' (Fernàndez 2008: 220), it might not seem fertile ground for the development of a queer aesthetic. Pons's own account of the dynamic at work in *Carícies*, as a deliberately negative representation (until the end) of 'aquello que es absolutamente positivo: el amor' ('what is absolutely positive: love') based around 'todo tipo de relaciones: homosexuales, heterosexuales' (Campo Vidal 2004a) ('all types of relationship: homosexual and heterosexual') chimes with Mira's perspective on Pons as the epitome of the normalising film-maker, making no distinctions between homosexual and non-homosexual narratives, issues or relationships while nonetheless leaving room for homoeroticism and subcultural allusion (Mira 2008: 547). However, what might otherwise have been the assimilation in the name of 'love' of queer concerns gains an edge of resistance from two sources. One is the sheer theatrical strangeness of the homosexual relationships in the two films so far discussed, as well as in the English-cast, English-language *Food of Love* (2001); another is the directness with which the films may be perceived to address or affect Spanish queer cultures. This directness is evoked by *Zero* magazine's interviewer (Esteban 1999a) who in one prompt to the director speaks of the authenticity of his 'approach' to homosexuality and suggests, perhaps, a return to the progressive mode of the heritage years in that:

> Hacía tiempo que no veíamos personajes tan reales de gays y lesbianas dentro de historias tan conmovedoras como éstas. Parece algo

revolucionario en un tiempo que están tan de moda películas un tanto petardas. (97)

(It is a long time since we have seen such true characterisations of gay men and lesbians set in such moving stories as these. It seems revolutionary in a time when somewhat crude comedies are so in fashion.)

Between these 'real' characters, however amplified and typically representative (in *Carícies*, in modernist style, they have no names) they may be, and the difficult dialogue or the esoteric psychological positioning of key characters, there are productive tensions. These are enhanced by emotional extremity, the reflexive camerawork of the sort Pons alludes to in talking about *Carícies* above, the conventional theatrical device of planting grief, dissension, sexual and emotional frustration and failures of communication in the bourgeois home and city, and above all by performance. A similar process is in operation in the queerer films of Almodóvar, of course, with a more film-melodramatic turn.

Forasters (*Strangers*) (2008), subtitled 'melodrama familiar entre dos segles' ('a melodrama of a family across two centuries'), after the play of Sergi Belbel, has a gay man as the link across the generations (one of the 1960s, one of the early 2000s). Josep, as adult, is selling the flat in which the story takes place (Manel Barceló plays the adult); the teenage Josep (Dafnis Balduz) grows up in the knowledge, as his terminally ill mother puts it to him as he washes her in the bath, that, though a good boy, 'tens aquesta tara' ('you've got this defect'). As the immediate scenario plainly suggests, it is not Josep who needs to wash away the stains and defects; rather, in a classic gesture of homophobic scapegoating and displacement the voice of wider socially received ideas – relayed by the mother (who else, for psychodramatic effect?) – blames the boy for showing symptoms of its own malaise, one which manifests in xenophobia (towards the family upstairs in the 2000s) and patriarchal repression and violence (in the family upstairs in the 1960s). From the perspective of the narrative present, Josep clearly never took his mother's stifling advice to stay in the closet and get along with girls. The film discretely shows his boyfriend and an implied life after closetry; in the closing arrangements over the sale of the apartment, a queer life is, indeed, leaving its mark for posterity.

The relationship built up in *Amic/Amat* between the professor of medieval Catalan literature Jaume (played by another major figure on the Catalan and Spanish screen and stage, Josep Maria Pou) and his brilliant but recalcitrant student David (David Selvas) is nothing, at one level, if not a classic bourgeois set-up and a highly conventional dramatic device. What explodes it – queers it – is the pressure of intellectual questions of inheritance and sexual desire, or, as Fernàndez puts it (2008: 215), 'the paradoxical juxtaposition of the body and its legacy [placed in the context of] Catalan culture' and a directness in the representation of non-normative homoeroticism. This directness, with David selling a sexually charged image of himself to clients and audience alike and

Jaume providing frank detail of his homosexually promiscuous earlier years, is not without its paradoxical reversion to, if not the normative, nonetheless the typical. On the one hand, Fernàndez's sense of the two men as 'very distant from the usual cinematic stereotypes of gay men' (2008: 221) and the film's 'neutralisation' through them 'of modern discourses of homosexuality' (220) is convincing for an audience focused on the pedagogic-paederastic model Fernàndez helpfully sees the film as exploring (216–24). On the other hand, an audience looking elsewhere might see in them little more than variations on an old theme in queer Spanish film heritage (in Eloy de la Iglesia, Jaime Chávarri and Pedro Almodóvar through the one-man-teaching-another motifs of *La ley del deseo* and *La mala educación*). This other audience might also see a realistic representation of two contrasting ways, from two different historical periods, of men managing the business of having sex with, and falling in love–hate relationships with, younger men. David, so handsome, so well (and sometimes so fetishistically) dressed and so masculine in his posturing, is the typical object of desire of popular gay consumer culture (although David the character is not 'gay'). Jaume is, basically, the older or more learned gay man who is the protagonist narrator of many a Spanish novel from those of Eduardo Mendicutti (see Chapter 5) to others constructed around unequal erotic capital and notions, such as in Pedro Jiménez Ariza's *La noche en que me enamoré de River Phoenix* (The Night I Fell in Love With River Phoenix): 'Debe ser hermoso proteger a alguien, me dije. Sí, lo es. Y también era hermoso ser esclavo a su lado' (Jiménez Ariza 2003: 153) ('It must be beautiful to be someone's protector, I said to myself. And it is. And it was also also beautiful to to be a slave at his side').

Josep Maria Pou's negotiations in performance between grief-stricken awareness of the undesirability of his body and the uncertain value of his intellectual production, between creepiness and urgent purposefulness, continually shift the perspectives for the audience. The typically gay and the extraordinarily homoerotic are shown as intertwined; the sexual and the social matrices of power are overlaid. David is a heterosexually identified rent boy for men with a pregnant girlfriend, Alba (Irene Montalà) and a violent aversion to homosexual love: but he needs a man, a father-figure. Jaume is – like the friends of his generation – dulled and in crisis precisely because of social and professional success, but he is reignited by the bizarre conjunction in his life of medieval thought on salvation and masochistic homosexual love dressed up in modern kit. He seems to need a (younger) man and a sense of loving, but all he really needs is a sense of futurity. It is Pons's recent attraction to the representation of this sort of undecidability, as well as an undeniable quotient of 'messy and overwrought ideas' alongside intensity and originality (Lim 2000), that brings into such high relief the queer pleasures, for Pons, of visualising the male body (Fouz-Hernández 2009). It makes his output – despite its inherited narrative and dramatic conventionality – curiously radical. It also contributes to his high profile at festivals and relative success in the international DVD distribution market.[6]

As already noted in Chapter 2, Pedro Almodóvar – another radical tradi-tionalist, in recent years at least – constitutes a strong personality-based line of contact with the LGTB past in Spain; Smith (2000a), writing during the early 1990s, had made the crucial link, too, with queer cultures, suggesting that 'Almodóvar anticipates the critique of identity and essence that was later to become so familiar in feminist, minority and queer theory' (3, also 170) and that his 'pursuit of pleasure' (in his early films) 'might be read as political', in the sense later taken up, for example, by Gracia Trujillo in her discussion of the radical ludic and the imperative for a lesbian-queer politics to stake out a playful, pleasurable occupation of marginal positions (Trujillo Barbadillo 2008b: 109). Medhurst (2009: 125) frames him as 'pre-eminent[ly] queer'. However, just along the terminological line, Mira reports that his informants in the blog questionnaire feeding into his book *Miradas insumisas* reiterate and consolidate a supposition long floating free in the Spanish and the worldwide press, that 'la estética almodovariana es lo que los espectadores gay consideran epítome de la "estética gay"' (Mira 2008: 416; and comments thread to 'A queer one/Julie Jordan' 2006) ('Almodóvar's style is what gay audiences con-sider to be the epitome of "a gay style"'). This positioning of Almodóvar as gay auteur and cult figure is certainly borne out in popular reactions as mediated in the gay press: *Zero* magazine in 1999, still in its more cultural-political mode before the turn to the style-and-glamour emphases which preceded its demise a decade later, ran an eighteen-page feature on the director, with an interview, comments and photos (Barón et al. 1999). '¿Cuánto le deben los gays españoles a Pedro Almodóvar' ('How much do Spanish gay men owe to Almodóvar?') is the significantly obvious leading question, with the tag, 'y viceversa?' (Barón et al. 1999: 56). The feature alights on affinities and aesthetics as the 'rasgos definidores [y] marcas de la cultura gay de este fin de siglo' (56) ('defining traits of gay culture at the end of the millennium'). In the entry under H or Homosexualidad in the feature's A to Z, the coordinating editor notes how

> los gays, . . . en su progresiva salida del armario [desde la *movida*] habían aprendido a sofisticar su imagen y tomaban lecciones de su director favorito. (Esteban 1999b)
> (gay men . . . as they continued the process of coming out [since the *movida*] had learned to refine their image and were taking lessons in sophistication from their favourite director.)

As well as aesthetics and affinities, then, there is a political effect surrounding this director, but not one arising out of emulation or, indeed, out of any real-istically assimilable life lessons. In the same pages in which he is lauded as the bestower of mixed cultural and political capital – how to be queer (male) but cool, perhaps – Almodóvar refuses to self-identify sexually, or allow his films to be, as he sees it, pigeonholed (Barón et al. 1999: 63). This is the customary position for him (Mira 2008: 419–20).

Since that pre-1999 period when Almodóvar was, as it seems, teaching Spanish men how to come out in style, he has increasingly tended to make films reflecting on and reworking favourite genres, or his own *oeuvre*, or focused on the objects of desire of world cinephilia (the essays in Epps and Kakoudaki (2009) give some recent sense of this range). Only *La mala educación* (see Chapter 2) in this period has a plot that pivots round an unequivocally homosexual man. When lesbianism is explicitly returned to, in the relationship between Huma (Marisa Paredes) and Nina (Candela Peña) in *Todo sobre mi madre* (*All About My Mother*) (1999), it is set to one side of a complex process, as Bersani and Dutoit argue (2009), of the 'desexualising and depsychologising of homosexuality' (265). This process works in favour, rather, of a rich form of sociability between women (in which Nina has no part); alternatively, it is there more for melodramatic and intertextual effect than for making an argument about desire between women. The characterisation of the gifted, glamorous older woman who allows her life to be ruined by a feckless, drug-using and unfeeling younger lover is formulaic (except, that is, in performance – Paredes circumvents this). Although it represents very much the opposite of presenting a positive role model (and so might be thought of as queer), it is not even empowering by way of perversity, as it might otherwise have been, in a queer masochistic manner. It contributes to the risk of the film becoming one of 'exotic trappings' that audiences might appreciate but without 'necessarily identifying with Almodóvar's gender dissent' (Maddison 2000: 270). This is in contrast to the film's queerer, if highly stylised, attention to transgender in the characters of Agrado (Antonia San Juan) and Lola (Toni Cantó) and to that project of enhanced sociability within a wider plotting of gender dissent (276–8). The queering of the somewhat heteronormatively structured lesbian relationship, which might otherwise make it part of the film's 'radical inclusion of resistant identities' (282) and help audiences think their way out of gender power relations structured around men, is in very many ways unavailable.

Actors (II): Newer Names

Almodóvar's appeal for a younger audience segment is perhaps at best retro in character. However, a number of young actors in recent films have found conscious and unconscious commonalities with the style of early to middle period Almodóvar. I want now to return to *Chuecatown* – which makes an old favourite of Almodóvar's central to its plot: the combination of violent death, farce and incompetent police men. Pablo Puyol, in the character of the murderous Víctor, has a particular resonance for audiences in their twenties and thirties, partly through prior roles and partly for his career in music and dance. One of the most prominent of the short films of the early- to mid-festival years boom in LGBT short film production in Spain was *En malas compañías* (*Doors Cut Down*) (Antonio Hens, 2000) in which Puyol had played the hunky garage mechanic, Asier, from late-teen Guillermo's (Israel Rodríguez) neighbourhood. Guillermo's matter-of-fact account of his desires, his cruising the shopping centre, a forcible coming out and his parents' reactions is one of its most radical and enabling features. The relationship with Asier which he finally strikes up beyond the toilets of their first encounter works as a narrative counterweight to his father's comment – on seeing a besotted older man hanging around outside their flats – that 'hay mucho maricón suelto por allí' ('there are a lot of queers on the loose out there'). It is also a vibrant visual contrast to the deathly silence that overcomes family life after Guillermo is caught in bed at home with his male English teacher. On a trip back together to the shopping centre, both looking good, both looking confident, Guillermo gives Asier a lingering sexy, public kiss in full and defiant view of the security guards who had once enforced his prosecution for cruising. The voice-over comment 'me siento bien con él' ('I feel good with him') makes Asier/Puyol a token of liberation, a handsome prince, for Guillermo. What Rodríguez is representing in this characterisation is a common enough set of experiences and anxieties for young men who have sex with men. The poster image of the two of them – still in circulation on the web – is like a cheeky little medal of empowerment, with Puyol the knowing lure. In *Zero* magazine's review of the line-up for the 1999 Madrid and Barcelona festivals (Esteban 1999c) it is Puyol's head, seductive glance and tattooed shoulder which (with the image reversed) occupies more than half the lead-in page (67).[7]

By the time Puyol played the straight-acting hunk of a market warehouse-boy, Raúl, in the flamboyant musical *20 centímetros* (*Twenty Centimetres*) (Ramón Salazar, 2005), he was already 'a heart throb' (Fouz-Hernández and Martínez-Expósito 2007: 194). Raúl is the problematic love interest for Marieta (Mónica Cervera) who is transitioning but currently stuck with the eponymous twenty centimetre-long obstacle to her full sexual happiness, though, amusingly and disruptively enough, it is very much part of her charms for Raúl. Carnivalesque overturnings of established gender and sex roles and of homo- and heterosexual behavioural boundaries are abundant in the film. At one stage Marieta observes to Raúl 'muy activo no te veo' ('you don't look much like a top to me') as they attempt anal sex, but he also plays his part in their relationship like a young, heterosexual and rather straightforward gallant, courteously looking out for Marieta's safety (as well he might). Puyol's first beautifully lit, almost slow-motion appearance, with a box of strawberries on his ample shoulder, is a resonant set-piece, in harmony with the film's borrowings from the great film musicals and their showiness: it sets him up as an object of desire and positions him in a highly equivocal play of ideas around the phallic (Fouz-Hernández and Martínez-Expósito 2007: 193–6), getting a queer fix on him. The one-joke, two-dimensional treatment of him in *Chuecatown* was, then, unfortunate: in the end it is the vision of his dead body which allows his role to speak most interestingly there, as a satirically exemplary end. Despite the mildly allegorical import for the times of the film's release of Víctor's body fascism and clothes snobbery (on which see Fouz-

Hernández 2010: 90–2, 98), Puyol is not enabled by the film to bring forward much of the disruptive material attaching to his spectacular image in previous appearances.

Like Puyol, Carlos Fuentes – who plays Rey in *Chuecatown* – has a prior association with the sort of compact and intense treatment of LGBTQ issues which the short-film format allows, as well as with the kind of camp perspectives on marginality that Almodóvar so effectively focalises. In the short *Ricardo: Piezas descatalogadas* (*Ricardo: Discontinued Items*) (Herman@s Rico, 2005), Fuentes plays a taxi driver, Ricardo, whose voice-over monologue introduces us to the rejects in life referred to in the film's title. One of the snapshot lives is Carlos (a.k.a. Nano) (Paco Becerra), who is astringently introduced to us as 'maricón, pero no como los de hoy' ('a queer, but not like those modern ones') – the modern ones being ones you cannot tell are queer and who come on to you. For Ricardo, Carlos 'no es gay ... es maricón' ('is not gay, he's queer'), and Ricardo sees the *maricón* in this sense as 'in a minority'. However in a minority Carlos might be, he has strong and radical views and a forceful way of putting them. In a cameo conversation in the cab – another Almodovarian touch (Allinson 2006: 116–18, 131–2) – he objects, for example, to over-made up and complacent television presenters talking routinely of homosexuality as 'an accepted fact': he, Carlos, is happy enough with the fact, but objects to the acceptance. This stand against poorly informed condescension would have pleased the radical thinker Paco Vidarte (1970–2008), whose complex thesis in *Ética marica* (2007) has as one of its bases the conviction that the particular politics of acceptance constructed in Spain around the time of the changes to the marriage laws are violently (neoliberally) exclusive, leaving aside – with Lesbian and Gay politics in league and inhabiting a 'Disgayland' (Vidarte 2007a: 22) – the practical totality of queer subject positions and queers (46–62), falsifying the ideas of community or solidarity and disallowing the formation of a sense of 'ourselves' (19–21).

Fuentes' character becomes involved with a bitter-sweet celebration of the sort of anti-normalising radical queer that is associated not only with contemporary oppositional thinking such as Vidarte's but also, in tone and look, with the politics of some sectors of late 1970s sexual politics in Spain, as encapsulated in the figure of José Pérez Ocaña, as presented in Ventura Pons' *Ocaña* (1978) or in the magazine of the short-lived Coordinadora de Col·lectius d'Alliberament Gai, *La Pluma* (Mira 2004: 455–60, 485–6). The end of this short film is certainly queer enough – in an old- and a new-fashioned sense – as Ricardo drives the taxi off down through the underpass, with the city lights above, and does his 'cock-thing' to please Carlos in the passenger seat: the trick is to steer hands-free with a readily sprung erection at the wheel, and this he cheerfully shows and does. In one direction there is the comedy of scandal of the *movida* (and the much-loved 'erecciones generales' ('general erections') sketch in Almodóvar's *Pepi, Luci, Bom y otras chicas del montón* of 1980), with its own roots in music hall variety smut; in another, there is the new(-ish) ludic representation of the homosocial continuum along whose stretch, here, men meet giggling halfway between homo- and hetero, as united by the cock-thing as they are by their grief at the recent death of Ana (Silvia Giner), whom Ricardo had fallen for precisely because she was terminally ill – a personal tragedy which is intersected by the narrative strands of social disempowerment and exclusion.

Lastly, of *Chuecatown*'s collection of minor or not quite major names, there is Pepón Nieto in the role of Leo. Nieto already had the attention of a mass audience for his role as Mariano Moreno in the police drama *Los hombres de Paco* (Paco's Men) (Antena 3, 2005–10), whose plot-line involving Pepa (Laura Sánchez) and Silvia (Marián Aguilera) and their wedding was a major lure for an LGBTQ audience segment (Antena3 2011b). An earlier role as José Antonio Aranda in *Periodistas* (Journalists) (Tele5, 1998–2002) had seen him associated with the series' 'self-conscious dramatisation of social issues' (Smith 2000b: 188). Ten years previously, Nieto had played the flamboyantly queeny Carlos in *Perdona bonita, pero Lucas me quería a mí* (starring with Jordi Mollà) in a performance that Mira (2008) finds 'perfectamente creíble' (512) ('perfectly believable') and true to life, despite, he notes, being not to the taste either of gay audiences (too 'marica') or straight (too 'gay') (513). Not to the taste of most LGBTQ audiences, it might be imagined, is the tenor of Nieto's reply when interviewed about the prize awarded to him in recognition of his work at the third Festival del Sol in Las Palmas (2008). Asked by a historically disingenuous reporter about his taking on gay roles, 'cuando no estaba bien visto' (Ayala 2008) ('when doing so was so not well regarded') – in 1997 and 2003, no less – he replies 'Bueno, en verdad, sólo he hecho tres mariquitas en todas las producciones . . . hasta la fecha' ('well, in fact I've only played gays three times in all until now'), reiterating this in his next response for all the world as if, actually, doing so were still not well regarded (by Nieto at least). The too 'marica' and too 'gay' mode had been reprised by Nieto in *Los novios búlgaros* (*Bulgarian Lovers*) (Eloy de la Iglesia, 2003) with the role of Gildo, most of whose dialogue is a string of catty jokes using the feminine form for talking about men, and whose gestures and movements Nieto renders with restless cockings of the head, spreadings of the hands and general heavyweight shimmying. To this extent Nieto becomes an anti-model, playing a type the recognition of whom triggers perhaps a rather anachronistic laugh but mostly the registration of a mental note to avoid the perpetuation of such shallowly adopted social roles. Nieto as Gildo becomes a useful reminder by negative example of how to measure the distance between radical camp of the sort discussed by Mira (2004: 142–75, 525–9) or displayed, low key, by Marta Balletbò-Coll in *Sévigné* (see Chapter 2), and the performance of camp as a hollow, much repeated and inappropriately stagey joke. Nonetheless, the representation in *Chuecatown* of Leo as the cosy, more or less low-key, hard-working and early middle-aged 'bear' living a modest life in Chueca is, for 2007, perfectly believable if we remove the frame of comedy. It chimes with some elements in *Cachorro* (again, see Chapter 1) and there are some distant visual matches.

POPULAR FILM-MAKERS

By 2001, and the release of *I Love You Baby*, the writer-director team of David Menkes and Alfonso Albacete were already being discussed online in terms of a recognisable and reiterated style (J. O. 2011 [2001?]) – as auteurs – and along with Dunia Ayuso and Félix Sabroso (see Chapter 5) they represent a fairly wide niche market in gay Spanish comedies. One online reviewer (Martínez March 2001) notes that *I Love You Baby* shares with *Sobreviviré* 'el mismo espíritu de llevar a cabo una comedia liberal [y] romántica . . . tolerante con la variedad de gustos sexuales del personal' ('the same willingness to make a liberal-minded, romantic comedy [showing] tolerance towards the sexual preferences of those involved'). As they had done with *Sobreviviré* the directors (and their co-writer Lucía Etxebarria – see Chapter 5) combine elements of everyday social realism with extravagantly unlikely emotional scenarios. Marcos (Jorge Sanz) is a simple village lad, come to the big city to work in his aunt and uncle's bar. Marisol (Tiaré Scanda), who falls for him, is from the Dominican Republic, working in Spain to make money to help bring up the toddler she has had to leave behind. The traditional Madrid bar, her shared flat, a hairdressing salon where she works, the dance venue-cum-community bar, La Americana – all these venues give the film a mixed look of the retro (this is the Madrid of 1960s popular comedies or of nostalgic TV dramas) and the topically social realist (the salon is a site for precarious employment for immigrant and transient populations – as also in *Princesas* (*Princesses*) (Fernando León de Aranoa, 2005) and *El dios de madera* (The Wooden God) (Vicente Molina Foix, 2010)). On the other hand, the central premises and the pivotal moments of the plot are far from believable. How could Marcos – for all that he later reveals that back in the village he had always fantasised about going to bed with a man – so easily and quickly fall for Daniel (Santiago Magill), lovely though his eyes, his ideals and his young man's beard might be? How could Daniel not heed warnings from Carmen (Veronica Forqué) that it is all too sudden and that Marcos might be just experimenting? How, particularly, should Marcos's abrupt switch back to heterosexuality (and Marisol) really be due to a karaoke-bar accident with a glitter-ball? When Daniel decides that the best way to win Marcos back is to cross-dress and pursue him, and when a some-years-later coda reveals that Daniel is now the lover of his longtime idol, Boy George (whom we are reminded was also a victim of a glitter-ball accident, and who makes a strange little personal appearance in the final minutes), one has to laugh. If in its ordinary moments the film almost has something to say about difficult comings out, precarious working conditions and (by example) the dangers of living in ignorance of queer lore, in the extraordinary moments it is an interesting muddle. The interest comes of the commercial success of these two directors (see below) and from speculating about which of the 1,080,029 paying viewers who went to see *Sobreviviré* and the 115,548 for *I Love You Baby* (MECD 2012) were true successors to those queer viewers of 1960s and 1970s comedies who also might have found themselves not knowing whether to laugh or to resist (Melero 2010: 160).

The film is reinforced by three key players with strong associations for different segments of the LGBT audience. Santiago Magill as Daniel would have been familiar to a younger segment for his role as the (initially) closeted protagonist Joaquín in the Spanish-Peruvian co-production *No se lo digas a nadie* (*Don't Tell Anyone*) (Francisco Lombardi, 1998), a film which, in the coming-out-and-finding-oneself sub-genre, is an intense and at times powerfully erotic recapitulation of the dramas of patriarchal control, homophobia, closetry and the influence of traditional Catholic teaching. It is also a film which explores (in a way which Albacete and Menke's film fails to do) some of the intricacies of queer migration (Subero 2006: 189, 196). It involves reinventions of the self and renegotiations of sexual desire (190), as well as meanderings between the experiential territories of the hetero- and the homosexual (192–8). Joaquín, in the Peruvian film, becomes reinstalled in a closeted life, 'tak[ing] a position within heterosexism itself' (199); in the Spanish film, Magill's character reverses the situation, as an out (if naive) gay man witnessing it all played out in the ostensibly conflicted Marcos.

Jorge Sanz brings with him for a slightly older audience segment connotations of his former self as sex object (Perriam 2003a: 145–72): heterosexual in *Belle époque* (Fernando Trueba, 1993), homosexual (for pay) in *Hotel y domicilio* (*In Calls and Out*) (Ernesto del Río, 1995), semi-comical heterosexist in a host of comedies through the 1990s (Perriam 2003a: 158–63) and cross-dressed in *Almejas y mejillones* (*Mussels and Clams*) (Marcos Carnevale, 2000). However, his performance is lacklustre – seeming to take far too literally the scripted denominations of him as *paleto* (bumpkin) – and registers nothing of the conflict or the joy which might more usually be associated with the drama of a first gay bonding, kissing and sex (tellingly, not shown), let alone the drama of getting all this wrong in the first place. As one informal web critique put it:

> Jorge Sanz vuelve a repetir como portador del estandarte pro-cambio de la identidad sexual, como ya hizo en *Almejas y mejillones* y vuelve a estar igual de insustancial que de costumbre. (chueca.com 2001)
> (Jorge Sanz repeats his role as a standard-bearer for sexual identity change, as in Mussels and Clams, but once again he is as lacking in substance as ever.)

Veronica Forqué as Carmen, Marcos's gay-friendly best woman friend, appeals to the Almodóvar fans on the one hand and, on the other, to the fans of *Reinas* (see Chapter 1) as well as to those of the only slightly unconventional, and decidedly straight, *¿Por qué lo llaman amor cuando quieren decir* *sexo?* (*Why Do They Call It Love When They Mean Sex?*) (Manuel Gómez Pereira, 1993), where she works with Sanz and Rosa Maria Sardà. The Forqué of Almodóvar's *¿Qué he hecho yo para merecer esto!* (*What Have I Done To Deserve This?*) (1984) and *Kika* (1993), as Cristal the prostitute next door and as the eponymous psycho-sexual blank slate, respectively, can bring to the lighter roles of later films such as *I Love You Baby* a trace of enjoyable perversity, a queer association. But it more than risks dilution.

Mentiras y gordas (*Sex, Party and Lies*) (2009) consolidated the relative commercial success of Albacete and Menkes, and was a substantial early box-office success taking first place for takings (€1,793,314) in the first weekend run in Spain (28–29 March 2009) with 220 copies in distribution and beating Almodóvar's *Los abrazos rotos* (*Broken Embraces*), in its third week of its run, into third place (Fotogramas 2009). It too exploits the associations and prior roles of its actors, but at a different level and for a different generation. It has the studio-and-manageable-locations look, and the episodic style, of light television drama (though with a portentous, high soap opera finale), and its cast includes some small-screen grand celebrities of the younger generation.[8] One commentator predicted that the unexpectedly grim perspectives on the lives of twenty-somethings in Spain in the 2000s meant that 'no es la película que esperaban los fans de las series que han hecho populares a sus protagonistas' (Vall 2009) ('it is not the film that was hoped for by the fans of the television series which made its characters popular') and that this could adversely affect its takings (he was wrong). Built around familiar patterns of friends, flatmates, lovers, crushes and infidelities, as in the earlier, cult generational film *Historias del Kronen* (*Stories of the Kronen*) (Montxo Armendáriz, 1995) the film juxtaposes pleasure and disillusion against a backdrop of political and economic crises of confidence (much more penetratingly explored in the earlier film). Of the half a dozen or so combinations of close friends, ex's and couples, two are of particular interest to the LGBTQ audience (the physical charms apart of Ana de Armas and of Hugo Silva – who, with the TV presenter and comedian Eva Hache, opened the 2008 Madrid Pride celebrations). These are Tony (Mario Casas) and Nico (Yon González: with a role, as Iván, in the quality Antena 3 series *El internado* (The Boarding School)), and Marina (Ana María Polvorosa) and Leo (Duna Jové).

The two young men are bonded by a long-standing power play in which Tony, until the narrative span of the film at least, has silently suffered from his strong homosexual attraction to Nico, and in which Nico only half-consciously uses this constantly to get Tony to do as he wants (such as get involved in casual dealing). What goes on between them is significantly enhanced by their small-screen prominence and heart-throb celebrity status beyond the film. Casas was already a well-known figure for his role as Aitor Carrasco in *Los hombres de Paco* and as Javi in *SMS: Sin miedo a soñar* (Not Afraid of Dreaming, TxT) (La Sexta, 2006–7). One Mario Casas fan site (now closed) covered his early career with particular dedication, and is superseded (by mariocasasfans 2012) and supplemented by a smartly designed new Forum (MarioCasasWeb 2011a, 2011b). Winner of the Shangay prize for the best performance by a Spanish actor in an LGBTQ-themed film (MarioCasasWeb 2011b) he was rapidly – hastily, indeed – claimed for gay iconic status (Giraldo 2009). This has subsequently been consolidated (despite no further gay or queer roles) by a co-starring role, with María Valverde, in *3 metros sobre el cielo* (*Three Steps Over Heaven*) (Fernando González Molina, 2011) and a range of cultural interventions, new roles and performances (MarioCasasWeb 2011a).

As for González, the crafting and the fan and audience impact of *El internado*, as Smith (2010: 309–12) has pointed out, was substantial and intricate; the series launched his image as 'uno de nuestros guapos oficiales' ('one of our officially recognised heart-throbs') – as well as his career (Antena3 2011a). Before *El internado*, like Casas, he had had a major and continuous role (as Andrés) in the series *SMS*. Like others on the cast of *Mentiras y gordas*, he already had a highly active web fan-base (El Internado 2008; Cascales 2010b: 15), and was able to use the role as 'a stepping-stone to cinema' (Smith 2010: 309) and to further television work (though in neither case as solidly as Casas). He has also become a gay pin-up, whose presentation on the front of *Shangay Style* in the summer of 2008 as 'no longer a boy' is as indicative of career trajectory as it is bluntly suggestive (Cascales 2010b; see also Yon González 2011).

The two women, Marina and Leo (whose name is one of the lies of the title) are engaged in a passionate relationship not the least of whose problems is their evening-after-the-night before mutual decision that neither is really lesbian. Their negotiations of their differently motivated refusal of the lesbian label constitute a strong exemplary sub-narrative. Ana María Polvorosa, as Marina, works vividly through the emotional difficulties of coming to lesbianism by way of attraction to an apparently much more knowledgeable and worldly woman and in ignorance (as so often in these feature films) of the community and social networks of possible, lesbian-specific support (she relies on her not very wise friends, and on instinct, for direction). Polvorosa was awarded, along with Casas, the prize for Best Performance at the 2009 LesGaiCine festival. Their roles, in the words of the festival press release, as 'dos personajes homosexuales' ('as two homosexual characters') were seen – perhaps rather problematically, or, at least, insufficiently – as contributing 'a la visibilidad de jóvenes gais y lesbianas' (DosManzanas 2009) ('to the visibility of younger gays and lesbians'). Polvorosa has worked on the television series *Aída* (Telecinco, in her role January 2009–ongoing) and has a substantial presence for fans there, as well as being involved in a crypto-lesbian screen kiss with television personality Belén Esteban, making a guest appearance (Series 8, Episode 18 (143)) – a moment whose premise in the script is that kissing another woman will help you become famous. (Esteban had also had a cameo role, as a cleaner, in the short *Petunias* (César Vallejo, 2005), a zany piece focused around the quickfire, yet deadly serious, dialogue of three drag queens reviewing their lives as they get ready to go out on stage.)

The connections to television of the other actors include: Ana de Armas (Carola) in *El internado*, alongside González; Hugo Silva (Carlos) in *Los hombres de Paco*, alongside Casas (from 2007); Asier Etxeandia (Cristo) in *Herederos* (The Inheritors) (TVE, 2008–9) and *Los hombres de Paco*, along-side Casas (from 2010); Maxi Iglesias (Pablo) in *Física o Química* (from 2008 to 2010) and *Los protegidos* (The Protected Ones) (Antena3, from summer 2010), in which much is made of his bare torso (just as in *Física o Química*, his character, Cabano, had used his body for work in web pornography: in Series 2). These domestic small-screen personalities and names in print and at social networked fan locations become, then, cross-associated through their involve-ment in the film with two dramas of queer indecision: one lesbian in all but name, represented with visual directness but not much purpose; the other a tale of the precarious borderline between homosociality and the cruelties, in Nico and Tony respectively, of casual and internalised homophobia.

Casas's acting in relation to this politically crucial issue is frequently excel-lent in embodying the discomfort and yearning felt by Tony whenever he is near Nico. However, the potentially queer discourse which an audience might unpack is sabotaged by pat and universalising instances in the script, such as Tony's assurance to a tearful Carola, in love with the sexually unfaithful Carlos, that being in love is 'una mierda' ('shit'). Similarly, any specificity that the acting might have endowed is effectively erased in the film's finale, first by an extended sequence in which Casas must stagger bewildered around the dance floor, and second by his ultimate collapse and death from danger-ously combining different recreational drugs. His end is unfortunately close to being a classic killing off of the queer as a tragic figure, not only because it is associated through montage with what should have been a liberating (though possibly bareback) sexual encounter with a very handsome stranger but also because of a clumsily overused musical number 'Tony el Mesías' (Juan Sueiro and Juan Carlos Molina) that sets Tony up as screen sacrifice. Nico's genuine horror and the belated release of his conflicted emotions as he embraces the dead Tony out among the parked cars is strongly affecting, and might animate a critique of the restrictions of heterosexual masculinity were it not for this structural self-sabotage. The sequence makes too prolonged a use of slow motion and of muting out the ambient sounds of urgency and distress; it also wants to draw too much on the generic homosociality of the cinematic fallen buddy. That Tony only gets to be properly embraced by Nico when he, Tony, is a ghost – on the seashore at dawn in a poorly established epilogue fantasy sequence with an oddly dispersed point of view – does nothing to cement the realities of learning to be queer in contemporary Spain. As for Marina and Leo, they are just looking in on this final drama of doomed queer masculinity, and looking sad, and looking good. The young actors, and what they might embody and convey for a queer audience, have had to struggle with what some commentators have seen as not so much the positive and career-amplifying effects of popular auteurism with a genuine new take on the dynamics of exclusion as mere repetitiveness, sexploitation and lack of directorial talent (Focoforo 2009; comments in 'robgordon' 2009).

Mira (2008) posits the existence of a number of popular gay auteurs working within a process of 'desarmarización' ('coming out of, or removal of, the closet') which he sees as opening up creative possibilities (546), tapping into direct personal experience, free from a 'repertorio construido desde la perspectiva heterosexista' (548) ('a repertoire built around heterosexist perspectives') and contributing to a signature style or set of preoccupations (545–6). As well as Menkes, Almodóvar and Pons, he cites Miguel Albaldejo, Antonio Hens, Juan Luis Iborra, Ramón Salazar and (surely less 'popular') Gerardo Vera and Agustí Villaronga (546). To this list should be added – as well as some of the actor-icons with whom this chapter has also been concerned – writer-directors Chus Gutiérrez and Marta Balletbò-Coll and, on the more restricted but equally 'popular' short-film circuit, Juanma Carrillo, Mariel Maciá, María Pavón and Rut Suso, and Jorge Torregrossa, as frequent presenters at the key festivals and with a recognisable touch. It is to the resonances of figures such as these, for different audience segments, that the next chapter will turn.

NOTES

1. In particular the page for Monólogos de bollería fina, <http://www.facebook.com/pages/Monólogos-de-Boller%C3%ADa-Fina/113973285309617> [last accessed 16 June 2011].
2. Available at <http://www.cinelgbt.com/peliculas>; <http://www.lesbianlips.es/fichas/>; <http://www.lambdaweb.org/cinema/ca/ediciones_anteriores.php>; <http://www.lesgaicinemad.com/ediciones_anteriores?ArkXP=q2d1pn6c10lq6ncvf29g1fuqf2> [all last accessed 21 May 2012].
3. This section on Abril draws on a longer study (Perriam 2007a). I would like to thank the editors of the *Hispanic Research Journal* for permission to re-use some of that material.
4. In the later feature-length *Carne de neón* (*Neon Flesh*) (Paco Cabezas, 2010) Pura is played by the equally iconic Angela Molina, and ex-rent boy Ricky by Mario Casas (see below).
5. The resulting photograph is available at <http://www.joancrisol.com/foto.php?sc=4&ss=21&id=3> [last accessed 21 May 2012].
6. The University of Colorado Denver's International Conference 'Ventura Pons: The Unconventional Gaze of Catalan Cinema' (4–6 October 2012) is also a sign of the continuing academic interest in his work.
7. These images viewable at <http://www.filmaffinity.com/es/filmimages.php?movie_id=703870> and <http://www.homocine.com/cortos/e/enmalascompanias/enmalascompanias1.htm> [both last accessed 21 May 2012].
8. A fan video was available on the OneMore Lesbian (OML) website during 2011, and survives at <http://mentirasygordas.blogspot.co.uk/> [last accessed 21 May 2012]. On the attractions of the male actors specifically, see 7pk2 (2009).

4. AUDIENCES

There are three sets of audience which this chapter intends to analyse: readers and LGBT bookshop goers who are also DVD buyers and cinema goers; web-based queer 'followings' (of film-makers and of types of film); and festival audiences. In line with the findings of Pujol Ozonas on cinephilia and antici-pating a straightforward assumption that underlies my next chapter – that no queer person's cultural participation is dedicated solely to cinema – I begin by looking at queer cinephiles who are also readers or, at least, browsers and purchasers of books and magazines as well as DVDs. The notion of an inter-pretive community, indeed, famously surfaces in modern critical discourse in relation to texts (Fish 1980) and is later extensively used in discussions of science fiction, and other fan-targeted narrative genres in print and fan fiction on the Internet (Hellekson and Busse 2006; Hills 2002). Attention to the web-based audiences allows a mapping of the formation of queer interpretive com-munities, and the festivals offer an entry point for considering also 'wished-for interpretive communities', audiences, that is, 'wish[ing] to be part of certain kinds of community', a wish which 'shapes how they want to employ their imaginations around the film[s]' (Barker 2011). Both sets of audience manifest and construct identities and differences prompted by questions of taste, desire, commitment, political inclination, wish or fantasy in line with the dynam-ics of cinephilia (Pujol Ozonas 2011: 17–19); they might also be expected to resist the heteronormative context of mainstream cinephilia, which Pujol Ozonas argues is particularly acute in Spain (19–21) and which privileges the codes, tastes, habitats (the Filmoteca art houses and resources) and the sense of humour of the straight male (19). If it is axiomatic that 'ningún espectador es un solo tipo de espectador' (89) ('no viewer is just one sort of viewer'), then this is even more the case in the context of a strategic and wished-for engage-ment with films and their byproducts and sources as part of that polyvalent viewer's range of queer cultural experience. As Pujol Ozonas suggests specifi-cally of the popular cultural context:

[s]ituar el cine en el campo de la cultura popular contemporánea significa estudiarlo en relación con otros objetos de esa cultura [incluyendo] las culturas del tiempo libre y del ocio. (23)

(to place cinema within the field of contemporary popular culture means studying it in relation to other objects in that culture [including] leisure and free time.)

The Bookshop Image

I start, then, with the retail (and coffee-shop) spaces, the stock, online events postings and distribution of catalogues through e-listings by Berkana, the major Madrid-based LGBT bookshop, Cómplices (also Barcelona, and partner in the publishing enterprise Egales) and Antinous in Barcelona, at the serious and more bookish end of the spectrum. At the more visual end of the spectrum are boyberry.es/tiendaonline (mainly for film) and A Different Life. Berkana has made of itself an emblematic space at the heart of Chueca, that much filmed and written about – and much changed – neighbourhood in central Madrid. Like its predecessors in other countries (Reger 1999) – and in common with other such stores and feminist bookshops in Spain – Berkana has powerful connections to the lesbian and gay movement, to community projects and preoccupations, and to visibility in a period of intense struggle for social change. New books, artwork and films have been habitually presented in the bookshop's cafe area in its larger premises (between 1993 and 2011), involving some high-profile cultural figures as well as speakers from community groups and political organisations. It also sponsors events such as the local cultural events of Chueca Pensante (Thinking Chueca) in June 2011, or the blog and literature prize as part of the II Festival Lésbico MíraLes (November 2011). Its founder owner, Mili Hernández, is both a high-profile cultural promoter and political activist, having been General Secretary of the FLGTB and spokesperson for COGAM, among other roles (Herreo Brasas 2001: 312). In a conversation on 24 May 2011 Hernández saw the shop as having intervened directly in the lives of LGBTQ Spaniards and as a channel for the importation of new ideas, images and stories from outside Spain.[1] As a typical 1990s style LGBT bookshop, it is 'an essential part of the "ecosystem" supporting lesbian communities' (Reger 1999: 126) as well as gay ones. As Carlos, the narrator of Eduardo Mendicutti's *California* notes as he starts to put the heady, sexy days of porn shoots and sugar daddies in Hollywood behind him, back in Madrid the store is 'un refugio amable y lleno de otras voces' ('a friendly place of refuge, full of other voices') countering the deafening roar of the past, and of the noisy, flashy street outside in Chueca (Mendicutti 2005: 226). Egales, the linked publishing company (at <http://www.editorialegales.com/index.php>) has a strong list of commissioned translations of fiction and theory out of other languages, particularly English, and the stock on DVD ranged on the shelves has, over the years, made strikingly visible the commercial dominance of non-Spanish film entertainment for gay men and, even more so, for lesbians in a kind of double-edged cultural gift (cutting one way to make nice fittings of the imitative, comedic type discussed in Chapter 2 or of the youth culture or same-sex romantic products discussed throughout; cutting in another direction to shape an independent, resistant culture pushed in the main part into festival and web presence, and short or documentary format). The store has a stall at the annual Feria del Libro, a fact of visibility brought to a particularly interesting point in 2010 when Queen Sofía's visit to the stall made front-page news. Pilar Urbano's recent interview-based follow-up to her 1996 biography of the queen had cited her making apparently homophobic comments attacking Orgullo and same-sex marriage, widely leaked and protested in the autumn of 2008 (Mucientes 2008): 'Hernández took the opportunity to upbraid the monarch and present her with a very pointed gift: a history of gay culture in Spain [Mira's] *De Sodoma a Chueca*' (Hedgecoe 2011).

Linked to Berkana via Egales, Cómplices, in Barcelona, labels itself inclusively as a 'librería gay, lesbiana, transexual y bisexual' and, unlike its Barcelona rival Antinous, avoids listing its categories of merchandise on its website alphabetically. Instead, lesbian fiction in Spanish and lesbian fiction in translation come first, with queer theory seventh and transgender and transsexuality not too far down the list. (In the DVDs frame, transgender still comes after lesbian and gay, but these two have their priority reversed). Its blog site advertises its seventeen years promoting 'la cultura homosexual' and its commitment to 'la integración y la igualdad de derechos de gays y lesbianas de todo el mundo' (Librería Cómplices 2011) ('the integration and equal rights of gays and lesbians worldwide') whereas in a less 1980s style the links frame amalgamates (this time alphabetically) community and political organisations with magazines, leisure guides, commercial advertisements and catalogues. Here, the socialising is virtual, with no coffee-shop space but link-ups by way of the channels lesbianasviajeras or Nextown Ladies, for example. Antinous, like Berkana until 2011, has been able to make use of the bookshop/coffee-shop model, however, and now (since November 2008) also runs a blog. Although this store targets perhaps a less eclectic, slightly more bookish (and more male) clientele, labelling itself simply as a 'libreria', recent events have included a question and answer session with director Isabel Coixet, on the one hand, and a reading organised by the Col.lectiu Gai de Barcelona of Javier Sáez and Sejo Carrascosa's radical essay *Por el culo (Políticas anales)* (Arsewise: Anal Politics) on the other, as well as its own book club's sessions on Emili Teixidor (author of the novel *Pa negre*, the film version of which is discussed in Chapter 2) and on Federico García Lorca. The blog site's top page has, in its bottom left frame, clear links to a number of community help and activist groups, including the Casal Lambda, the veteran Front d'Alliberament Gai de Catalunya and the Associació de Famílies Lesbianes i Gais. Here it is more directly political in its linkages than Cómplices, with its more pluralistic and layered contextualising and chanelling of the experience of its LGBTQ users.

As physical and virtual spaces, these stores combine text with film and facilitate a mixed mode of consumption and production of Spanish queer culture. Queer cinephilia in Spain has in these spaces, at least for the most unrepentant of users of pirated material (although these do seem to be many), one of its most important points of reference and (self-defining) community interaction. As prominent novelist and film critic Vicente Molina Foix (see Chapter 5) notes, Berkana was 'donde tantos hicimos la "mili" de la mejor literatura y cinematografía gay y lesbiana' (Molina Foix 2009c) ('where so many of us did our MILItary service, drilled in the very best of lesbian and gay literature and film').

All these stores – and more so the websites – also keep the business running through the sale of items which would not fit Molina Foix's bill so well. Mugs, flags, kitsch souvenirs, calendars, high price-tag photographic erotica and pornography on disc and page mix with light and middle-brow fiction, boxed sets of *The L-Word* and *Queer As Folk* (both versions) as well as with the heavyweights Javier Sáez, Beatriz Gimeno, Luis Antonio de Villena, Agustí Villaronga (in this latter case, even at Boyberry, but alongside more straightforwardly salacious offerings). Even the relatively high-minded Antinous's alphabetical listing starts, by happy accident, with Accesorios. These stores and sites, while central to queer Spanish cinephilia and to the wider cultural and community ecosystem, are by no means exclusively spaces for radicalising cultural consumption and exchange. As Robbins observes (2011), even the community-minded and politically aware Berkana, in its larger Calle Hortaleza premises at least had a layout that 'at times favored the male consumer', forefronting 'erotic postcards and comics designed almost exclusively for men' and a women's narrative section with a backdrop of coffee-table photo portraits of male nudes (158). Cheerful pluralism (celebrating the Madrid leisure scene's smart management of a mixed lesbian and gay, queer and straight culture) has tended to rub shoulders, then, with effective monopolisation in this regard. In particular, in the mode of display and promotion of films on DVD (and leaving aside gay pornography, which is a more or less prominent lure in the different stores), commercial necessities understandably trump the immediate needs of community commitment, while also sustaining, in various and unexpected ways, an anti-normative discourse. The customer in search of the serious Spanish gay or borderline (male) queer art film might have to look for them stacked thinly side-on behind and around the comedies of custom and youth drama or reality-lifestyle films (such as *Mentiras y gordas*: see Chapter 3) propped up proudly facing front.

Regular DVD holdings of films for women also require of anyone in search of the lesbian a significant amount of looking behind the covers. In Antinous, Cómplices and Berkana the predominance is in popular titles of the sort that Tasker (1994) once noted are 'deemed interesting [for a lesbian perspective] and yet found wanting in quite complex ways' (172), wanting not least, that is, for their lack of radical social realism or ability, as De Lauretis (2007) has it, in her contrastive discussion of *She Must Be Seeing Things* (Sheila McLaughlin, 1987), for their lack of willingness to '[to pose] the question of desire and its representation from within the context of actual practices of lesbianism and cinema' (38). On the shelves of Berkana and the web lists elsewhere in 2011 both *Chloe* (Atom Egoyan, 2009) (among the English-language offerings prominent) and Julio Medem's *Habitación en Roma* (*Room in Rome*) (2010) were placed to outshine other more reliable and formative classics. The familiar tactical choices lie between delicious temporary complicity and determined resistance – one as queer as the other.

The Glamorous Lesbian Image

Several of the critical arguments presented in Chapter 3 about the theatrical adaptations of Ventura Pons identify a strong potential for redirection of the attention of audiences away from the comfortable, straight problematics at their dramatic surface. This happens either through the production, through the acting, through disturbances of feeling or through certain rebarbatively anti-normative elements in script and plot. The director-adaptor, moreover, has a fan base which adds its own rebalancing weight, away from an interest in the melodrama of the distraught but empowered and towards more socially and sexually marginalised subjects who are precarious but radically impassioned, who are in some ways queer. By contrast, Medem's film, while not a theatrical adaptation (rather a remake of the Chilean director Matías Bize *En la cama* (*In Bed*) of 2005), normalises the lesbian by redirecting attention away from 'the actual practices of lesbianism' (although, half paradoxically, it does so by extensive sex scenes) towards a rather generalised surface of secretive, intense and unexpected romance amplified by the much re-borrowed and markedly heterosexual device of the lightning affair – an in-cameo infidelity – played out in a holiday location or, as here, a luxury hotel. Medem does go through the motions, however, of some 'actual practices of . . . cinema', and the film has a visually luxurious treatment of bodies, urban structures and interiors, light and textures which, if they do not convince the viewer of their real connection to lesbian reality, certainly might make her wish she was there. Perhaps ironically (the film and the echoes in the director's idiosyncratic *oeuvre* make it hard to judge), however, Rome seen from the hotel balcony is heavy with the exotic stuff of classic films featuring, well, Rome and women.

The city is packaged for cinema, made into yet another in a long line of aestheticised 'cit[ies] of containment, of objects' on screen (Shonfield 2000: 133). This gives rise early on to fears of a matching commodification of the women and their bodies. Seen schematically on a map of the Roman city and via a Google Earth mock-up, it is also – true to one of Medem's auteurist predilections – a quirky microcosmic and spatially inverted arrangement designed to make the emotionally impelled action both tiny (fascinating) and portentous (involving) at one and the same time. This swamps what might have been the radically exciting core event – 'Alba' (Elena Anaya) and 'Natasha' (Natasha Yarovenko) making up stories about, and names for, themselves in order to demolish their outside identities better to enable a night of lovemaking which for Natasha is initiatory and for Medem is clearly envisaged as spectacular and an extension of his previous practice of representation of women-focalised, but heterosexual, sexualised romance. The sex in the room is so staged (and so unrealistically hasty, though reiterated) that the effect is one of chill detachment as Arce (2010) notes, interpreting this as an act of tactful respect for the subject matter. As another online critic quite rightly, but disingenuously and incompletely, remarks (Casañas 2010), the fact that the film as a remake swaps a man-and-a-woman pairing for a woman-and-a-woman pairing makes no difference. Casañas is using this to make the comfortable and widely applicable old point, that the film is interested in being 'una historia de amor con independencia del género de sus integrantes' (2010) ('a love story where the gender of those involved is irrelevant'). To this extent – the extent imposed by normalisation – the lesbianism makes no difference, and Anaya's compelling acting (particularly), and her positioning of herself as an actor in this empowering spot for her lesbian audience, has the sting taken out of it, in this suite of rooms, at least. However, as one blogger notes, 'Además, que una de las protagonistas sea lesbiana de verdad me parece que aporta más que realismo a la historia' ('Graciela' 2010) ('And the fact that one of the characters is lesbian in real life too gives the story a more realistic feel, I think'). Anaya was outed in the summer of 2011 by the gossip magazine *Cuore* and her inclusion in *El Mundo*'s ('La otra crónica', June 2011) annual list of the fifty most influential Spanish LGBTs (despite, as several collectives noted, having never addressed the issue in public). She had already become an object of fascination or a cause for frustration. Many fans were, by this stage, 'asumiendo el hecho' ('KAT' 2011) ('taking it for granted'), although the 'hecho' in question still refers ambivalently to bisexuality or lesbianism. Her suddenly heightened visibility as a public and screen personality with LGBT associations helps to rescue the film from some of its more outrageous and politically damaging gestures of normalisation and their parallel, fantasising tactics of the artificial isolation and intensification of the hotel-room affair in Medem's film.

Out and away from the ersatz glamour and the room that Natasha prefers should stay their secret (their closet), Alba has a story of her own to make a difference. On the very small screen of a digicam her story unfolds: there by a chilly, Northern stretch of water, is her Basque lover Edurne – no less a figure of extreme sexual beauty, much exploited in independent Spanish cinema, than Najwa Nimri – pictured with her young children. The recent accidental death of the youngest disrupts the idealising Roman narrative obliquely in much the same way as the drowning which underlies *Don't Look Now*'s (Nicolas Roeg, 1973) narrative of a Venetian getaway (not so much romantic as redemptive, but erotic nonetheless). This off-screen story is the true centre of gravity as far as the lesbian audience might be concerned (although the film's DVD presence on the shelves and lists of LGBTQ retailers in Spain, and its sales, possibly owes more initially to the prospect of Anaya and, though less famous, Yarovenko naked). This is not just because it is a sign of the two women laying their souls bare – a valuable dramatic device noted by at least one blogger ('sergiomora' 2010) – but also because it is an indication of a connection, albeit tenuous, with the real world of lesbian parenting and commitments; as González observes (2011: 259), the majority of Spanish feature films with lesbian characters are interested only in one class of person (urban middle class), and this film is exaggeratedly in line with this. If beyond the room grief, decisions, affections, betrayals and different lives all clamour for attention, they are countered by the middle- to highbrow feel and held off by the (very prolonged) dramatisation of the lightning love story, as well as – again, who knows if ironically – by a literalisation of Alba's being love-struck. Cupid's arrow leaves the frame of one of the many stodgy artwork reproductions in the suite and pierces her in the bath, sabotaging any effect that the film might be deemed to have on the enhanced visibility of lesbian lives and issues in Spain (*pace* González 2011: 232, who argues that the in-camera scenario does not make the women or the issues invisible at all). As one blogger had it, 'La música, insufrible. Los cuadros, pedantería pura. La duración, insufrible una vez más . . . en fin. Dan ganas de hacerse heterosexual' ('avendetta' 2010) ('The music is insufferable; the paintings [on the walls of the suite] pure pedantry; the length of the film, again, insufferable. All in all, it makes you want to turn heterosexual'). On the other hand, those commenting on their viewing of the film in the forum lesbiana.es (2011) are unanimously enthusiastic, giving a sense of a memorable, empowering and enjoyable night out for those happy to watch – or even go along with – a tendency in recent Spanish cinema to 'mostrar a lesbianas en historias más íntimas . . . obviando el discurso panfletario/reivindicativo' (González 2011: 261) ('to show lesbians involved in more personal stories . . . and to avoid the pamphleteering, politicised approach').

Early in the encounter, on the hotel balcony, the looks of desire between the two women are self-consciously noted through the acting and are visually underscored. They are reprised with increasing intensity and eroticism through the film, offering the potential for the activation of a gaze structured around 'different cultural competences' (Evans and Gamman 2004: 213; Wilton 1995) in relation to lesbian imagery (of which the film is full for those viewers able and willing to bypass the sexploitative – and thus de-lesbianising – connotations of much of what is shown). This redirection of the hegemonic gaze, and the sideways glance at the reality of lesbian family life in San Sebastián, as referred to above, both contribute to a politically effective underpinning to the positive, loosely identificatory reactions of some viewers.

Rut Suso and María Pavón's short *Ester* (2004) also uses the confinement of a bedroom to dramatise lesbian desire and to take risks with the potential in the representation of the youthful, beautiful body on screen to neutralise the politics of lesbian sexuality. A voice-over attributed to Ester's partner in bed offsets the immediacy of sensual caresses and close attention by the camera to both women's bodies, however, with a triple narrative account of how this moment of contained visual and sexual plenitude has been reached. In one strand, the narrator tells of meeting up one night a month ago with Ester (her first experience with a woman); in another, going further back, she tells a familiar story of a mother resigned to a loveless marriage asking when her daughter might herself get married, and of worries about finding the right man in a long search following a five-year relationship with one Fernando who had proven obtuse on the matter of what the narrator sexually desired and on why she had to leave him; in the third, a romantic novel Fernando clumsily gives her leads to the conclusion that that you must always trust what your own skin tells you. The narrative soon catches up with the visual grammar of sensual compatibility and the mingling of two bodies: Ester's hands – she recalls – seemed at once like her own; their first kiss has lasted the whole intervening month; she verbalises her fascination with the texture of the other woman's skin; touching Ester is like touching her own body.

There is an interesting mingling here of universalising images of love as fulfilment and oneness and the specific shock of skin on skin that is at the core of the narrator-contemplator's highly visible flight from heterosexuality. These mediated bodies interlace a soft version of 'el follar lesbiano [como] proceso de desnaturalización de las prácticas sexuales' (Preciado 2005: 131; after Wittig) ('lesbian fucking as a process of denaturalisation of sexual practices') with the closetry and the limitations associated with just 'sexo entre mujeres' ('sex between women') (rather than 'el follar lesbiano') (Preciado 2005: 131). Ester is akin to some women in the television dramas analysed by Platero Méndez (2011), who, after being in a heterosexual relationship, find that they are attracted to women but can fit neatly into a heteronormatively defined place as 'lesbian' (93–5). 'Hallando reunidas todas mis fantasías en este mismo lugar' ('finding that all my fantasies had come together in this one space'), the voice-over narrator constructs the bedroom and Ester's body in it as a simple and direct metaphor of the sudden realisation that neither narratives nor sensations on the surface of the skin account for the free recognition of love: the shock – she says – is deep in the soul. (The portentousness of this final narrated remark is to an extent then dissipated by an extended epilogue where hands and fingers drum, intertwine and play to the soundtrack of Björk and the Guðmundar Ingólfssonar trio performing 'Gling Gló'.) The space of the bed and bedroom in *Ester* prefigures in a number of ways the space of the water in Suso's videoart piece *Les étoiles* (discussed later) as also does the interlinking of a closeness of regard on the body with voice-over narration (in the case of the videoart piece, lyrical) drawing attention to the meanings and textures of the surface of the skin.

More radicalising, because of a humorous undercutting, is the last of the seven dialogues which make up Miguel Albaladejo's compendium film *Ataque verbal* (Verbal Attack) (1999). In a different exotic bathroom to that in Rome, all eyes are on the dark, wet skin, perfect face and striking smile of the singer Lucrecia, there in the bath, in Cuba, and illuminated by the hot sun through the open window above. A mistaken identity trope whereby her character Cari, in the bath with Elkita (Marta Fernández-Muro), turns out, in fact, to be Diana, Cari's younger sister is a more straightforward and elegant playing with false identities than that used in Medem's film. It brings into play, in the quick-fire of the dialogue, pointed questions about race, objectification and coloni-alising desire, but lightly and ludically. Half-angrily but half-teasingly Cari/ Diana accuses the very white Elke of imperious inability to discriminate among black women, and more angrily resists Elke's suggestion that she is playing the role of the *jinetera*, the woman seeking to escape the island by hitching up with a rich tourist. Resisting this positioning by Elke, and with the role resisting a wider spectatorial imposition as an object of masculine desire (Argote 2003: 15), '[Diana] es una mujer que ... se ha transformado en sujeto con deseo femenino' ('Diana is a woman who has ... become a subject with her own female desire') as part of a wider project of disassembly of representational strategies of disempowerment in terms of race, ethnicity, gender and migratory provenance (15, 18). Elke, whose naivety and goofiness is prettily played up by Fernández-Muro, moves bravely on through anger at Cari and Diana's ruse, at Cari's move into a heterosexual marriage arrangement, and at herself – 'lo mío es muy fuerte' ('mine's a pretty heavy story'), Elkita laments, in the mode of a number of Almodóvar's anti-heroines. Having wanted to be a scriptwriter and failed, Elkita is now, indeed, a professional ventriloquist – a projector of alternate personalities. Using a flannel to substitute for her puppet, she reca-pitulates one of her acts, winning Diana back to her, opening herself up to honest acceptance of the absurd precariousness but enjoyability of the present situation, and, what is more, opening wide the episode to concerns elsewhere in Albaladejo's compendium. One of her puppet characters, Gustavito, is a gay boy scout who has got a friend pregnant, and whose high-pitched tag-line 'soy bisexual' ('I'm bisexual') is a gentle parody of a clumsy, teenage confes-sion dramatised in the fourth of the film's dialogues. So is Diana/Cari, but Elkita, although she knows she is lesbian, is thrown into confusion as to why exactly she is in this bath. Is the Cari speaking through Diana telling Elkita that her desire is – was – just for a look, a body (a black one, any black one, Diana angrily proposes)? Is the Elkita who has been so ardently speaking as if to Cari an authentic Elkita? Where is the voice positing and positioning sexual identity coming from? These questions are lightly, sharply, floated in the piece, a queer mini-comedy of mistaken, and therefore more thoroughly understood, identity. The glove puppet is also making a gentle caricature of a character in the compendium's fourth dialogue where, again, intimacy had been built out of half-truths and things left unsaid, out of an emotional skating on thin but exhilarating ice (see, briefly, Chapter 5). This witty bathroom episode allows queer questions about identity and power to be floated on visual, lesbian, pleasure.

In Spain, as in other Western cultures, mediatised lesbian chic of the sort which in 1980s magazines saw 'languid ladies draped and intertwined together, but desiring who?' (O'Sullivan 1994: 80) is a prominent cultural phenomenon (Platero Méndez 2011: 72–9). It has fed demand for cinematic and televisual representations of the gorgeous lesbian. One likely catalyst is the success of the North American series *The L-Word* on television (Platero Méndez 2011: 77), initially on pay-to-view (Canal+, from January 2006), as well as in boxed-set sales. One web commentator enthuses that 'me encanta que sean femeninas, guapas, inteligentes y divertidas' ('marylyz' 2009) ('I love the way they are all feminine, beautiful, intelligent, and fun'); another only wishes such images had been on screens earlier in her life since these women, though they might be not always realistically presented and are definitely socially advantaged, are shown in so open a way that 'significa mucho para todas nosotras' ('Ex-usuaria' 2009) ('means a lot to all of us').

Lately, such images abound (although they were hardly absent from the earlier films of sexploitation: see Chapter 2). In *Los dos lados de la cama* (*Both Sides of the Bed*) (Emilio Martínez Lázaro, 2005) the lesbian affair between Marta (Verónica Sánchez) and Raquel (Lucía Jiménez) has a lightness of application to the comic plot which is enhanced by the studied easiness on the eye of the two women and their getups (see Chapter 2). Even in the otherwise meticulously on-message *Spinnin'* (see Chapter 1) Jana and Luna are, if not chic or glam, certainly very photogenic. Lázaro (2008) notes the significance of this trend in television in Spain, making the somewhat odd linkage between conventionally beautiful telegenic lesbian television actors and the politics of visibility (a link Mili Hernández, interviewed, is co-opted into making too, but with due caveats and distinctions).[2] The eponymous, bohemian co-protagonist of *Eloïse* (Jesús Garay, 2009), in an interesting and more or less intentional twist, is mildly radicalised precisely by her own sexiness. She is glamorous in the sense of aloof and arty, as well as dressed in flowing materials, elaborately made up and interestingly coiffed. All this means that, when first spotted by her future lover Asia's college friends, she is branded as too noticeable, too attractive: '¡Qué chica más rara!' ('She's weird'), is the plot-establishing call. As I have begun to show, short-film production can also find itself making room for the photogenic woman's body and a concomitant political freighting. In *Buenos días* (Laura A. Cancho, 2008) (with 3,016 views on YouTube), two good-looking (but in this case not over-young) women Silvia (Emma Álvarez) and Katy (Inma Gamarra) wake up in a bedroom after their first time (ambiguously either together or in a threesome), both feeling strange about what has happened, but both in elegant lingerie that normalises the scenario with a touch of what in another culture would be the look of Marks & Spencer. In Eli Navarro's *Naranjas* (Oranges, or Couples) (shown at Zinegoak 2011) and *A oscuras* (In the Dark) (both 2009) Mar (Marra Barros) and Lucía (Elena Gómez) play out problems of closetry (in Mar's case) in a context where conventional good looks assist passing, and (in *Naranjas*) Lourdes (Bego Isbert) is attracted to Cris (Celia Arias) because Cris has, in Lourdes's view, broken free of conventions and of labels – 'somos Lourdes y Cris; y no una pareja de bollos o lesbianas' ('we are just Lourdes and Cris; not some pair of dykes or lesbians'); Cris is 'normal' and, the implication is, looks it.

One figure of resistance to the glamorous lesbian is the admirably unconventional one. This is a strong feature of literary representations by writers such as Isabel Franc and her alias Lola Van Guardia or Libertad Morán (Castrejón 2008: 143–81; Collins 2009; Norandi 2009; Vosburg 2011) but might also (at first) include the character of Maca (Patricia Vico), the young doctor in the prime-time series *Hospital Central* (Tele5), who very publicly fled her own heterosexual wedding in the conservative South (Jerez de la Frontera) to come out as lesbian; this model of behaviour underlies the representation of the free spirit Silvia (Áurea Márquez) in *En la ciudad* (*In the City*) (Cesc Gay, 2003). Alternatively, and in short film, there is the mode of satire. In the fast-paced and indignant short *Bañophobia* (Fear of The Ladies) (Blanca H. Salazar, 2009), the exaggerated sexiness of one woman whom the narrator-protagonist remembers happily bumping into in the toilets is quickly defused by the woman's crass assumption that the protagonist is a young man (she is thus aligned with two other exaggeratedly heterosexist and housewifely women encountered in the toilets and forcefully denounced as 'machistas'); in another short, the slow, wry *Turistas* (Tourists) (Marcos de Miguel and Isabel Coll, 2008), an older woman sitting on her cottage bench in rural Fuerteventura is given an earnest little lecture on being gay and lesbian by the adolescent son of two lost tourists. When they all leave, she wanders happily hand-in-hand into the sunset with her woman (perhaps trans) lover, asking 'did you know we were lesbian?', out-normalising normalisation and making the closet and its anxieties an amusingly irrelevant 'cosa de turistas' ('touristy thing').

FILM, CULTURAL ACTIVISM, VIDEOART

As an alternative to the feature film or innovative television drama, short film and videoart production provide audiences with some of the more complex, more questioning and more aesthetically queer materials of resistance. This can be seen not only on the festival circuit (discussed in the next section) – often with repeat opportunities through traveling showcases and, in the smaller events, recourse to retrospective programming out of economic necessity – but, increasingly, online. Some non-narrative works have a presence in galleries and multi-format exhibitions, as well as in the videoart slot at, for example, LesGaiCineMad. I want now to turn to three cases. These are Mariel Maciá's EnikPro, the creative production agency Volando Vengo and the work of Juanma Carrillo, generally under the production name of EmocionesProduce.

Favouring a directly narrative and thematic intervention in contemporary lesbian cultural politics in Spain are the two films presented by EnikPro (Enik Producciones: Proyectos CulturaLes). This self-styled 'asociación' is the brainchild of cultural activist, director and scriptwriter Mariel Maciá. Maciá has a following beyond film production and promotion through her 'Monólogos de bollería fina' (The Lady Finger Monologues).[3] The 'monologues', performed as a compendium play in small theatre and cabaret spaces, deploy humour to send up heterosexist assumptions, refining the audience's sense of what, and how amusing, it is to be lesbian. As stand-up turns, they are both topical and oriented to a popular cultural experience of lesbian reality, designed to combat stereotyping and show that 'lesbians are everywhere', 'integrated' (EurOut 2010: 26). They can adapt to circumstances and events, for example with a series, in a tailor-made sub-entity 'Bollería Fina Super Exprés', in various Madrid venues for Orgullo (Pride) 2010, and with a new monologue at the alternative venue MicroTeatro Por Dinero in Madrid as part of Orgullo 2011. Maciá's role as artistic director (Industry and Marketing) for the promotional arm of LesGaiCineMad, SFM (Spanish Film Market) in 2009 and 2010 and latterly as a *vocal* (representative) on the Junta Directiva (board) of CIMA (Asociación de Mujeres Cineastas y de Medios Audiovisuales) (along with well-known names in Spanish film-making such as Icíar Bollaín and Helena Taberna, and with Chus Gutiérrez as Vice-Chair) align her work centrally with contemporary cultural intervention in a feminist frame.

Four years prior to the premiere of the monologues and their offshoots, *Flores en el parque (o los primeros besos)* (*Flowers in the Park, or Those First Kisses*) (2006), however, while theatrical and to a certain extent integrationist, had been gently serious in tone. With more than 500,000 online views by the end of March 2012 across three YouTube channels (one official, two not), it has a far wider audience than the monologues and more than most of the short films being considered in this study. In Spain the film won the awards for best Spanish short and best Spanish film overall at the 2006 LesGaiCineMad festival, and best short film award at the 2007 CineGaiLesAst festival. Two young women have arranged via an Internet chat room to meet in the park: Ana (Diana Díez) has her doubts while Lola (Isabel Sánchez) courts Ana with single roses on their first and third encounters. Ana's reaction to the gift of the flower is a comically abrupt 'pero yo no soy lesbiana . . . bueno... un poco' ('I'm not a lesbian . . . well . . . a bit'). For the first day the staging and framing keep the two women apart from each other, geometrically positioned on a bench in what is emotionally a stiff and unequal encounter. Ana gives this everyday, realistic scenario a light reflexive spin as she makes as if to run away but asks Lola if she is not supposed to say something like, 'stay a while', and notes that 'se supone' ('we can assume') that Lola is the one who knows how these things work. Despite this, and her no-show on day two, Ana leads: she is the one to initiate standing up and moving away from the bench, she insists on day three that there be no further kisses, and she it is who on the first two occasions moves out of the tight framing. Only on day four does the scene shift, fifty metres away, to the steps. Here Ana confesses to her own uptightness, gives Lola a jokey cloth flower, and the camera finds a more fluid mode, tracking back, then panning to follow the two as they walk – hand in hand now – out along the path. As a representation of a small but significant moment in the lives of young (or new) lesbians the film – with its simple visual effects underlining restriction, self-censorship and tentative alignments – has been extremely well received. As well as the prize already mentioned, and its success on YouTube, when relaunched on Facebook (EnikPro 2010) in August 2010 it prompted fifty 'likes' and a year-long string of comments. 'Maria Oliva' (2011) sees aspects of herself reflected in the character of Lola; 'Esme Baltasar' (2011) notes that 'yo no kiero más Anas en mi vida' ('dont want any more Anas in my life!'); and 'Veruska Morales Roa' (2010) remembers having seen it the first time round, and remarks 'que putada de estados transitorios' ('these transitional states suck'). It is this sort of identification which Maciá's narrative here encourages, as part of an overall impulse towards a non-lesbian-specific openness to the structures and small comedies of everyday emotional life.

A domicilio: o incluso también el amor (At Home: or Love As Well) (2007) won the award for best short film at LesGaiCineMad 2008 and at the Festival del Sol in Las Palmas. Also shown at the 1ª Muestra de Cine Lésbico de Madrid (First Madrid Lesbian Film Showcase) in March 2010, it recasts in lesbian mode an old topos in gay cinema and popular literature – the experimental awakening to homosexual desire of the hitherto straight-identified, paying punter. Rosa, a married professional woman (Mónica Vic), has engaged Flor (Marina Vradiy) as an escort for the night (see Figure 8). As Flor approaches the apartment and Rosa anxiously waits, the split screen signals the distance between their two situations; the simple dramatic unity of the evening of antic-ipation, the night together (sushi, a bathroom scene, bed) and the morning after also splits Rosa into an anxious and uptight pre-lesbian and a joyful, relaxed new woman. It is an unassuming feel-good piece, crafted neatly to its limitations and good-humouredly brisk with any potential contradictions to its message of self-liberation (such contradictions might be, of course, the use that Flor is put to, the lack of negotiation with Rosa's past with her husband, Rosa's butch-coded attire, and Flor's tight little black dress and glamorous appeal). Maciá's work is carried out in the triple context of market disadvan-tage for small, independent film-makers (EurOut 2010: 29), the predominance in Spanish film-making of male scriptwriters and directors (as also worldwide) (CIMA 2011), and the need to respond to an under-recognised lesbian audi-ence and to the lack of lesbian points of reference in Spanish cinema (González 2011: 251; InCinema 2011). In a conversation on 20 October 2011 Maciá used the terms 'pluralidad' and 'integración' in elaborating on her strategies as a scriptwriter and film-maker in relation to her target audiences. Her brief filmography has real audience impact, in the relative terms of this mode of output, and has begun to find a popular on-screen lesbian image that responds to the limitations hedging it about.

Rut Suso and María Pavón (see the discussion of Ester, above) are the

Figure 8 Rosa (Mónica Vic) discovering herself with Flor (Marina Vradiy) in *A domicilio: o incluso también el amor* (Mariel Maciá, 2007). Image provided by Mariel Maciá/Enik Producciones; reproduced with kind permission.

creative directors of Volando Vengo, a Madrid-based audiovisual production company working in videoart, documentary and fiction film, as well as commercial advertising. It describes itself, in its English-language self-presentation, as 'following an open feminist policy' (Suso and Pavón 2009). The agency's visual points of reference are predominantly the material conditions of women's lives and the bodies of women in movement or locked in intimacy as performances and images 'que consiguen despertar el conocimiento emocional del espectador' (volandovengo 2008) ('that are able to awaken the emotional intelligence of the viewer'). Explicit links into queer politics and activism come in their montage of the HIV-AIDS awareness visual arts exhibition and campaign 'VIHVO' (November–December 2009) and associated video spots (2009 and 2010),[4] and the making and web distribution of the music-dance video 'Orgullo Nacional' with its anti-identity politics message (though with its paradoxical original commissioning for Mr Gay Pride España). The ongoing projects Confessional Room and MyCookingFilms deploy respectively documentary testimony in a feminist social framework and disruptive eroticism and satire in a loosely radical queer aesthetic.[5]

Volando Vengo's film-making work ranges from the work just described, through narrative film – notably *Ester* – to video art (with Belén Paton joining the team, in the case of the 2011 piece *La escalera*). Their second short fiction film, *Pasión por el fútbol* (A Passion for Football) (2007), is a playful decon-

Figure 9 Two new fans (Ángeles Maeso and Itziar Miranda) in *Pasión por el fútbol* (Rut Suso and María Pavón, 2007). Image provided by Volandovengo; reproduced with kind permission.

struction of gender stereotypes and a gentle, dramatic exploration of coupledom drifting into tedium because of masculine insensitivity and obsessive behaviour. Once the camera's view floats down from the treetops that denote a park on a sunlit day, it reveals first, in jokey obviousness, the separate, distinguishing entrances of the toilets in the park. Nearby a woman sits listlessly reading (*Metamorphosis*): we follow her gaze to the signs over the doors, first for the women's, then the men's: immediately there follows a side profile close-up of a man with a transistor radio close to his ear, enthralled; the tinny sounds of football commentary are audible. The woman's eye is caught by another, leaning against a tree (see Figure 9); another day, the scenario is repeated, but the two women go together to the toilets, passing the sign jauntily proclaiming that the facilities are 'Provided Free to the Public', and with fond intensity they make out. The sound of bongo drums being played by another woman in the park, as if by way of a pantheistic chorus, weaves in and out of prominence on the soundtrack. The sensual, and football chatter-free choreography of caressing and undressing is interrupted by the man and his raucous radio: but his girlfriend or wife covers up what she and the other woman are doing, he moves off and they resume, more passionately. With the possibilities of lesbian desire having transformed the woman's park life, in a final set of substitutions the man is now repositioned – literally, as he is now leaning against the tree where the first same-sex seductive glance originated. The previous relationship is clearly over; the reading woman has turned her sexual page; another woman is now on the bench, with her own commentary-enthralled male partner. The man leaning against the tree lightly but sensually touches his upper chest, becoming aware of his body, his availability and of the world beyond his football interest, whose blaring accompaniment has caricatured gender fixity. Although his glance crosses with that of the new, smiling woman on the bench, the play of bodies changing places, shifts in objects of desire and the gently amusing, open

Figure 10 Self-encounter in *Alguien se despierta en mi cama* (Rut Suso, 2008). Image provided by Volandovengo; reproduced with kind permission.

suggestion that the episode is going to repeat itself heterosexually but based on a lesbian narrative premise, makes things, as it were, perfectly queer. The film had had 22,198 plays on YouTube as at 24 May 2012.

The much more niche-targeted videoart piece *Alguien se despierta en mi cama* (Someone Wakes Up In My Bed) (2008) – signed by Rut Suso only in this case – has a poetic commentary over a visual meditation on the body of the artist herself, with shoulder, upper torso and head shots predominating, with slow arcs traced by the camera and mirrored images in a glass whose frame is invisible against a black background (see Figure 10). Words and visuals construct the mirror as a lens for projecting abstract notions of love, as well, more conventionally, as a means of reflecting on the fragmentary, fleeting or plural nature of identity. The glass and the tight framing overall also act to make a confessional space, with the speaker identifying complicated defects in herself, including having loved in some wrong way. Confined, she finds that 'cuando alguien te mira con amor es para poseerte' ('when someone looks at you with love it is to possess you') but her movements show a mix of desire for this, or acquiescence at least, and anxiety. The 'someone' who looks, and who awakes in her bed, is a corollary of the speaking subject's farewell to herself: 'ya no recuerdo si es mujer u hombre' ('I can't remember now if it is a woman or a man'). What the narcissistic proximity of the filmed artist to the reflected image risks is, as Doane (1992: 231) puts it in speaking of narrative cinema, 'a certain over-presence', a problematic narcissisism (231) and '"closeness" to the body' (232) which might disempower (Doane is using Luce Irigaray's strategic notions of proximity and distance and the structural placing of the female subject philosophically and politically in a position of absence). The piece also uses this risk to celebrate a polymorphous, yet still narcissistic gaze, which is perhaps an element in that 'open feminist' strategy, highlighted by Suso and Pavón on their web page: the script and images suggest a dissolving of difference and a fantastical, seductive confusion made of the direction in which desire might be projected.

Les étoiles (2011) takes a similar radical-lyrical angle on the female body and combines single-location footage of a woman (again, the artist-director herself) swimming offshore with on-screen text and a single-number musical soundtrack, the eponymous song performed by Melody Gardot. The video suggests a viewing context variously as: that of a family album (a glimpse of a beach, an older woman hugging the swimmer – the artist's mother); of a playfully erotic but also estranging exploration of 'la arquitectura del cuerpo como refugio' ('the architecture of the body as a hiding place'), as part of the captioned text has it; and as a more abstract treatment of how swimming is the closest one can get to 'volar en la tierra' ('flying on earth') and the best mode of seeing the stars (the glinting air bubbles here). The narrative arc from personal memories through sensitivity to corporeality and on to the floating non-meanings of the look and sound of the water is the move away from consciousness of self: 'me deshago de mí / al fin' ('I rid myself of me / at last'). However, as Suso's Vimeo channel biography makes explicit, 'Todas sus obras se distinguen por estar unidas a la investigación sobre el deseo y la sexualidad de la mujer' (Suso 2011) ('a distinctive and unifying mark of her work is its exploration of women's sexuality and desire'). As such, the water and the stars have some specific sexual political points to them. *Les étoiles*'s attention to the female body occupying liquid space caught up in its soundscape – of quiet subaquatic murmur at each end of the music – and the words of the song pull in this direction. The question is: can, indeed, the body speak? For a twenty-second sequence prior to the song's reprise the bubble stars and the floating body as a whole are replaced by a singular and close-up nipple – its own star or haloed planet – bobbing happily close to the lens, and bringing the erotic back into play, or, rather, into synch with the mood of the song through the words ('Dites-moi, étoiles, qui vous donnera l'amour?' – 'Tell me, stars, who will give you love?'), a smoky voice and bossa nova style. The presentational text quoted earlier also suggests that all Suso's work is undertaken 'desde un punto de vista político y pedagógico' (Suso 2011) ('from a political and pedagogical point of view'). That politics, consciously or not, is informed aesthetically by the feminist poetics of fluidity of Julia Kristeva and Hélène Cixous; the watery, maternal and sensual scenario of *Les étoiles* is very like that 'space [in which] Cixous's speaking subject is free to move from one subject position to another, or to merge oceanically within the world' (Moi 1985: 115).

The third example for this section, Juanma Carrillo, has one of the more substantial filmographies of the short film-makers under discussion here, and a substantial portfolio of videoart and music video productions (Carrillo 2011). His work had a one-night retrospective at the FIRE!! 2011 festival (Giraldo 2011a) and he led a round-table discussion on his work at Zinegoak 2012

– the two major alternative LGTBQ festivals in Spain. Although his (experimental) move into black comedy in *Fuckbuddies* (see Chapter 1) has increasingly magnetised audience attention, it is his far less relaxed, more demanding work – and its crossover qualities – which best represent his output. *Muro* (*Wall*) (2010) had around 3,750 viewings on YouTube and Vodpod combined as at the end of March 2012 and has been exhibited at the prestigious, open-competition web-based Notodofilmfest as well as LesGaiCineMad and Zinegoak. It is on the one hand a simple snapshot of the end of an affair; on the other, in its attention to duration, affect and empathy it (and a companion piece, *Andamio* (Scaffolding), in development in 2012) lays experimental ground for the later medium-length *Esperas* (Long Waits) (2011) – less disseminated at the time of writing – into which its own narrative of waiting is spliced and interspersed as one among nine others. In *Muro* a young man waits anxiously, in his neat, clean shirt leaning against a wall on a demolition site; the blank wall allows for a gently sexy iconographic placing of the subject, and the smiling restlessness of the performance of the waiting all point up the materiality of 'sexualidad, cuerpo, carnalidad, intimidad' ('sexuality, body, physicality, intimacy') as the typical point of departure, for Carrillo, in the encounter with the other (Román 2011). Another man arrives, to the relief and delight of the first, but he immediately answers his mobile and engages in a smiling and flirtatious exchange with someone else. He becomes progressively cooler towards the one who had been waiting and who has to have it spelled out on the wall behind him: 'I Don't Love You Any More'. At the end (in *Muro*, but not in *Esperas*) he adds his own message on the wall, accusing the other of emotional cowardice (in *Esperas* an end-title supplies different information: that he has to wait another five years yet until the affair is well and truly over). The film is enriched by visual echoes of José Luis Guerin's *En construcción* (*In Construction*) (2001) and by allusions generally to silent cinema. There is sound – construction work and the city's ambience hollowing out but also amplifying the drama (as also in *Esperas* for all the episodes) – but no dialogue. The two mismatched lovers mime their small drama, exaggeratedly, in black and white.

The aesthetics of anticipation and the choreography of physical approach also inform *Caníbales* (*Cannibals*) (2009). With exhibition at six Spanish and several more international festivals, this is a richly textured, half abstract, half narrative piece in which the camera – a constant, roving POV – explores visually the space of cruising for sex 'en el que', as Carrillo has observed, 'se maneja un lenguaje universal que nadie te enseña y que, sin embargo, aprendes enseguida' (in Giraldo 2011a) ('where you expertly use a universal language without anyone ever having taught you'). As one blogger observes, 'le sobra y le basta con una cámara para atrapar al espectador y lanzarle al abismo' (Linares 2010) ('a camera is more than enough for [Carrillo] to capture the viewer and tip him into the abyss'). As in Carrillo's other work, visual intensity is privileged, and a certain vertigo is produced by the insistent movement through and into bushes, branches, twigs and glaring open clearings alive with sex or its anticipation. However, as the camera structures its quest it also wryly takes in the variously shy, provocative, jaded and in-your-face reactions of the men it brushes past. It also registers its own embarrassment and excitement through abrupt turns and, as it were, averting its eyes (in a witty shot of a statue an angel is seen doing the same, heavenwards); more obviously, it keeps closing in obsessively on certain scenes, building up to its final drama and the abandonment of relative abstraction. It is clear from the soundtrack early on that a metaphorical charge is in the air, as well as '[lo] crudo y morboso a partes iguales' (Giraldo 2011a) ('coarseness and perverse fascination in equal parts'), as the cicadas and crickets open up the soundscape of silence in the obvious summer heat in much the same way as the famous and equally human-body obsessed, allegorical classic *La caza* (*The Hunt*) (Carlos Saura, 1965). In queer cultural terms, of course, the subject of casual open-air sex has a long and radical pedigree (in Rainer Werner Fassbinder, Pier Paolo Pasolini, Thom Gunn, Pedro Lemebel, Lluís Fernández, Jaime Gil de Biedma and others). The resonances of the Casa de Campo park on the west side of Madrid, where the cruising takes place, and the conflictedness and risk which can accompany the quest for casual sex is also powerfully recorded specifically in Carlos Armenteros's popular novel *El Lago* (The Lake) (Armenteros 2000: 45–56). In the film's last minutes the abstraction-laden voyeurism of the camera is supplanted: a man being fucked on all fours looks up in what first seems to be the indignation at the invasion of intimacy which the camera had met before several times but this turns to horrified guilt as the fuckee is revealed to be looking into the eye not of the camera but of a spectacularly out of place and smartly dressed woman – the man's wife. She, now, is the camera's final objective as she looks on wordless but filled with harsh understanding. An epilogue stages a staccato melodrama as still photographs of the couple's wedding, first child and general happy coupledom go up in flames in sequence (and colour intervenes in the film for the first time, in the flames only). The sounds of need and nature are replaced in this epilogue by the high artifice of Arvo Pärt's 'Da Pacem Domine' for choir and string orchestra. In some ways this is a curious departure, disruptively out of tune with the main body of the film; in other ways, by centring so emotively on guilt and the significant banality of the tragedy of closetry, it obliquely politicises the whole.

Perfect Day (co-directed with Félix Fernández, 2010) won the Madrid LesGaiCine prize for a videoart piece but, as with much of Carrillo's work, has wider repercussions and crossovers into the non-thematically restricted festival and art exhibition circuits proper, due, in part to 'la contundencia en forma y fondo' (Pérez Toledo 2011) ('the strong impact of form and content') that characterises the videoart pieces, and this one in particular. While the subjects of *Esperas* are constituted as themselves by the postponement of connection with the other person (and are in some cases destroyed by the resolution) the focalising figure of *Perfect Day* (artist, co-writer and artistic director Félix Fernández) is constituted as lacking by the rapid sequence of partners and

Figure 11 Guadalupe Lancho, Félix Fernández and Juan Gómez in *Perfect Day* (Juanma Carrillo and Félix Fernández, 2010). Image provided by Juanma Carrillo; reproduced with kind permission.

homo- and bi-combinations (see Figure 11). In the abstract, the piece is about the imperfect matches of the body to the contortions – or, in Román's word (2011), vertigo – of desire. *Une sensation de vide* (2011) is a videoart project on dance, and partying – and rage – whose gentle involving rhythms of movement and light, and a semi-ethereal musical soundtrack from Bell Orchestre, at first offer a useful counter to the rough and noisy treatment of the club scenario to be found in *Mentiras y gordas*. However, as the music progresses into a Dave Clarke mix, a drama of violence breaks out between two of the men dancing (it is sparked by a spilled drink), and as the editing becomes fast, the music more urgent and the lights flash, the violence spreads (see Figure 12). Bloodied, one man falls to the dance floor and the piece closes open-endedly (in contrast to the melodramatic certainty-cum-unbelievability of the death scene of *Mentiras y gordas*), adding to the vertigo of the dance a haunting sense of narrative and motivational nothingness turning on the vacuity of human rage. In *Las flores también producen espinas* (Flowers Also Yield Thorns) (2007) Saida Benzal's character (adopted name Hana), whose voice-over internal monologue constructs her as emotionally damaged, wonders if her male lover (played by Iván Sánchez) may also be empty inside, and the piece has a shock ending in which he has indeed been bled out. *Cuerpos deshonrados* (2010), presented at, and made for, the web-coordinated multi-country Optica festival, is again without spoken dialogue and is choreographed to an intricate and rhythmically insist-

Figure 12 Precarious ecstasy in *Une sensation de vide* (Juanma Carrillo, 2011). Image
provided by Juanma Carrillo; reproduced with kind permission.

ent soundtrack. Soundscape and tightly framed movement-performance lead
from an apparently everyday passionate encounter between a naked man and
a naked woman through an incrementally intense drama of domination and
into a savagely ritualistic, initially surreal emanation of blood (in the manner
of Buñuel's *L'Age d'Or* (1930)) eventually covering the man's body entirely.
The scene ceases being human, emotions become affects, the bodies become
what they were striving to be in the work from the start – forms.

In its deconstruction of the erotic dyad, whether male on male or female on
female, and in its borderline obscenity, the videoart work develops an auteurist but radically resistant aesthetic which references sexual political issues of
import.

In as much as this mix of sensibilities and effects inflects also the semi-
narrative films, with their disruption of easy expectations about fulfilment,
communication, sexual completion, love or commitment, then they correspond to what in other cultures would be attributed to a 'queer director'.
Carrillo himself quietly hopes this might not happen to him – 'no me importa',
he says (in Giraldo 2011a), but queer is not what he has set out to do. In a
conversation on 19 January 2012 he took a similar line while not excluding the
usefulness of the term for the kinds of political art and performance emerging
in Spain in 2011 around the unfolding crisis over debt and public finances, the
Indignados movement and the electoral platform – and victory – of the Partido
Popular in November of that year.

Figure 13 Programme cover, LesGaiCineMad festival, 2009. Photograph by Pablo Bordenabe, design by Martin Casanova; reproduced with kind permission of Fundación Triángulo/LesGaiCineMad.

Festivals

In the Introduction I sketched the LGBTQ festival scene in Spain. The range, to remind ourselves, runs from the relatively high-attendance LesGaiCineMad (selling 15,000 tickets by 2008) (LesGaiCineMad 2008 – see Figure 13) and its, albeit short-lived, positioning of itself as a marketplace (through SFM, the Spanish LGBT Film Market) through more radically focused events such as Zinegoak and FIRE!! to specifically targeted events such as the 1ª Muestra de Cine Lésbico de Madrid (March 2011) and A Coruña Visible (a multidisciplinary festival which concentrated on film from 2011). The latter, supported by the local Social Services department, resumes in direct terms the general objectives of the LGBTQ festivals which concern me here:

Queremos que los gays, lesbianas o transexuales aparezcan en algunas de la imágenes que consumimos ávidamente en el cine, la televisión o el

ordenador, contando historias como las demás, pero diferentes [y] pro-
ponemos una primera cita con un cine diverso, divertido y reivindicativo.
(Visible Cinema 2011)
(We want images of gays, lesbians or transexuals to be among those we
so avidly consume [on screen], telling stories like those of any others, but
different; [and] we propose a cinema of diversity, of fun, and of dissent.)

This element of local but cosmopolitanised festivity enhances engagement by
the audience, programmers and (to a certain, demand-led, extent) film-makers
with the politics, and the fantasies and desires, of everyday queer life. The
Spanish festivals, too, are intersectional in a way that is typical of the queer
film festival as studied by Zielinski ([2008] 2011), who suggests that:

> While general international film festivals operate within a very well
> defined network, the added categories of sexuality and community cru-
> cially and fundamentally change the relationship of the films screened to
> the festival, films and festival to audience, and the festival to any network
> of distribution.

These vectors are clearly in play in the Spanish queer cultural network of
festivals. As Suárez (2006: 602) observes, the festivals 'contribut[e] to the
circulation and visibility of queer concerns and work [and] have served as
well to bring together queer and nonqueer Left political actors in temporary
alliances.' Connections between the festivals and the self-identified experiences
of their particular audiences are patent and can be registered in modes from
the plain and simple – LesGaiCine Madrid in 2003 being described as 'un
festival útil' (De Zero a 100: 2003) ('a useful festival') – to the more complex
and wide-ranging, such as Ugarte Pérez's sense (2008: 142) of the mission of
the festival offering as being not the presentation of yet more queer characters on screen but the production of '[una] mirada [que sea] interna' ('a view
from the inside') through which 'los personajes lgtb experimenten la realidad
a través de sí mismos, con sus deseos inquietudes y actitudes' ('LGTB people
can experience reality through their own eyes, with their own desires, anxieties and attitudes'). (The complexity comes, of course, in the questions that are
begged here of agency and imaginative projection: Ugarte Pérez's 'personajes'
interestingly conflate those acting on screen – or writing the script, or programming the festival – with those just watching.) The implicit utility that is part
of that 'mirada interna' of the festival is enhanced by the inclusion of round-
table discussions, question-and-answer sessions with film-makers (introduced
to the Madrid festival programme in 2000 and a core aspect of FIRE!! and
Zinegoak) or of publicity which is issue-based or linked to sponsoring or other
organisations' campaigning. In addition they share the customary qualities of
being 'precious, unique, live events' (Triana Toribio 2011: 220; after Harbord
2002), with a sense of their own back history to transmit (220–2) and altering

temporarily the city locations (or the venues) where they take place and with whose cultural politics they interact (222–7, 230–3). No less than any others, these Spanish festivals constitute a 'happening [that] creates a managed site of specialised knowledges' (Harbord 2002: 68). The rarity value of such events, and of their particular combination of content, as discussed by Triana Toribio (2011), combine with the particular community demands and expectations relating to an LGBTQ festival (Straayer and Waugh 2005, 2006). In Spain, as Maciá (2010) has pointed out, '[a] pesar de lo que se pueda pensar el público LGBT es muy exigente, genera sus propias estrellas, sus propios autores y su propio mapa de eventos' ('contrary to what might be thought, LGBT audiences are very demanding, creating their own stars, their own auteurs and their own mapping out of events'). That is, they manage the very managed site itself.

Not the least of the specialised knowledges and celebrity-making skills are those pertaining to the articulation between the film's narration or visibilisation of concerns and feelings with those true to queer life. Such knowledges and skills help build a substantial and diverse Spanish queer cinephilia, perhaps answering part of the question surfacing and resurfacing in the blog forming part of Mira's project *Miradas insumisas* (Mira 2008) about 'la falta de un concepto de "cultura cinéfila gay" en nuestro país' ('A queer one/Julie Jordan' 2006) ('the lack of the notion of a "gay cinephile culture" in this country [Spain]').

A questionnaire circulated to the film-makers involved in the 2004 LesGaiCine Madrid festival sought to widen this sense of 'community' and began by asking if an LGBT cinema 'movement' was thought to exist as such (Palencia 2005): none were able to say unequivocally that it did; one identified an obvious 'circuito de cine de temática LGTB' (54) ('a circuit of LGBT-themed cinema') fostered by festivals and characterised by a rise in the number of short films being produced; and four respondents (including the first just cited) thought it would be best if the category ceased to exist and their production integrated into film production more generally. None, on the other hand, questioned the use of the term 'colectivo' when asked how an LGBT cinema can reflect accurately the real experience of the LGBT collective, identifying the qualities of plurality, diversity and openness as factors in a proper film-making practice. The social utility or relevance of the films was taken as given in that, when asked if there was a need for 'un cine LGTB político y social' ('politically and socially committed LGBT cinema') none demurred, while the responses alluded to the need to work to close the gap between equality in the law and social equality (55–6). The larger festivals allow space for documentary (and experimental) films of which the most notable (in addition to those discussed in previous chapters) are: *Homo Baby Boom: Famílies de lesbianes i gais* (Homo Baby Boom – Lesbian and Gay Families) (Anna Boluda, 2009); *Guerriller@s* (W@rriors) (Montse Pujantell, 2010), which is a testimonial and theorising piece on gender identity; and the interview-based *El muro rosa* (*The Pink Wall*) Enrique del Pozo, 2010) addressing the memory of persecution and corrective 'therapy' under Francoism of gay men and transexuals as well as contemporary trans- and homophobic violence. Regional, publicly sponsored events on a smaller scale may also include this type of material. At the fifth CinegailesAST 2011 Xixón/Gijón, five documentaries were shown, including *Homo Baby Boom*; the Muestra de Cine Gay, Lésbico, Bisexual y Transexual de Fuerteventura (into its tenth run in 2011), supported by the Cabildo de Fuerteventura through the Altihay collective, has also made room each year for a documentary strand.

As early as 1999 *Zero* magazine was able to draw attention to another element of the intersectionality of the nascent Spanish festivals, their ability to link up two cultures – 'quienes salen de noche [y] quienes salen de día' ('those who go out at night [and] those by day') – and to mediate between 'comercios rosas locales [y] firmas comerciales de primera fila' (42) ('small local businesses in the pink economy and front-rank commercial brands'). Where major world festivals participate in and reactivate the 'culture of international commodity flow' (Harbord 2002: 70) the niche LGBTQ festival, competition or event can easily mimic this in proportion. The new micro-festival MiMi (Barcelona) has behind it the beer manufacturer Estrella Damm, Axel hotels and local clubs and businesses; the thirty-title, five-day Festival de la Luna (in 2010) – expanded to thirty-six titles and ten days in 2011 – claims to make Valencia 'capital mundial del cine gay y lésbico' (GayValencia 2010) ('the world capital of gay and lesbian cinema'). It mixes local government support with that from mainly Spanish gay businesses. The Pequeño Certamen de Cine de Ambiente (La Pecca) (Compact LGBT Film Competition), organised by the Seville-based group De Frente, has run since 2006, screening seventeen titles then, rising to twenty-seven in 2011, nearly all Spanish. Its two prizes, the Peccas de Oro or Plata (gold or silver) in 2012 were worth €1,000 and €500 respectively, with the competition backed by the community bank Cajasol. The award of the Pecca de Oro in 2007 to *¡¡¡Todas!!!* (*All!!*) (José Martret, 2003), in 2009 is an interesting example of how the smaller competitions can afford to register the significance of films well established on the micro-circuit as much as that of new work.

Mira (2008) points to a Spanish perspective (from film-maker Antonio Hens) on the limitations created by market perceptions of LGBT cinema as single-issue, or closed-themed, with very different films, both feature-length and short, misleadingly bracketed together (64). The festivals – despite their respective labels – can unpick this and encourage a differentiated and differentiating viewing. In order to demonstrate this in some detail in the final part of this chapter, I move now to accounts of two of the most heavily attended festivals, the independent Festival Internacional de Cinema Gai i Lèsbic de Barcelona (FICGLB) and the NGO-affiliated LesGaiCineMad (one chief programmer of which until 2001, Xavier Daniel, is now the director of FICGLB).

The closing event of the FICLGB on 3 November 2011 showed something of the 'constellation of overlapping economies, discourses, cultural practices, and spaces' posited by Zielinski (2011). Held (like the whole festival) on the prestigious premises of the Filmoteca de Catalunya's technically and decoratively well appointed theatre on Barcelona's Avinguda de Sarrià (prior to its move to a new site in the Raval district of the city) – the event drew an audience of some 160. A cafe bar aligned with the foyer and on the same frontage facilitated (for those who could fit in) a welcoming and informal transition space, with festival organisers, invited guests and a mixed-age public to mingle speaking Catalan, English, Italian and German. Moving on towards the theatre, for a showing of *Going Down in LALA Land* (Casper Andreas, 2011), audience members passed displays of posters attesting to the centrality and continuity of the Filmoteca as a cultural institution within the polity of the Generalitat de Catalunya, as well as showcases of academic film books (more visible on the way back out). Speeches from representatives of the Directorate of the Filmoteca and of the cultural office of the Generalitat de Catalunya gave formal and formulaic support to the festival while a more immediate note was struck by the announcement of prizes for short films by a jury of film school students from the Escola Superior de Cinema i Audiovisuals de Catalunya, the Centre d'Estudis Cinematogràfics de Catalunya and the Escola de Mitjans Audiovisuals. Non-verbal reactions to the film itself during its showing – a polished, generic, romantic comedy (in American English) – belonged to a much less localised, and a less politicised, discourse. The happy ending to this sexy-picaresque tale, lightly spiced with the politics of celebrity outing, involves a well-performed but caricature re-enactment of the stock figure of the gay boy's straight and sassy best woman friend who is something of a forgivable devious hogger of the vicarious limelight. We were all happy enough, the men at least it seemed, to laugh at this before filing out quickly past the displays of Catalan and cinematic cultural history on the stairs and in the foyer.

The following night's selection of gay shorts included only one Spanish film, *Sígueme* (*Follow Me*) (Alejandro Durán, 2011). The film moves radically away in setting and tone from the urban glamour or outdoor thrills of more standard treatments of the intensity of casual sex and the emotional pull it can have for a community. Explaining to the audience prior to the film's 5 November 2011 showing at the FICGLB, director Durán highlighted a parallel in the completion of the film with issues in his own life, creating an effective context of expectation. The film, indeed, dramatises the strain put on the relationship between young married couple Julia (May Melero) and Rubén (Jacinto Bobo) with its windy, winter setting on the Atlantic coast of the province of Cádiz and with its apparently non-linear montage of events, and it illustrates it with its low exposure look and emphasis on sand, yellow stone on a ruined wall and low cliff-top castle. Rubén's intense and suddenly intimate session of casual sex with a runner (Paco: Daniel Enríquez) one afternoon in the ruins leads to his losing his wedding ring, picked up on as if by instinct by an already moody Julia that night, as if she smells another man on him. In a move forward, the film's last minutes see Rubén, Julia and their baby (pregnancy and birth have been elided) approaching the same sandy area of the original sex scene. Rubén's choice of a picnic spot 'éste es un buen sitio' ('this is a good spot') echoes the earlier, raunchily intended words of Paco, making an interesting queer clash, but also a matching up: this queer space adapts to show, properly enough, that it contains permutations of desire beyond the same-sex dyad. Julia is fully accepting of the situation, and Paco, while hesitant (with the audience nicely tricked into thinking that he has simply come across the happy family in dreadful error) is soon smilingly integrated into the picnic in the wind.

Coming between the experimental Mexican-Canadian *Vapor* (Kaveh Nabatian, 2010), which linked coming to sexual awareness in middle age to death and dying, and the oddly names *Blokes* (Marialy Rivas, 2010), which linked an adolescent boy's yearnings for his older neighbour and classmate with the political repression and killings of the early Pinochet years, *Sígueme* shifted the evening into a more ordinary and present-day mode. Its gently dramatic social realist feel and its refusal of the gay male dyad also put into perspective the comic playing on drag and effeminate stereotypes in two of the other films, and the variations on the narreme of the precarious or risky one-night stand in two others.

The second evening of short films, this time of lesbian 'thematics' (as the favoured terminology in Catalan and Castilian rather problematically has it) had two Spanish shorts in the central part of the programme, *Dos maneras y media de morir* (Two and a Half Ways to Die) (Ruth Caudeli, 2011) and *Luz* (Pablo Aragüés, 2011). The first of these looks back, as it were, into the heritage years for its generic hook, turning the merging of homosexual and heterosexual bonds into a triangle of tragic inevitability rather than a space of open possibilities. Against the soundscape of a cover version of 'Doing Something Wrong' performed by Tania Gómez (who plays Ali), bisexual Paula (Georgina Latre) is drawn away from her relationship with Salva (Gonzalo Pastor) by his sister (Ali), but not so definitively as to prevent Ali's murderous jealousy and a melodramatically staged stabbing of Paula in a dark, wet street and the subsequent poisoning of Salva. The piece thus recycles the cliché of the murderous lesbian and that of the bisexual woman as treacherous in an unusual, non-parodic, recourse to the damaging imagery of previous years. *Luz* started out in a more modern vein, with a quick paced montage of Luz's work as DJ in a nightclub and her many one-night stands, crosscut with scenes in a hospital where her mother (played by Assumpta Serna) lies dying. One bed trumps the other, in successive images, as rebellious sexual energy is set off against the emotional rejection of – and by – the biological family, and Luz joins other on-screen representations of queer and angry youth. However, this originality, depending on how the audience might take it (on the night nobody audibly groaned; many laughed), is either compounded or confounded when Luz – in a shock twist of plot and genre and tone – dies in the arms of a glamorous vampire, without having been able to make peace with her mother, and decides to make amends by vampirising her mother too. Suddenly, though parodically, we are back in the world of Spanish lesbian vampire movies (Melero 2010: 52–77; Pelayo 2009: 281–91) and of lesbophobic narrative mechanisms 'que encuentra[n] terror en la diversidad sexual' ('that find terror in sexual diversity') and horror in homosexual attraction (Melero Salvador 2010: 76), where lesbianism is represented as 'un mal terrible . . . y el posible placer que produce está siempre envenenado' ('a terrible ill . . . and the pleasure it might bring is always poisoned') (75).

LesGaiCineMad 2011 – unfortunately timed to coincide in 2011 with FICGLB (or the other way about) – occupied not one prestigious space but several. Three of these at least have substantial cultural and political cachet: the trade-union founded Fundación Ateneo Cultural 1º de Mayo (for the opening four days); then, further down the grand central boulevard of Recoletos, the Casa de América, its proud and elaborately dressed corner frontage sharing the limelight opposite the iconic Post Office building on the east side of the Plaza de Cibeles; and the much dingier but intellectually just as respectable Ateneo Científico, Artístico y Literario de Madrid in the narrow but central Calle del Prado. This latter was the venue for two sessions of non-Spanish language short films on 8 November, creating by this fact alone an interesting dissonance with the emphatically bookish look (and remit) of the institution; moreover, the small audiences for the two sessions (one of 'temática gay', one of 'temática lésbica') were able to mill gingerly around the unpolished floors of a dusty main gallery outside the grand hall set up as the cinema, looking at the generally dark portraits of worthy male intellectuals of the past (but also feminist intellectual Emilia Pardo Bazán) and noting, in rudimentary glass-fronted display cases, the seemingly arbitrarily displayed and catalogued representatives of the Ateneo's extensive library. Catching the eye at catalogue number 20 – alongside some hefty canonical materials of the eighteenth to the twentieth centuries – was upmarket lesbian/crypto-lesbian writer and editor Esther Tusquet's *Confesiones de una editora poco mentirosa* (Confessions of a Scarcely Mendacious Editor); the *Diccionario de estudios de género y feminismos* (Dictionary of Gender and Feminist Studies) edited by Susana Beatriz Gamba was at number 35; and at number 65 were the poetry and prose of the queer Barcelonan Jaime Gil de Biedma (see Chapter 5) in the Galaxia-Gutenberg edition by Nicanor Vélez introduced by James Valender. This spatially enhanced collage effect and its clashing cultures (also mirrored in the staff of the festival's reception desk facing, two paces away, the club's own habitual portering and reception staff) proved an analogue for the typically mixed collection of films to be shown within, under the startlingly painted high ceilings and busy hangings. For the men (about two dozen only), the range was from the movingly dramatic, in *We Once Were Tide* (Jason Bradbury, 2011) to the quirkily musical *Skallaman* (Maria Bock, 2011). In contrast to the erudite accuracies of the Ateneo and its collected volumes, some of the films were very poorly translated and subtitled, from the English and the French at least: much of the mistily, island-based symbolic point of *We Once Were Tide* was jettisoned with a misreading of 'tide' as 'tied'; motive and narrative chronology came across as inappropriately opaque in *Breach of Etiquette* (Mark Levine, 2010); and there were isolated instances of misunderstood idioms or verb tenses in other films shown. Pressure of time and diminishing resources that afternoon piled oddity on oddity in this corner of an international festival. For the women (again, some two dozen) the range on offer was from satire in *Fluid* (Dara Sklar, 2011) to grim drama in *Alice in Andrew's Land* (Lauren Mackenzie, 2011) and included the interesting cross-L/T 'themed' *Pokerface* (Becky Lane, 2011), itself an amalgam of narremes – of coming out with a twist, a revelation of a non-lesbian past, and of rejection and acceptance of transgender transition.

The audience of some 225 attending the session of Spanish short films at the Sala Berlanga on 9 November 2011 were in more conventional surroundings for such an event (a smart, fringe theatrical venue, a fair way out from the centre of town). *A los que gritan* (*Sara's Shout* [or, To Those Who Shout Insults]) (Juanan Martínez, 2010) dramatised the issue of homophobic abuse on the street, and before the end titles displayed statistical evidence of such cases in Spain in recent years. It began with a strong triple impact of the sudden appearance, out of black and close-up, of Sara (Anna Allen) and her girlfriend stepping out onto the street, the shout of '¡Oye! ¡Tú!' ('hey, you!'), and a slap delivered to Sara following her angry confrontation of the abuser. At home, by way of explanation of her bruising, she takes her father through hypothetical everyday scenarios where insult and reaction might be provoked. This psychodramatic exercise in 'what-would-you-do?' ends, in a good, swift twist on the coming out narreme, in her bringing her lesbianism to the table and her father to either stunned or thoughtful silence. With its credited support from COGAM, the film is of the dramatic-didactic sub-genre which gains impact through its treatment of lesbophobia rather than the more usual gay-bashing, which, as revealed in Q & A with the director, had indeed been the original focus (with the shift to women being actor Anna Allen's idea).

Two of the films, *Turno de noche* (*Night Shift*) (Carlos Ruano, 2011) and *Muy mujer* (*So Womanly* [or, Very Much the Woman]) (Luis Escobar, 2011), made imaginative play with some standard entertainment industry tropes – respectively, horror and the dream-within-a-dream – creating an interplay between specifically queer scenarios and the general imaginary of the filmgoer. In *Turno de noche*, a young male window dresser in a shopping mall, Pablo, strikes up a tentatively erotic acquaintance with the straight-acting (if preening) security guard, David. Their timid journey towards almost acknowledging their mutual sexual attraction is centred around the underground storage room where the mannequins are kept. These, and their body parts – particularly their hands in half open grasp – are fetishised by the camera, with occasional sly matches to Pablo's hands and, in a cloakroom scene, David's bare torso. Pablo, inappropriately for his job, is uneasy in their presence – rightly so, as the film takes the horror turn that its music and chiaoscuro had already humorously suggested and, half-fuddled by the drugs he has shared with David in what should have been a lead-up to their finally making out, Pablo gets shut in the basement, the dummies come at him in scary, static, stop-motion leaps, and he dies at the hand of one of them. David too, as the film ends, seems set up for the same fate. By constructing parodically a fable of punishment for sexual transgression the film neatly shunts such a fable's presuppositions away into storage and instead entertains, slightly chills and also charms with its representation of the tenderness and immediacy of the normative scenario of the straight-acting, working man and the sensitive younger man (as also deployed, more raunchily, in *En malas compañías* – see Chapter 3). It also draws lightly on the sub-genre of queer horror, like *Luz*.

Muy mujer was designed, as director Luis Escobar told the audience, with a happy ending in mind as a counter to so many films with grim ones. It deployed a double *mise-en-abîme* combining the dream trope with a sub-plot of drag performance in order to entertain its audience. Susi, in stable lesbian coupledom, dreams a dream in which Andrés, himself in a gay marriage, also dreams that he is a straight man holding out on (straight) Susi by not telling her of his parallel life as a drag queen, SophiStykada (or of a one-off bout of sex with the bear-style masculine drag club owner). In a kaleidoscope of strikingly staged cameos, and with the well enough withheld surprise of the double dream, the film pays lively homage to the culture of the *travesti*, makes some carnivalesque points about masks and identity, exploits the trope of moral courage and integrity in adversity and wild absurdity – like *El Calentito* (Chus Gutiérrez, 2005) and its many parallels and forebears – and has some complicated fun at the end with the idea of heterosexuality as a messy and incoherent nightmare.

Between these two films had come two others requiring completely different modes of response: *Doble fila* (*Double Parking*) (Olaf González Scheeneweiss, 2011) and *Voces* (*Voices*) (Eduardo Fuembuena, 2010). *Doble fila* had a directness of treatment of the difficult transition from one relationship to another – the temporary double-parking of the the title. With a traumatic event at its core, Empar's hospitalisation after a car crash, the film stages in the filter-enhanced but already bright blue Valencian sunshine beyond the hospital bed of its premise a familiar, difficult conversation between an ex (Maribel) and a new lover (Alicia). The cars stand in for some simple, key ideas here. What the women need to get through – in an analogue of Empar's recovery from her injuries – is as straightforward, if irksome, as shunting a double parked car out of the way, and when Maribel cuts off in mid-flow the heightened drama of La Lupe singing 'Puro teatro' on the car's sound system when she gives Alicia a lift, what is signified is the no-nonsense recognition of what they have in common, and of what she, Maribel, must give up. The film is deft, simple and adult, and Empar recovers to drive, and park, again.

Some of this simplicity, though, comes from the director's desire – which he attested to in the Q & A after the showing – to 'normalise' the representation of same-sex desire. Indeed, despite the quirkiness of the parked car motif and the camp presence of La Lupe, there is little of disruptive effect in the treatment of these women beyond the neatly alternative repositioning as lesbian of a standard drama of relationships discussed in cars and in the Mediterranean outdoors.

By contrast, *Voces* was dark and convoluted in its mediation of queer desire. An overwrought and poorly acted drama of regret staged around a story of a triangular, late-schooldays relationship between Marcos, Adrián and Cristina it is another short film with repressive shades of the past in the mode of the films discussed in Chapter 2. At a crucial moment in the past, near a strangely chill patch of walled-in ground twice returned to by the film, Marcos had forced a kiss on Adrián, in long pent-up frustration, and after many fey sideways glances and meaningful looks. A horrified Adrián had reeled back in shock and – the film elliptically suggests – thus began his spiral into the insanity leading to his eventual death. The moon seen through clouds in a dream and the recitation voice-over of verses translated into Spanish from Cavafy's elegaic 'Φωνές' ('Voices'), as well as the chill anger of the knowing, bereaved mother, make the film a pseudo-gothic and very literary melodrama of tragic insufficiency, fixation and sexual dishonesty ('no soy así' ('I'm not that way')), is Marcos's tearful summary of his guilty, grieving feelings at the end). In a different mode to the sunlit and no-nonsense lesbianism as survival of *Doble fila*, this short too offered its audience that night normalisation through treacherous universalisation. In Valencia, the audience might be led to think, lesbians negotiating the emotional double parking effect might just as well be no different to other realigning couples. In the inland, northern woodland and in Adrián's parents' bourgeois home it is precisely what is different and cannot be given voice (the possibility of queer desire) which constructs around itself a set of stereotypical reactions and subject positions set up around the notion of same-sex desire as wrong and paralysing – a walled-in, haunted place. The quiet and eerie presence of Assumpta Serna (again) as the grieving mother reluctantly receiving Marcos in her home – bitterly half aware of, and suppressing articulation of, the nature of the closeness felt by Marcos to the dead Adrián – is a tonal match to the chill in the walled in patch of ground. In *Luz* (as just discussed) Assumpta Serna as the mother had been involved in a ludic attempt to exorcise the image of the ultimately disempowered lesbian vampire; in *Voces* she sees ghosts.

This chapter has indicated something of the contextual range of images available to the LGBTQ cultural subject as she picks her way through leisure time or negotiates urgent socio-political moments to join with others in becoming audience or community. The texts and films on offer present tactical choices or decisions of taste, frames for constructing affinities or building resistance. The short films in particular, and the sporadic visual event of the festival, represent an ephemeral but also potentially cumulative and coalescing effect for their audiences of feeling that they are part of a queer and variegated picture.

Notes

1. Verificatory user comments are to be found, for example, at <http://11870.com/pro/libreria-berkana> and <http://www.yelp.es/biz/libreria-berkana-madrid> [both last accessed 24 January 2012]; see also Robbins (2011).
2. Scriptwriters' website abcguionistas (2008) reproducing (and acknowledging) this material substitutes an unequivocally lesbophobic header for Lázaro's original 'Ponga una lesbiana en su serie': 'Lesbianas, pero "sexy"'. This gives a particular spin to Lázaro's already outdated, caricature notions of a change from checked-shirt wearing lesbians to cool and stylish ones.
3. Maciá uses 'Fancy Pastries' as a translation. The title puns on *bollo* as signifying both lesbian, popularly, and cakes and buns, more conventionally.
4. Available at <http://vimeo.com/7642561>; and <http://www.youtube.com/watch?v=3LfEmsewuGc> [last accessed 24 November 2011].
5. Available at <http://vimeo.com/10459520>; <http://vimeo.com/4864228>; and <http://vimeo.com/4864270> [last accessed 24 November 2011].

5. WRITERS

There is now no monoculturally queer cinephile audience in Spain (if there ever was, or any more than elsewhere), and this book has been concerned with the interconnectedness of viewing, consuming, reading, surfing, zapping, cinema- and festival-going, borrowing and downloading. In this chapter the focus is on the traffic between popular literature and film and the role of cinematically connected writers in constructing queer culture in Spain – and in particular the role of the screenwriter. It also examines two biopics on queer writers. The connections between text and film in this context are several. Popular lesbian and gay literature has scriptwriter or actor protagonists and plot references to films and filmgoing. Two high-profile novelists – Lucía Etxebarria and Vicente Molina Foix – are also a screenwriter and director respectively. Many screen- writers have a parallel activity as producers of popular fiction and journalistic essays and, as one of the novelist-directors studied in this chapter has reminded his readers, 'los escritores [hoy], unos por cautela y otros sinceramente, con- viven con el cine, cuentan con él en su repertorio imaginativo' (Molina Foix 2009a) ('nowadays writers, whether as a precautionary measure or genuinely, make cinema part of their lives and their imaginative repertoire draws on it').

Off-the-Shelf Middlebrow Lesbian and Gay Imaginaries

Far from uniquely in urban cultures where LGBTQ life has a commercial presence, Spain's specialist bookshops mix the sale of DVDs and books. The two together have formed a substantial cultural field of entertainment and of group identification. The outlets already discussed in Chapter 4 contribute, in their combinations of stock and in their roles as community forums as well as retail sites, to the writing of the script of queer cultures in Spain. As Robbins (2011: 154) observes, 'gay and lesbian bookstores have traditionally not only been business establishments but also spaces in which people could congregate for political or purely social purposes.' Indeed, a continuing pro- gramme of book presentations and cultural discussions in the Madrid book- shop on which Robbins concentrates and the small cafe space in which these are held are witness to this (despite a marked downturn in footfall by 201, as Mili Hernández affirmed in conversation on 24 May 2011).[1] Building on queer social and cultural theory's elaboration of concepts of spatial practice from Lefebvre and Certeau, Robbins examines 'the image of lesbian Madrid' and the city's '"queer literary spaces"' as having 'transformed and been transformed by queer social and cultural practices, including literary writing and reading' (Robbins 2011: 149, 150). She also analyses the uses made of, and the tensions and exclusions imposed by, the Chueca neighbourhood (151–3, 167) and the Berkana bookshop in particular (153–7). The latter typifies the traditional mix of commercial social purposes identified by Robbins, above. Robbins also focuses on the publishing practices of Egales, the joint venture by the Berkana and Cómplices bookshops in Barcelona. Noting omissions in the list for women (particularly in the area of general feminist interest, but also in coverage of Latin American and chicana writers), she nevertheless recognises the collection's strong commitment to essays (including many in translation), anthologies and 'entertaining, easy novels, that [have] normalised and legitimised homosexuality for gay and lesbian readers and thereby eased the coming-out process' (155). It is this mix of reading material that, according to Berkana's lead proprietor, Mili Hernández, has 'changed' and even (figuratively) 'saved' lives (Hidalgo 2011).

These establishments, institutions and support mechanisms set out with the purpose of providing familiar narratives to fill a gap in a community's awareness of its own history and character in the wake of Spain's long dictatorship (Pertusa and Vosburg 2009b: 37). Castrejón (2008: 276) identifies a strand of 'costumbrismo' (localised realism) in lesbian writing, responding to this need in the Spanish context, and this can be traced through even the post-1998 selections by Pertusa and Vosburg (2009a). Castrejón's key example is Libertad Morán, whose protagonists she sees also as creating 'sus propios códigos' ('their own codes'), but rather than being recondite or private, these are 'comunes, representativos de un colectivo visible' (Castrejón 2008: 280) ('common currency, representative of a visible community'). Morán's novels, published with Odisea, present a lesbian subject who, far from being invisible, 'irrumpe en el ámbito sociocultural' ('bursts onto the sociocultural stage') to recount in explicit terms her experience as a lesbian and to reclaim her rights (Collins 2009: 164). Breaking away, in *A por todas* (published 2005), from the image of the lesbian as isolated and disoriented, the protagonist Ruth offers a sense of collective experience and agency (Collins 2009: 152). *Mujeres estupendas* (Morán, 2006) has a range of narrators engage in discussions about parenting and alternative family structures and includes a wry take on attendance at LGBTQ film festivals. *Una noche más* (Morán 2007) offers a version of a Chueca that is more accessible for lesbians than might be suggested either by their relative invisibility in the standard Chueca-set novels and films of popular gay culture or by ethnological observation and sociological critique (Gimeno 2007a; Robbins 2011: 152–3).

The collection in which these novels are marketed, Odisea's Safo, has a remit to provide accessible, entertaining realism as does its mainly male-oriented counterpart Inconfesables, as noted by Pertusa and Vosburg (2009b: 37). Their mix of characters and situations with which to identify, and erotic scenarios around which to fantasise, is typical of a whole product range (Pertusa and Vosburg 2009b: 38; Robbins 2003). This has developed beyond the juridical watershed of 2005 into an extensive production of writing that seeks to give an integrated sense of lesbian desire as inscribed in everyday experiences and love lives (Pertusa and Vosburg 2009b: 39–44). By contrast, it is an economically and culturally driven characteristic of film production by and for lesbians in Spain that such a relatively extensive and, to use Pertusa and Vosburg's terminology, normalising new wave has not made an impact on screen beyond television.[2] Even the popular, web-disseminated *Chica busca chica* (by TerraTV: 2008–9) – a sort of lower echelon *L-Word* (in terms of the social mix and habitats of the characters involved and of production values themselves, of course) – had, at the time of writing, only survived one series, with a feature-length sequel compilation promised for over a year via a precariously structured site with little in the way of direct assignation of responsibility for the project (Chicabuscachica 2011).

Popular lesbian writing offers numerous examples of the ludic shake-up of received ideas about queer and lesbian thought and experience, and of the relationship between them. In Susana Guzner's collection of short stories *Punto y aparte* (Start the Next Sentence) – an Egales publication – the narrator of 'Carta a Raquel' ('Letter to Raquel') observes with rueful irony Raquel's decision to leave her for a man, noting that, of course:

> la exclusividad lesbiana va a contramano de la vanguardia política y no sé cuántos ditirambos teóricos que resbalan sobre mi piel como gotas de aceite. (Guzner 2004: 27)
> (being exclusively lesbian goes against progressive politics and who knows what other theoretical choruses whose sounds run like oil off the surface of my skin.)

In 'El otro espejo' ('The Other Mirror'), in the same volume, the drug-fuelled, comical fury of the focalising character Teté directed against a male-to-female transexual slow in exiting the women's toilet develops into a rant against queer political correctness when an earnest, bespectacled young woman in the same agonised queue objects to Teté's use of the term 'travestón' (37) ('big trannie'). Such texts have an affinity with the playful-serious takes on sexual orthodoxy to be found in the films, for example, of Balletbò-Coll or Blanca Salazar. In another direction, Pertusa and Vosburg (2009a) note how elements of humour in Marina Mayoral's short story 'Antes que el tiempo muera' ('Before Time Itself Dies') in the collection *Recuerda, cuerpo* (Body, Remember) (published 1998) 'naturali[zan] la expresión de la sexualidad femenina' ('naturalise the expression of female sexuality'); the story also explores lesbianism in a rural context and the paradoxically enabling aspect of invisibility, allowing women's desire for women to pass unnoticed precisely because it is unimaginable in certain social contexts (Castrejón 2008: 117). A reader who had enjoyed this tale might readily have gone to *Nacidas para sufrir*, which also has a ludic element to it (see Chapter 1), or followed the story of Axun in *80 egunean* (see Chapter 2).

The parallel tradition of novels by men for men takes place in the different socio-political context of longer established visibility and, to judge by their only partly idealising content, greater – almost unlimited – access to leisure resources and time. It occupies a different cultural space in which the novels, though often hyperbolic, are seldom in serious search for a new language to express new subjectivities (as in the opposing case of successful lesbian writers such as Flavia Company (Pertusa-Seva 2011)). These are by default notionally realist and accessible representations of the lives of men who have sex with men in a country now prolifically supplied with spaces for the practice and embodiment of non-heteronormative desire. Their socio-cultural positioning vis-à-vis a fairly confident, fairly young male readership already in possession of some room of their own, and a range of treatments that is strongly flavoured by translations in from the American English tradition of gay literature (as the catalogues of the various retail outlets readily attest) place many of them in the liberal middle. Like the lesbian or gay strands in the post-heritage comedies discussed in Chapter 2 and the Chueca- and Gayxample-based dramas (notably the online series *Gayxample*), or the version of a comedy of manners *Mariquita con perro* (Queen with Dog) (Vicente Villanueva, 2007) (on how to be a Bad Gay), they form a version of the social, commercial and taste-dictated phenomenon of the Anglo-Saxon early-to-mid-twentieth century, the boom of the middlebrow, but with a fun, contemporary twist and – in *Gayxample*, for instance – abundant sexual interest. For, like the products of that particular boom, these Spanish novels in general set out to entertain and instruct, delight their readers through mirroring their problems and their sense of being out of kilter with or unheard by the dominant culture, and sell a way of living. There is at the base of these texts a realist urge behind their choice of topic, setting, protagonist and tone, a sense of an ethos to be delineated and tested, a set of social practices to represent, new configurations of desires and older stories and voices to be reconstructed. As David Bergmann (2003) points out in relation to the writers of the Violet Quill group of writers of the 1970s, they 'did not represent how all gay men lived, or even how most gay men lived, but they did make visible a certain image of gay life that spoke to a large number of gay men and formed the fantasies of even more' (19) and had 'a keen awareness of how the pressures of society impinged on their stories' and an awareness of 'just how unsettled the problem of gay representation was' at the time (20). Queer Spain, in the small and mainly middle-class cultural space in which these novels have been solicited, produced, read and talked about, has witnessed a particularly intense taking stock of 'the pressures of society' and has formed distinctive 'geographies of sexualities', to use Bell and Valentine's term (1995). These are cross-mapped in text and on screen.

Like some of the poetic or experimental short films previously discussed – but not alike in form – there is an anxiety at large in some of the novels to validate experience by reference to ostensibly higher cultural modes, names or practices. So, in Pedro Menchén's *Una playa muy lejana* (A Far Distant Beach) (1999) the story of mismatched lovers moves briefly twice to the historic city of Cuenca. Like certain amateur photographers, as studied by Bourdieu (1990) – 'halfway between "vulgar" practices . . . and noble cultural practices' (97) – the narrator's tightly accurate but artistic descriptions of the visual prizes of the city, navigated with the help of his dead father's patina-endowed copy of *Ciudades pintorescas* (Pictureque Cities) and an anxiety to set himself apart from the other snapshot-taking tourists (Menchén 1999: 25–37) all are meant to serve to give (perhaps ironic) temporal depth and broader cultural meaning – a certain distinction – to the otherwise shaming and tawdry affair set in a flat in Benidorm which forms the substance of the novel. The text, characteristically, teeters uncertainly around the poles of the noble and the vulgar, activating questions about value and taste.

It has been observed of British and North American writing of 1920s to the 1960s that readers wanted access to a 'ready-made tradition' through a literature made more accessible by publishers 'responding to the demand for culture in organised, manageable packages' and responding also to the demand for pleasure (Rubin 1992: vi). What was wanted, and marketed, was a text 'both cultured and enjoyable' (Humble 2001: 255). In the Spanish texts there are many examples of the mixture of the enjoyable read and the cultured experience. This occurs in a manner reminiscent of the early novels of British novelist Alan Hollinghurst in Juan (1999), obsessively in Jiménez Ariza (2003) and parodically in the chapter 'Follar no es un acto cultural' in Morte (2004) ('Fucking is not a cultural event'). In Luis Melero's *El espejo líquido* (Melero 2001) (The Liquid Mirror) a well-muscled country boy and male stripper (Diego, a.k.a. El Cateto Atómico) (The Atomic Bumpkin) likes reading Steinbeck and Faulkner (because of his country upbringing), is recommended Miguel Delibes (for the same reason) but also fixates on Gore Vidal's highly cosmopolitan memoirs which provide him with a means to work through his, to him inexplicable, visceral attraction to a gym buddy. Ortiz (2003) uses film cultural reference and Greek mythology (as well as Shakira) to get the narrator through a painful, thoughtful story of doomed desire, whereas art cinema is used simply to enhance the sexual cachet of the narrator-chronicler of city life in Rei (2005, 2007).

Treatments of disappointment, humiliation, confusion and misinterpreted friendship tend towards the well-worn metaphor and link this form of writing to problem-page journalism in a way which is typical of certain segments of the romantic middlebrow while also jeopardising the equally middlebrow project of creatively constructing basic new cultural formations and guides to living. On love itself in these novels (as in the films) there is a very broad range of advice and a scattergun approach to the target readership with huge variations in the expectations of level of readerly or actual experience.

As important to these texts' uneven project of the construction of taste and identity, however, is history itself (as in some of the documentaries and queer heritage films I have been discussing). This is a strand studied by Martínez-Expósito in relation to more upmarket texts and films (1998: 1–28, 59–83) – that of the delineation of a consciousness of identity as the product of specific historical moments and social configurations. Personal gay histories are imagined or transposed and reconstructed; experiences of oppression and self-repression are simulated. The reader learns how to be a good homosexual, or at least a wary or a wise one. Alberto Ciáurriz's *El gran salto* (1999) (The Big Leap) – the first Odisea Prize winner – flavours its story with warnings of 'un nuevo oscurantismo' (Ciáurriz 2002: 41) ('a new obscurantism') brought about by a younger queer generation's ahistoricised lifestyle politics. Miguel Fernández's *Yestergay* has flashback sections documenting fictionally the homophobic police brutality of the Franco years, and constructs a provincial urban Spain of the 2000s where the old ideologies, coupled with traditional family structures, still allow the normalisation of acts of violent dismissal of non-heterosexual life experiences as 'cosas de maricones, lo peor de lo peor' (Fernández, M. 2003: 169) ('queerboy stuff: the worst of the worst'). In Carlos Armenteros's *Las aves del caos* (The Birds of Chaos) a bereaved gay lover's moral right to inheritance is contested by a family (whose most violent and vociferous member is dangerously closeted and conflicted, tellingly enough): 'Era evidente que para ellos [yo] no era una persona, no era un igual, era solo un intruso' (Armenteros 2006: 185) ('it was clear that for them I was not a person, not an equal, but just an intruder'). This is the kind of social structure of exclusion explored in the short film *Lala* (Esteban Crespo, 2009), where Jesús, returning to his village and the funeral of his grandmother (whose death has been kept from him), is confronted at the door by a group of one-time school bullies whose homophobia is still in sardonic evidence, and inside by a mother who tells him that there is nothing here for him, that he has, after all, gone off in search of a new life (abroad, in fact, and as a university lecturer).

More specifically, some of these books make a distinctive queer contribution to the well-documented boom of the early-to-mid 2000s in narratives of historical memory in Spain (Resina and Winter 2006). Alberto Ciáurriz's *La terraza de enfrente* (The Balcony Opposite) involves a transition from the voyeuristic fascinations of a Madrid apartment balcony via an extravagantly complex blackmail plot to the Spanish Civil War and to memories of 'una posguerra eterna . . . como una vieja película en blanco y negro' (Ciáurriz 2006: 130) ('an endless postwar . . . like an old black and white film'). The fourth Odisea prizewinner, *El viaje de Marcos* (Hernández 2005; in its fourth edition) (Marcos's Journey), is set in the high summer of 1970, in a village in

La Mancha where the intense romance of young homosexual love in the late Franco years is juxtaposed with the activities of a vigilante group, the Hijos del General (The Children of the General) (one of whom is, in a conflicted way, queer) on a mission to keep Spain clean of communists, masons and queers ('maricones') (154). The narrative is highly dramatic, full of set pieces and lit by storms and hot sunshine. It would have made a good B-movie in former years.

Sometimes the painful complexity of being queer in these Spanish contexts breaks through instructively into the space of textual form itself, either by way of bewildering intricacy, insistent symbolism and frantic cultural allusion, or by way of more sober representations of the feelings of marginalisation. Thus in Carlos Armenteros's *El Lago* (The Lake) (a finalist in the 2000 Odisea competition) the narrator Pedro uses cruising as a means to forget but instead comes to know, through its dynamics, the strangeness and ungraspability of the self, as well as rejection by family and heteronormative society (Armenteros 2000: 45, 56), as is also dramatised in the epilogue to Carrillo's film *Caníbales* (see Chapter 4).

SCREENWRITERS: LUCÍA ETXEBARRIA, ELVIRA LINDO, ÁNGELES GONZÁLEZ-SINDE

The invisibility of the screenwriter in the post-Hollywood Golden Age – an old topos – has been duly revisited as an issue in Spanish contexts by the organisations ALMA (the Union of Scriptwriters) (ALMA 2008) and FAGA, a new forum for screenwriters' associations (Rivadulla Corcón 2010). Most accounts of LGBTQ feature films, indeed, go direct to director or content. However, at the precarious end of production, in the conception and creation of short films, as well as in their circulation and discussion, the indivisibility of writer and director is to the fore. Most short films, particularly debut ones, are, self-evidently, the produce of the sole writer-director. At the other end of the spectrum, Almodóvar's *La mala educación* (see Chapter 2), with its doubly reflexive treatment of a director-screenwriter in search of a story, was a reminder of this iconic director's creativeness in writing characters who are often neither fully heterosexual nor homosexual, not politically lesbian or gay, not containable in coupledom, who are trans but not part of a trans community. The well-known speech by the character Agrado in *Todo sobre mi madre* (*All About My Mother*) (Pedro Almodóvar, 1999), in the context of a sub-plot about learning old lines and new roles, also dramatises the obvious links between sexuality, textuality, visuality and gender politics.

The mid-to-late 1990s inheritance of box-office targeted comedies, as discussed in Chapter 2, had established a modest stable of screenwriters for feature films made for (or, sometimes, about) the lesbian and gay audience. Two already established comedy screenwriters, Yolanda García Serrano and Juan Luis Iborra, came together to write and direct their first completely gay-plotted film *Amor de hombre* (*The Love of a Man*) (1997), with García Serrano simultaneously publishing a novel based on the script. As Fouz-Hernández and Martínez-Expósito (2007) suggest, the film is scripted in a pedagogic mode, 'intent on "explaining" homosexual lifestyles to a mainstream audience', from a stereotyping heterosexual perspective, albeit with the pros and cons of the inclusion of 'a large number of gay characters with different and at times idiosyncratic understandings of their own sexuality' (125). This may well be (as these critics politely imply) because the script itself does not understand them, and this is a situation which is only partly ameliorated by the time García Serrano came to work on *Reinas* (see Chapter 2) in 2005, though now with Manuel Gómez Pereira and Joaquín Oristrell, two experts in rough-and-ready comic psychological verisimilitude.

Some very prominent figures have been involved in developing scripts for LGBTQ film in Spain. Lucía Etxebarria – a regular presence on the 'New In' display tables of the major bookshops and in the cultural media – was an important focal point for consumers of novels and films alike in the late 1990s. She has since moved steadily away from fictional engagements with what is probably best described as queer-light sexuality and has, in her own life, settled into a heterosexual marriage (in June 2011), to take disingenuous and far from obviously feminist delight in such things as attending summer jazz festivals where

> [M]e regalo la vista con negros y mulatos de una belleza comparable o superior a los que paseen por playa caribeña alguna. (Etxebarria 2011b)
> (I feast my eyes on black men and mulattos as beautiful as any to be seen on a Carribean beach, if not more so.)

Her debut novel *Amor, curiosidad, prozak y dudas* (*Love, Prozac and Other Curiosities*) of 1997, with its young lesbian character Gema as a catalyst for feminist rethinking of family bonds, was adapted (*Love and Other Curiosities*) (Miguel Santesmases, 2001) with a script by her and Santesmases; *Beatriz y los cuerpos celestes* (*Beatrice and the Heavenly Bodies*) (1998), a novel of self-determination through politicised sexuality (Castrejón 2008: 128–42) which also explores a language of reinvention (140–1), gained widespread media attention (in part because it won precociously the prestigious Nadal prize that year); *Nosotras que no somos como las demás* (We Who Are Unlike the Others) (1999) consolidated a process of 'self-commodification – both of her own image and her fiction – [which] has provoked much controversy and unfavourable criticism' (Tsuchiya 2002: 79). The 'abundance [in *Beatriz* ... of] passages in which the character, as the author's spokesperson, presents disquisitions on feminist issues in a way that would be digestible to the general reading public' (Tsuchiya 2002: 83) extends to Etxebarria's other writings. This chimes both with the burgeoning male tradition of middlebrow popular writing in Spain and with a prominent sub-type of LGBTQ film which over-neatly packages up issues of relevance.

One such package is *I Love You Baby* (2001) (see Chapter 3), co-scripted by Etxebarria, with its tour of some traditional questions in sexual orientation, masculinity and bad faith. Another is *Sobreviviré* (*I Will Survive*) (Alfonso Albacete and David Menkes, 1999), again co-written by Etxebarria, which, like the early novels, might be seen to 'debunk the presupposition of a clear disjunction between hetero- and homosexuality (or between hetero- and homosexual desires)' (Tsuchiya 2002: 85) and yet also to 'reinforce normative conceptualisations of gender and sexual identity' and power 'within the colluding structures of patriarchy and compulsory heterosexuality' (84). This later film's characterisation of Iñaki (Juan Diego Botto) as sexually ambiguous, and its uneven struggle with a 'structural problem [with] regulatory distinctions around sexuality and gender' (Perriam 2003b: 156), seems very much to show Etxebarria's hand. Botto's Iñaki is written as a livelier version of Sanz's Marcos in the later *I Love You Baby* (see Chapter 3), who appears to sleepwalk through a form of pared down, monogamous gayness back into heterosexuality.

Since 2001, Etxebarria has moved away from screenwriting and her essays and blogging (Etxebarria 2011a) only include cinema (and, indeed, LGBTQ issues) as one concern among a welter of others. For the screenplay of their next film, *Entre vivir y soñar* (*Searching for Love*) (2004), her collaborators Albacete and Menkes worked with Ángeles González-Sinde who had been screenwriter for *Segunda piel* (see Chapter 3). González-Sinde had won the Goya award for best original screenplay in 1998 for *La buena estrella* (*The Lucky Star*) (Ricardo Franco, 1997). She was President of the Academia de las Artes y las Ciencias Cinematográficas de España (Spanish Academy of Arts and Cinematographic Sciences) from 2006 to 2009 and subsequently became Minister for Culture (appointed in April 2009), responsible in particular for a range of measures against Internet piracy (controversial in a culture which had normalised and justified to itself this form of minor theft to a curious, and damaging, extent) (Fritz 2010; Agencia EFE 2011). González-Sinde, then, brought a certain cachet to lesbian and gay film and gave a very high public prominence to screenwriting. This, however, was not to consistently positive effect: hanging in the blogosphere there was a haze of resentment about policy and about the funding of *Mentiras y gordas* (see Chapter 3) on which she was co-writer (Fernández, Lara 2010). A received idea was formed that the script of this film was so poor that the connection ill-behoved a Minister of State (Jiménez 2009; 'marotorod' 2009; 'Tahamata' 2009; 'terrorinword' 2011). Nonetheless, the very direct connection between the Ministry of Culture and the filmic narration of the everyday problems and concerns of a certain strand of young queer citizen has had a significant effect of visibility, in line with Tony and Marina's perseverance in the film against the heteronormative odds.

I have referred, in Chapter 3, to suggestions that much of the box-office and digital-circulation success of *Mentiras y gordas* was due to the casting, with its appeal to a youngish audience attuned to the television careers of its good-looking actors. Additionally, there is a certain appeal in the skill with which its intricate, episodic structure is saved from incoherence or mere predictability by the dynamics of dialogue, the patterning of the appearances of the different pairings of characters, and the relative delicacy with which the old topic of the lonely gay boy with a crush on his straight friend is threaded through the film (even if his dramatic demise ties the story up more like a stranglehold). The crush that Tony has on Nico, to go back to the narrative but now to concentrate on the screenplay, is given dramatic and psychological substance in two well connected, consecutive scenes (*c*.38–41 minutes). Sitting on the beach side by side, the two young men play out the defining dynamic of their friendship, providing one of the most used promotional images for the film.[3] Nico tries to persuade Tony to come in with him on an amateurish drug-pushing enterprise, using a direct, no-nonsense style ('no pasa nada' ('there's nothing to it')) appropriate to the situation and to the minor youth crime genre being exploited here. Tony resists with realistic, common-sensed responses (what if they get caught? what about his college fees?), the script having him register the gloomy recognition that he is yet again to be seduced into doing something he does not want, and that yet again what he does want – Nico – is not for him. Casas's acting has Nico register guilt as much as frustration, but Nico goes for the kill with a well-timed 'podemos hacer . . . de todo; tú y yo' ('we can do exactly what we want; it'll just be you and me'), referring to the trip the two could make together on the proceeds of their dealing. They savour and swap that word 'todo', Tony repeating it looking longingly at Nico's lips, Nico with pushy enthusiasm. When Nico has registered Tony's look, and is satisfied that he has him hooked, he ends with 'hazlo por mí' ('do it for me'). An immediate transition to a kitchen scene between Tony and Marina is sutured by Marina's 'y ¿se lo has dado?' ('so you gave him the money?'), neatly back-converting the preceding drama into one of the many interleaved stories told in the film.

The script's treatment of Marina's own story – of her first night with Leo, of her doubts and fears – provides a neatly mismatched not-quite-lesbian echo of the would-be gay story on the sand. Tony's and Marina's thoughts are expressed in a fluent, slightly didactic-obvious mode proper to the style of the popular literature discussed in the first part of this chapter. Later that evening (the script observes a strict enough convention of unity of time and place and continuity) there is further solid, standard dialogue from Tony about homosexuality, religion, social exclusion (although that has nothing to do with his problem with Nico), the need to fight for the right for two people of the same sex to love one another, and the determination to be open, out, brave – 'no esconderme' ('not to hide'). All the right screenplay-based mechanisms for a film of this ambition are in place, perhaps because of the absence, in the cases just discussed, of attempts at comedy; perhaps because the queerness – in sexual, affective and political terms – of these moments is where the film's heart really is. The writing points this up deftly.

On the other hand, there are signs of haste, superficiality, an over-dependence on light comedy and sheer lack of in-depth understanding of the issues, cultures and individuals being represented. Not all the episodic jumps and edits are motivated or linked by narrative or by a verbal style – and even less by a deliberately queer aesthetic. Much depends, instead, on bridging via the musical soundtrack (justifiably enough, given one of the target audiences, although few young LGBTQ clubbers and leisure listeners are likely to deem the music – and certainly not the dancing – cool). As well as numerous intrusive small jokes on themes of sex and rebellion, one strand of the story depends on an absurd premise on the effects of ecstasy, whereby Paz (Miriam Giovanelli) – with a poor self-image, and representing the *gordas* (fat girls) of the title – and an astonishingly unfocused law student (a joke is intended) Bubú (Alejo Sauras) fall helplessly in lust and love with one another and, under the drugs' effects, carry on fawning over one another way into the following day. In a different plot strand, the story of Marina and Leo is robbed of substance by insufficient characterisation and back story. Despite the exemplary interest of the not-quite-lesbian relationship between them, Leo, though twenty-nine, has a grasp of emotional life which seems closer to that of someone much younger.

A much more subtle and genuinely fragile sense of the complexity and depth of a bond between women – in this case in adversity rather than just adrift – emerges from the dialogue in *Una palabra tuya* (*One Word from You*) (2008), adapted from her own novel of the same name by Elvira Lindo, and directed, in this case, by González-Sinde. The relationship between Milagros (Esperanza Pedreño) and Rosario (Malena Alterio), two street-cleaners, is structured around the destabilising loneliness of Milagros and the hardship of the role first of carer for, then subsequently grieving for, a mother who dies in dementia. Stocked on the shelves of Berkana at the time of writing and listed on the usual retail websites, the film takes its intense homosociality and its socially aware exploration of the causes of isolation, poverty, dependency and emotional dysfunction far enough – in a context of tenderness and non-sexual physicality – to be queer. Indeed, one defining moment for the positioning of the two women in their personal as well as their working lives is their inter-pellation indirectly by the giggling of co-workers in the women's changing rooms, as Milagros gives Rosario a foot massage (with a nice mixed sense on screen of innocent sensual relief, fun and joshing). In bluff, friendly fashion, male co-worker Morsa (Antonio de la Torre) asks outright 'sois bolleras, ¿no?' ('you're lesbians, aren't you?'). However, Morsa's comment entails the less friendly heteronormative and machista view, attributed to another male co-worker, Sanchis, that all lesbians are virgins. This combination of a politicised sense of what controls, inhibits or normalises, and of the free ambivalence of the feelings between the two women – is it love or affection? asks one blogger ('Nacho' 2008) – underpins the words of Milagros to Rosario as the two walk through the dramatic framing and amplifying deep perspective of a stonework arcade: 'a cada uno le toca en justicia lo que le debe tocar . . . y a ti te he tocado yo' ('we each get what we properly deserve . . . and you have ended up with me'). Rosario, as somebody on constant alert and who understands the meanings – as Lindo puts it – of 'la falta de cohesión social' (Morgado 2005: 104) ('lack of social cohesion'), is well placed to relay to the viewer a sense of how the feelings of this moment, how the relationship between these damaged, working women, intersect with channels laid down by social exclusion, by prejudice and by the pressure to conform to heteronormative family life and workplace expectations.

The film has a short precedent in Albaladejo's *Ataque verbal* (see Chapter 4) where, in the sixth dialogue, or 'ataque', Lindo (who wrote the dialogue) herself plays Rosario, and where a similar, tacit but telling closeness is represented between the two women (though in a more comedic vein). In this case the workplace assumptions are that Rosario is 'una reprimida' ('repressed'), and she sees herself as someone whom men do not want. With an affectionate quick kiss she tells Milagros (Heli Albaladejo) that she is the only one who has ever shown her love. What the dialogue lacks in socio-political underpinning to give it queer intersectionality, it gains in its juxtaposition within the full film to the fourth dialogue (the scout camp) and the seventh (the Cuban bath), sharing with these a deft sense of the two-edged power of half-truths and indirection. As in the feature film, the discovery of a baby among the rubbish serves as a token of this bond and as a sign of desperate loneliness (the Milagros of the short dialogue uses religious superstition as a crutch for her emotional instability). Unlike in the feature film, where Milagros's anxieties about abandonment lead in tragic paradox to her allowing the baby to die jealously guarded at her home, the short version of the story of Rosario and Milagros ends ludically enough, with the two of them and their hand-pushed dust cart, baby installed, trundling off along the darkened path of the park they have been cleaning, still talking. The mock pram, the pretend couple, the non-leisure time walk in the park show the edge of the disempowerment which forces the two to do what they do, and disallows their doing what they might wish to do and say to one another. But it shows the other edge too, banter redeemed as tenderness, and what is not said turned neatly into eloquence.

Lindo is a well known opinion page contributor in the national press, though not writing directly for an LGBTQ readership. In one brief piece she spells out the links between the sorts of remark that both Rosarios are subject to in the films – embedded misogyny and continuing paternalism in the media (Lindo 2010a). On same-sex marriage, she registers indignation at the possibility of the Partido Popular's working to rescind the law, and denying the right, like Franco's annulment of civil marriages after the Civil War (Lindo 2010b), while a bitter-sweet evocation of pre-gay Chueca (Lindo 2008) layers the history of the place with grim memories of drug-users, dog mess, ambulances and police cars. These two novelist-columnists, Etxebarria and Lindo, and the public profile of González-Sinde, then, serve to write LGBTQ realities into the social script.

A-LIST NOVELISTS: EDUARDO MENDICUTTI AND VICENTE MOLINA FOIX

A ludic angle on the social realities of economic precariousness and marginality as well as an ostensibly satirical treatment of the dynamics of the older-man-and-kept-boy are to be seen in *Los novios búlgaros* (*Bulgarian Lovers*) (Eloy de la Iglesia, 2003). This film is based on the novel of the same name (published 1993) by Eduardo Mendicutti. Mendicutti might as easily have had a niche in the previous chapter on prominent celebrity personalities and their images. The fictionalised autobiography *El palomo cojo* (The Lame Pigeon) (published 1991) was adapted to the screen under the same name (Jaime de Armiñán, 1995) and has been shown on the flagship Versión Española (TVE) (9 August 2002). It has a strong crossover audience appeal, guaranteed by its heritage look and formative-years narrative premise, which long ago established Mendicutti (born in 1948) as a prominent, out-gay, cultural figure. As a novelist he is on the list of the prestigious publishing house Tusquets Editores and is a regular columnist and essayist in the gay and liberal press. In *Zero* magazine, *Shangay* and more recently (since November–December 2010) *Oh My God* magazine, his topics cover a wide range of cultural, lifestyle and LGTBQ political issues. Since the first appearance of the national newspaper *El Mundo*, he has written a column in the Opinion pages and summer diaries under the pseudonym of La Susi. Like the Venezuelan-born television personality, essayist and novelist Boris Izaguirre, Mendicutti has constructed a distinctive, and humorous, anti-conformist and often anti-heterosexist position on social issues and topics in cultural criticism. In short, 'aparte de autor es una de las voces más importantes del colectivo homosexual español' (Gallardo 2010) ('as well as being an author he is one of the most important voices in the Spanish homosexual community').

Mendicutti sees himself as 'un buen compañero de viaje' (El Castigador 2011) ('a good fellow traveller'). As an essayist, like Luis Antonio de Villena and Lluís Maria Todó, suggests Mira (2004), he has created a highly visible form of alternative cultural intervention (609) which reflects the marginalised subject and pays attention to otherwise silenced voices which now refuse to be subdued (609). His novels demonstrate 'el triunfo de la diferencia' (Mira 2004: 446–7) ('the triumph of difference'), deploying a subversive, strategically camp voice which has its roots in the radical dissenting cultures of the Transition (527, 536–9). As Pérez-Sánchez observes of *Una mala noche la tiene cualquiera* (Anyone Can Have A Bad Night) (first published 1982), its wry and counter-cultural take on the attempted military coup of 1981, the 'depiction of a transvestite as the most reliable witness of crucial historical events', is crucial (Pérez-Sánchez 2007: 104). It allows a transposition of notionally central and peripheral subjects and perspectives, a retelling of history, and 'a creative critique of heterosexism and dualistic gender norms' (105) (all these are also exploited in the film). It 'blends', in other words, 'democracy with queerness' (110).

In the writing, cinema is a constant referent and source of camp material as well as of narrative structure. In *California* (Mendicutti 2005) the first part is set in Hollywood (the character Gildo's special interest in *Los novios búlgaros*) and explores, from the narrative point of view of a handsome, heartless kept young man, how '[t]odo en California, aquel verano del 74, era *gorgeous*, encantador, delicioso, radiante' (34) ('everything in California, that summer of 1973, was gorgeous, delightful, delicious, radiant') while in Madrid friends left behind are condemned to the grimness of the long terminal illness of Francisco Franco, to persecution and imprisonment (in one case) and engagement in 'la beatería de cambiar el mundo' (120) ('ridiculous, pious hopes of changing the world'). *Mae West y yo* (published in 2011) also uses classic Hollywood cinema, and Mae West and other divas, to build a camp discourse from the position of the marginal (and in resistance to illness).

The novel *Los novios búlgaros* (published 1993) is varied in tone and combines the virtuoso comedy of a half self-deprecating narrator (Daniel) telling the tale of his explicitly foreshadowed downfall (Mendicutti 1998: 11) with sobering, if briefly glimpsed, perspectives on a world turned upside down by political upheaval and individual venality (69–75). Daniel, aware of the oddity of his own and his friends' enthrallment by straight-acting, rough young men, is also thus affected by the thorough pervasiveness of 'los discursos dúplices' (74) ('discourses of duplicity'), of 'pena' and 'horror' (75) ('misery' and 'horror') radiating out from the transnational into the personal sphere. The world for him is 'hecho añicos' (228) ('shattered') and in need of being put back together, albeit as a more modest 'lugar propio y habitable' (228) ('a decent and liveable place'). The experiences of the older (albeit wealthy) gay man, the precariousness of the undocumented, refugee migrant, HIV/AIDS (47–8, 66–7), crime and exploitation (113–26) are all seriously treated, despite the general tone of light comedic caricature and stereotype, as 'consistent with [Daniel's] conformist world view' (Ramos 1995).

When in the film Daniel imagines being Kyril's moll, the literalisation of the fantasy, with a stagily cross-dressed Daniel complete with cheroot, the action and the joke are paralysed for a full 25 seconds while the audience's laughter at yet another stereotypical image of old-style drag is hauled out of the repertoire like a bad pun, with slow pan in and across and out and fade to scarlet. The film's use of Pepón Nieto (see Chapter 3) in an over-the-top performance as Gildo also tips the film disproportionately into obviousness. Nieto's performance takes the character and his context much further towards plain misogyny, objectification and exploitation of men and internalised homophobia than the novel. In the film, Gildo shares the narrator protagonist Daniel's cinephilia, but converts it into an excuse to gather together Bulgarian and other immigrant young men at parties, and the film uses it as an excuse also to glamorise and objectify them. The shock value of bad taste in one particular party sequence (Daniel's birthday is the occasion) which conflates lost political ideals, capitalism and concupiscence is high enough to activate a queer resistant reading in all but the most obstinately out-for-a-laugh film viewer. In a distorting parody of Marilyn Monroe's rendition of 'Happy Birthday To You' to president John F. Kennedy a well-built, young, blonde Bulgarian is placed on a pedestal, bathed in golden light, pawed by Gildo and encouraged to sing 'The Internationale'.

Although it employs would-be reflexive looks to and addresses to camera by Daniel and although the camera occasionally stands back to allow the narrative to gather depth, the film is mostly happy to depend for it effects on a colourful scene of ostensible playfulness, sexual compliments directed at younger men and the use of feminine pronouns and agreements applied to men. Mendicutti does habitually play with such traits in his writing, and he has his narrator in the novel use female nicknames for all the older men as well as describing himself at times from the start (Mendicutti 1998: 11) with the feminine adjectival forms. However, this is mostly undercut by indications of ironic distance and the balance of tones and concerns already indicated above. Above all, the novel engages in a more culturally far-reaching, slightly more cerebral, humour in its '[r]ich . . . allusions to Spanish classics', to picaresque literature and to novels of chivalry (Ramos 1995). It also uses the archness of the conventions of early twentieth-century novels of manners in the English tradition ('Sólo el alma del caballero es generosa hasta el final' – 'only the soul of a gentleman is generous to the last' – is the polite slant on the rather expensive farewell to Kyril) (Mendicutti 1998: 235). There is probably also a debt to the writer Álvaro Retana (1890–1970) (discussed by Mira 2004: 166–75 and Vázquez García and Cleminson 2011: 260–2).

Referring to the Festival de Cultura LGTB Visible Madrid, with a special event in his honour at the Instituto Cervantes, Madrid (Visible11 2011: 8–9), Mendicutti points out to his interviewer the importance of culture not only for developing personal identity ('para formarse uno mismo'), but for building a strong base from which to confront social and political changes, 'las vicisitudes que vayan surgiendo y que afecten a los derechos y la propia visibilidad' (El Castigador 2011) ('changed circumstances which might arise from one time to another and affect rights and visibility itself'). It is in this spirit that he appears as one of the subject-participants in the documentary *El muro rosa* (The Pink Wall) (Enrique del Pozo and Julián Lara, 2011) contributing to the oral history of gay life under Franco, as well as to the imaginative lives of (older) queer viewers and readers.

Vicente Molina Foix also has a substantial career as a novelist, taken up by prestigious publishing houses (latterly Anagrama) and winning the Premio Nacional de Narrativa for *El abrecartas* (The Letter Opener) in 2007, a novel which includes among its semi-fictionalised real characters Antonio Maenza (1948–1979) – queer, radical maker of independent (Valencian) films of the late 1960s – as well as the more well-known gay figures (as addressees) of Federico García Lorca and Vicente Aleixandre. He has combined novels with work as a drama consultant and translator and as a well-known film critic in the newspapers *Diario 16* and *El País* early in his career and for the magazines *Fotogramas y video* and, more recently, *Tiempo*. A prominent public intellectual, his writing in the large-circulation quality press has included opinion pieces on queer theory's advent in Spain (Molina Foix 1998) and same-sex marriage (Molina Foix 2006), wondering whether the former would be a passing fad in Spain or a step towards 'natural' acceptance of queer lives and, on the latter, accepting radical and philosophical arguments against same-sex marriage yet seeing them as utopian and against majority opinion. As can be seen in this summary, these pieces are cautious – conservative, even – but they also open out debates in original directions, pointing readers to key new ideas and writings (1998) or re-reading the theatrical, 'ostentatious' character of wedding celebrations as a useful borrowing by lesbians and gays from the straight cultural tradition, translating the conventional flamboyance of the ritual into a progressive project of making visible (2006).

On the so-called Wanninkhof case – in which Victoria Álvarez, released after unfounded conviction for the murder of Rocío Wanninkhof, her lover's daughter, was subjected to severe popular and media-led lesbophobic aggression – Molina Foix (2003) points to rumour, innuendo, self-interest and the homophobic activation of wayward personal beliefs or simple delinquency, identifying their crossing over into the actions and decisions in the judicial process, and placing himself firmly behind lesbian and gay organisations as those who should take the lead in protest. In his blog in *El Boomeran(g)* since March 2009 he has combined analyses of the work of some of the canonical figures of European and North and Latin American literature and film with occasional but sharp focus on aspects of LGBTQ culture: Chueca and the politics of Pride and oppression in Muslim countries (5 July 2010); the polemic around *El Consul de Sodoma* (28 January and 1 February 2010); and a piece written in memory of Leopoldo Alas Mínguez (26 November 2009). Further extending the range of his interventions in LGBTQ culture – though staying at a measured distance from direct or regular cultural activism in the lesbian and gay media, events or collections of essays – he has curated a retrospective of Spanish LGTB film at the Zinegoak festival in Bilbao (in 2006), marking his commitment to the (re)positioning of LGBTQ film in Spain.

In one of three entries in the blog on the making of his second film, *El dios de madera* (The Wooden God) (2010), Molina Foix (2009b) compares the practices of writing novels (the material unfolding sequentially, semi-planned), preparing a film script, and the way, during the shoot, in which the camera 'writes' odd parts of the programmed script to be put back together in editing. In the week of the film's premier at the Málaga Film Festival he returns to the question of being 'el escritor con apetencias de cineasta' (Molina Foix 2010b) ('a writer with a desire to be a film-maker'), highlighting the continued parallel activities of the writer, critic and film-maker. Writing on the film's second showing – sponsored, as he notes, by the publishing house Planeta – Molina Foix recalls how aware he was of a literary audience, and of addressing them 'como un tránsfuga o un transformista' (Molina Foix 2010c) ('like a deserter or a quick-change artist'). Molina Foix sees himself as bringing to films 'afinidades y coincidencias' ('affinities and coincidences') with the writing of novels, and to *El dios de madera* 'voluntad de estilo y . . . "libre invención"' (2010c) ('a distinctive style and creative freedom').

As in the case of some of the short films at the experimental and visual arts end of the spectrum of festival offerings (see Chapter 4) there is an attempt at the construction of a radical queer imaginary – new ways of seeing and new ways of narrating – in Molina Foix's first film *Sagitario* (*Sagittarius*) (2001). *Sagitario* was originally not a success on the general distribution market, and in 2009 a bad-mannered blog-site debate following a piece by Molina Foix in the magazine *El Tiempo* on the comic strip brought back to the surface in raw form some objections which might well have stood in the way of the film's success – that it was pretentious, vacuous, classist, unwatchable or mediocre (Barros 2009; 'Begoña' 2009, citing Alonso 2001; 'Espectador contrariado' 2009; 'fanhunter4ever' 2009). However, as a homosexually focalised piece, the film is interestingly at odds with the youth-and-humour trend of the Spanish gay cinema of the 1990s. It also carries forward from the 1980s and 1990s the strange charisma and even stranger acting style of Eusebio Poncela (see Chapter 3) in the lead role as Jaime. Jaime, refreshingly for some audiences, is in his forties; his ex (Héctor Alterio) is even older, and interestingly Argentine and intellectual rather than standard Spanish; less refreshingly (and, in fact, in a more reactionary, Spanish mode), by way of replacing the now failed relationship, Jaime hires a rent boy 'Omar' and falls for him, not just for his perceived foreignness (which turns out to be false) but for his passivity ('disponibilidad'). 'Omar' is in reality (and with more-than-Almodovaresque unlikeliness) a refugee from a pseudo-pederastic cult to whose leader he is still in thrall. Jaime's attention, and the visual interest for the viewer, is frequently entangled, though, with the fate of the rich, beautiful, embittered and abandoned Rosa (Angela Molina, in spectrally glamorous form) who thinks she loves him and wants his children. This aspect of the plot might have been productively poised between cliché and queerness (the latter for its intimations of non-bilaterally heterosexual parenting and its openness to bisexual desire) were it not for the elevation of Rosa up and out of any sort of real disadvantage or exclusion, the high bourgeois trappings of her life (as Molina's costumes opulently suggest) and a highly literary, teasingly enigmatic subplot involving a distant, leisured admirer of Rosa and the supposed workings of chance, destiny, instinct and horoscopes. The film was nothing if not earnest in its melodramatic and experimental opening up to the unconventional. It has now been delisted.

While *Sagitario* had, then, a certain strangeness and theatrical experimentalism to it, the second film responded more to the demands of assimilation and normalisation which Molina Foix acknowledged, for example, in presenting the Bilbao retrospective of 2006. There, the films of the 1970s and early 1980s are characterised as 'heroic' and 'pioneering', mould-breaking, whereas in 2006 what the reporter at the time called 'la temática' ('the themes', that is the issues and the images) 'se incorporan de una manera natural y llegará un momento en el que será normal y cotidiano' ('have become a natural part of the viewing experience and one day [this kind of cinema] will be completely normal and everyday'), making labels redundant (HoyCinema 2006). *El dios de madera* interlaces two Valencia-based stories. On the one hand there is a love narrative between Yao (Madi Diocou), a young and handsome Senegalese who has come to Spain in search of income from street-selling, and María Luisa (Marisa Paredes), a widow in her late middle age who now owns a chic little dress-shop but who once was a glamorously rebellious performance artist. On the other hand, there is a tale of queer sexual friendship between Robert (Nao Albert), María Luisa's (very) out-gay and sometimes cross-dressing son, and Rachid (Soufianne Ouaarab), an immigrant from Morocco on the verge of regularising his papers and the proud, no-nonsense, bisexual owner both of a hairdressing (and massage) business and a nicely muscled body. Although, by dint of the latter, Rachid is on occasion exploited both by the camera and by Robert, the film counterbalances this by making empowering its representation of Rachid's s rough-and-ready affection for and acceptance of Robert (whom he smilingly describes as 'un poco mariquita' – 'a bit queeny').

Robert's angry relationship with his mother and with his own inability to internalise the loss of his father underpinning a propensity to prissiness means that he does not seem to deserve this acceptance. Similarly, Robert's difficult personality is set against what his character allows the script to explore: the classic dynamics of an unevenly weighted erotic relationship. Rachid holds nearly all the cards and leaves in the end, matter of factly. It also explores the more unusual, but here integrated and normalised, dynamics of a cross-cultural meeting of the typically gay with the typically straight-acting where both involved are of the same age (thus like *Los novios búlgaros* but without the age gradient). Robert comes out of both sets of dynamics, for Rachid, as 'buen chico, buen amigo, buena gente' ('a good lad, a good friend, a good person'); moral good is the wellspring too of the cross-cultural relationship between the intense, sincere and emotionally attuned Yao and the conflicted, cautious, sad and unfulfilled María Luisa.

Her sexual and affective precariousness is (to an extent) salved by Yao; the precariousness of his position as an undocumented immigrant is (temporarily) attenuated for the duration of its functioning as an dramatic analogy of María Luisa's plight and as a token of a wider state of economic and political affairs. When a very straight and bourgeois suitor of María Luisa's refers tartly to 'tu hijo, el moro, y el negro' ('your son, the Arab, and the black') as a trio standing, implicitly, in his way, the issues of race, precariousness, sexuality, affective transformation, friendship and goodness, all come together as in a markedly queer structuring. María Luisa's dependence on the kindness of strangers recalls that of another of Paredes's characters, Huma in Almodóvar's

Todo sobre mi madre whose more or less queer echoes attach themselves to her presence in Molina Foix's film. The pairs of relationships are written into one another; the issues cross-refer. As Molina Foix has observed, the film reflects the need to change perspective, in the new order implied by the reality of immigration (in Spain), and to look 'hacia el rechazo o el amor' ('towards rejection or love'): it is 'una fábula de atracciones y miradas hacia los mapas de la piel' ('a fable about attraction, and about how looks are drawn to what is mapped out on the skin') (Agencia EFE 2010). In the overwhelmingly white context of Spanish LGTBQ cinema, these embodiments of racial as well as sexual and generational differences might have made a substantial impact. However, having lost its original distributors, Sagrera, to the financial crisis, and with only 4,887 ticket sales (MECD 2012), this was foiled; it was programmed as part of the Thirteenth FanCineGay festival (in Badajoz, 11 November 2010) but by April 2012 had all but disappeared.

WRITERS' LIVES ON SCREEN: FEDERICO GARCÍA LORCA AND JAIME GIL DE BIEDMA

In a discussion of the heritage sub-genre and queerness, Davis (2006) identifies a double edge in the openness of the sub-genre to the possibility of making the homosexual visible, on the one hand, and operating a regime of limitation, on the other; effectively it excludes queer forms of sexuality in favour of a commensurately older form of discourse, that of gay liberation (197–9). In this section I discuss two films whose audiences get caught up in the struggle between the gay and the queer in this sense, between responding to the heroic figure from the past whose life – or rather its mistakes – points the way to a neat teleology for identity of 'before and after "coming out"' (Neil Bartlett, quoted by Davis 2006: 205), and breaking through into the radical view.

The first of these is the British film (with Catalan co-production), *Little Ashes* (Paul Morrison, 2008; released in Spain, 2009, as *Sense límits* and *Sin límites*), which centres on the troubled relationship between Federico García Lorca (represented as in love) and the painter Salvador Dalí (represented as in denial). García Lorca's status as a queer writer is well established (Soto 2002, and bibliography therein) and the film makes strenuous (if at times sotto voce) use of lines from his poetry and, in the visuals, of motifs associated with García Lorca's early career writing (notably guitars and the moon). The casting is estranging indeed. Federico García Lorca is played by Javier Beltrán as a good lookalike for the younger Federico and sensitively attuned to the material, speaking in accented English (rather than the Catalan or Spanish of his usual career performances). Luis Buñuel, as fellow student in Madrid, is played by British television character actor Matthew McNulty (making an interesting leap from the BBC's *Lark Rise to Candleford* (2008) to an association with surrealist cinema). Salvador Dalí is played by Robert Pattinson, an actor with a definite youth queer fan lure attaching to him from a quite other area of film entertainment, the vampire films *Twilight* (Catherine Hardwicke, 2008), *New Moon* (Chris Weitz, 2009) and *Eclipse* (David Slade, 2010) and readily assimilated into the popular queer blogosphere and imaginary ('Flick' 2009; 'Despotorramiento feroz' 2009; Fernández, Lola 2009).

Despite Pattinson's declared problems with the love scenes ('Flick' 2009), the closeness of Federico and Salvador is gently enough built up to, especially in scenes in the Madrid Residencia de Estudiantes (Halls of Residence) where it picks up on a familiar sub-genre of lightly tormented, same-sex, college romance. However, any interest in the psychological oddity and specialness of the relationship is diverted by recourse in a Cadaqués-set scene to a moonlit dip by the two, and a long kiss set off against flashes of light on the water, with the whole scene blue-infused, and much underwater camerawork involving swirling limbs and gentle bubbles. What this does, along with similar, though less intrusive, romantic treatments of erotic entanglement, is to add power by contrast to the stern, fastidious manliness and homophobia of Buñuel as played by McNulty. There is a shocking directness to the character's name-calling of two men out on the street and the discomfort of Federico, even more so to his interestingly reluctant, guilty entrapment of a man out cruising in the park and his queer bashing. This representation of Buñuel directs a queer audience's attention away from an apparently easily discernible institutionalisation of homophobic violence in a vaguely understood fascism of the Civil War years and their aftermath, towards an understanding of the more pervasive homophobia subtending certain historical forms of masculinity as well as self-styled progressive artistic thought. It has a problematic treatment of the notorious execution of the poet – the resonant but intensely mythologised queer cultural moment of Spain's history is close to that in the filmed-for-television *El balcón abierto* (*The Open Window*) (Jaime Camino, 1984) as discussed by Smith in terms of its near coerciveness (1998: 106–14). A voice-off mutters about there being 'only one way to kill a queer' prior to the victim's being given the *coup de grâce*, with the camera's line of sight at the level of the fallen body, moving in from across the summer field where it has set up its observational point of pathos. In Camino's film, and Juan Antonio Bardem's serialised television drama *Lorca, muerte de un poeta* (*Lorca: Death of a Poet*) (six episodes 1987–8), as Smith observes, a 'mix of literalism and symbolism [tends] to erase the historical specificity of both work and life' (1998: 113). A similar process is at work here.

The second, and much more widely discussed, of the two semi-heritage biopics is Monleón's *El cónsul de Sodoma* (*The Consul of Sodom*) (Sigrid Monleón, 2010) (see also Chapter 3). The urbane and complex writings of its biographical subject have little or none of the popular appeal of that part of García Lorca's poetry and drama which misleadingly enwraps his figure in such colour, tragedy and – as Smith reminds us – vagueness of response. Though conventionally presented as a 'uno de los poetas españoles más celebrados del siglo XX' (López Manjón 2011) ('one of Spain's most celebrated twentieth-century poets'), Gil de Biedma remained relatively little known outside Barcelona (his home city and scenario of poetic writing), and beyond poetic or academic circles interested in the localised renaissance of gritty modern poetry around Spain's 1968 or in subtle representations of time and subjectivity (Vilaseca 2003: 241–324). However, his development of the 'poesía de la experiencia' ('poetry of experience') set up a creative position both at one remove from and at a slant to mainstream oppositional literary thought in Spain in the 1950s and 1960s – the 'social' novel and 'social poetry' (Villena 2006: 21–4). Gil de Biedma's writing of 'experience' is open to being engaged with by acts of reading for queer affinity, by Catalan and Spanish fans of his poetry and his life, even though he ends up being disappointing as a straightforward queer hero. Frustratingly for the politically minded he mingles outrageousness in life and text with cautiously elaborated secrecy (and collusive self-censorship). As an urbane, international businessman and cultural commentator, he seems in the texts so often the man's man; in the film the action takes place in a wealthy world of lavish *mise en scène*, travel, smoke- and gin-filled rooms with male writers and businessmen, one of whom is coaxed, in Hong Kong, into coming to a timely agreement so that Gil de Biedma can get back – he claims – to the beautiful woman awaiting him in Barcelona (he returns, the montage reveals, to urgent sex with his put-upon bisexual boyfriend). A sense of queer dissident history is there in the words, but the visual narrative mutes it or displaces it. The poet's highly charged sexual relationship with an ethereally beautiful and sensual wronged wife and mother of two – Bel (Bimba Bosé) – veers off into a melodrama of doomed hetero/bisexual love and remorse. As we have seen (in Chapter 3), the relationship with Toni (Isaac de los Reyes) is played in ways which give it the potential for rescue by a queer critique of a potential for commodification, denial and disempowerment inherent in domestic coupledom, but equally it brings to the fore effects of normalisation on various planes, effects that disallow a dissenting viewing of the film and draw the sting of the original writings. Gil de Biedma is, in short, one of the big names for queer Spanish heritage but in a conflicted, tension-ridden way.

His death from AIDS-related illness in 1990, kept as an open secret (Villena 2006: 33–4), re-established Gil de Biedma's fame, with a series of homages, re-evaluations and re-editions of his work. The film, for its part, later served as a restitution of a forgotten or unknown part of queer memory, of '[un] fascinante escritor, que muchos hemos descubierto a través de la película' (La Acera de Enfrente 2010) ('a fascinating writer whom many of us will have discovered by way of [Monleón's] film'), where the 'many' here are the audience, for example, of a local LGTB youth radio programme (in Elx, Alicante) and their friends. As another gay site encapsulates it (with the slightly misleading urgency of semi-professional web journalism), in Monleón's film 'El sexo, el amor, la literatura y la lucha política' are played out in a context of 'una época de rebeldía, violencia y el descubrimiento y aceptación de la identidad' ('sex, love, literature and political struggle . . . in a time of rebellion, violence and the discovery and acceptance of [alternative] identities') (Cristianos gays 2010). The poet's albeit problematically exemplary and dissident life can facilitate the taking up, by audiences, of what the Grupo de Trabajo Queer (2005: 26) identifies as that core queer 'posición desde la que responder políticamente a las normatividades múltiplemente impuestas' ('position from which to respond politically to the many forms of enforced normativity').

Of such forms of enforced normativity, the film very directly represents two: policing by the state and the expectations of the family. Both are amplified as elements in the plot by the distorting word 'maricón', as uttered by a detective who calls on the Barcelona family home one lunchtime armed with a list of names of leftist activists and a pamphlet and a poem by Gil de Biedma. He couples the term with another, 'inteligente': craftiness and sexuality are thus yoked together in a familiar and damaging politics of anti-intellectual reaction and control that is associated with at least the first twenty years of Franco's regime on the one hand (Pavlović 2003: 6, 22–3) and, more diffusely, internalised by the Church in the Biblical concatenation of same-sex sex, deceit, craftiness or debate, gossip and slander (Romans 1: 29–30). The words are used here in the classic, generic manner beloved of agents of authority irritated or befuddled by ambiguity and indirect connections to twist the hazy or recalcitrant material of contingency into a bundle of evidence. Similarly, access to the chairmanship of the prosperous family firm for Jaime, our subject – a state-controlled tobacco company, with trade centred in the Philippines – is blocked by an act of distortion in the form of the revelation to the board members of a set of compromising photographs of Jaime and a Filipino lad, previously designed for blackmail. For his father, the outgoing chairman, this strikes at the heart of family and legacy; for the firm, sexuality disrupts absolutely the possibility of the continuation of the proven rigour and rectitude of Jaime as the board's secretary to date – sexuality, that is, but with the amplifying distortion of homosexuality and of sex with the racial, postcolonial other (the Philippines were Spanish territory until 1898; as Jaime says in the script, the firm is essentially still a 'colonial enterprise', at least until 1972 and the declaration of martial law by Fernando and Imelda Marcos).

As do police and patriarchy, so too the biopic in aspects of its treatment turns and changes facets of Jaime Gil de Biedma through a generic and conventional urge to condense the life story into the 'legendary', 'the eminent and the exceptional; the charismatic and the heroic [subject] with a destiny' (Bingham 2010: 31–40). To a certain extent too the film is under pressure from the 'conventional thinking' that 'there is no point to a biopic . . . unless it shows why the world must rejoice in the subject's work' (49). This sets up further twists at the level of the reception of the film which involves, on the one hand, scandalised contemporaries (some of them made into characters in the film) lobbying, essentially, for more discretion (less gay sex, perhaps) and hankering for more eminence and exceptionality, and, on the other hand, a sense of the queer potential of the life story having been underplayed (a call, perhaps, for less complicity, less straightening out, less of a conventional narrative trajectory) due to distorting emphases on the subject's work. These emphases are produced from universalising angles that privilege literary value and a sense of generational belonging (where outsiderdom would be more appropriate) and from sensationalising angles that make the subject Gil de Biedma less queer, more gay, less disruptive of heteronormativity, more aligned with certain patterns of leisured lifestyle, comfortable toleration and even coupledom. These are angles such as those which have, for better or worse, nourished the 'liberal' in Spain's renowned liberalisation in social matters of sexual politics over the past twenty years.

Gil de Biedma – despite a predominantly masculine and conventional look to the poet himself and, above all, to the circle of (male) writers and intellectuals around him, as recaptured in images in some of the homages following his death[4] – has become a fascinatingly problematic meeting point for queer cultural concerns around both history (its reclaiming) and subjectivity (its structuring in relation to sex and ethics). His miscellaneous *Diario de un artista seriamente enfermo* (*Diary of the Seriously Ill Artist*) (published 1974) recording the year of 1956 in Manila and in the Spanish province of Segovia as part of a cure for tuberculosis, is used in the film and at times quoted to structure events as it also is in the biography by Miguel Dalmau (2004), one of the scriptwriters for the film. However, it has been studied critically for its complex disavowals of any possibility of a direct gaze on the subject of autobiography, for its enforced erasure, for the purposes of its 1974 publication, of all references to sexual desire between men (Ellis 1997: 57–74; Vilaseca 2003: 252–3). It has also been read for moments such as that, in David Vilaseca's words, in which 'something akin to what Lacan calls the apparition of the anamorphic "ghost" [in his discussion of Holbein's *The Ambassadors*]' presents itself when the narrator is 'traumatically confronted with an abhorrent "stain" in (the mirror of) the Other' (Vilaseca 2003: 254). Thinking he is looking at the handsome young Chinese John during some sex tourism to Hong Kong he finds that he is 'being looked at from a place I don't know' (254, quoting Lacan 1979: 88). The homosexual encounter, and the look of leisured, privileged desire, become, as Vilaseca says (adapting Bhabha), 'the embodiment of an "anxious absence" with which the subaltern subject manages to subvert the equivalence between identity and scopic mastery upon which the white, Western subject ultimately rests' (Vilaseca 2003: 256). In this intersection of homosexuality and postcoloniality, Gil de Biedma's '(illusion of) mastery and narcissistic self-transparency [as] established in a number of sexual adventures' is matched by his 'dream of perfect (autobiographical) self-mirroring *vis-à-vis* the "other"' which is 'doomed not contingently but *structurally* [in terms of the scopic and of subjectivity]' (Vilaseca 2003: 261). In an early scene set in Manila, as the poet walks home after a night with a trick, the camera establishes a line of sight between him and a coffin in the street. As Smith has observed, following Vilaseca, this points up tensions arising out of the proximity of homoerotic pleasures and the stain of death, and the difficulties of negotiating the fragility of the gay Hispanic self (Smith 2010b). That self is not only scripted, in this case, but further fractured in the transfers from poetic writing into life narrative (and from text into biopic). The dynamic of the proximity of disintegration has resonance for the narrative arc of the film (whose end, being a biopic, we know) and more widely: the film powerfully combines defiant eroticism with mourning and melancholia (Smith 2010b). The presence of images and tonalities of melancholy and regret (a powerful motif in the poems), while not adding up in any explicit way to an AIDS narrative, give the film that particular queer edge.

The film caused a tellingly clan-oriented moral outrage: in particular, the novelist Juan Marsé – perhaps oddly, given the uncompromising treatments of sexual experience and objectification which underpin some of his most famous novels – found fault with almost every technical aspect of the film, judging it to be 'desvergonzada, de título infamante y producida por gente sin escrúpulos' (Ruiz Mantilla 2010) ('shameless, with an insulting title and produced by unscrupulous people'). The director, Monleón, has insisted that it was impossible for the film to address separately from sexuality the main themes of Gil de Biedma's poetry – love, identity and the passing of time – and he dismisses critical concerns about faithfulness of characterisation and other matters by pointing to what he implies is the real problem behind detractors' remarks, an immature anxiety about representing queer lives in the way that, for example, British cinema has been able to do (Monleón 2010). Monleón is backed by one of Gil de Biedma's close associates and an expert on his mode of writing, Luis Antonio de Villena, who sees, clearly, that the poet's sexuality is 'pivotal' to his life (Izquierdo 2010). The outrage, indeed, might have been exacerbated had the producers gone with the original choice of director, Agustí Villaronga, whose idea, according to Miguel Dalmau, had been to 'destacar la faceta homosexual . . . prescindiendo del lado político y poético' ('D. M.' 2009) ('emphasise the homosexual aspect . . . leaving out the poetic and political side') – an emphasis that frightened off the producers but which Monleón does not underplay: however, perhaps true to life, the Gil de Biedma who emerges from the biopic is the one whose vocation for scandal (Villena 2000) made him something of 'un discreto militante por los derechos de gays y lesbianas' (Villena 2000, quoted in Izquierdo 2010) ('a discreet militant for gay and lesbian rights').

The writers and exchanges between text and film discussed in this chapter contribute to the production of a multi-mediatic, largely middlebrow queer culture in Spain and have a significant influence on the ways that the films in question are conceived and consumed. Cultural capital vired from one area of creativity into the other encourages higher profiles, wider audiences and more nuanced, more cross-referenced viewings and readings. The presence of LGBT film and film-makers in the scripts of the everyday – in blogs and newspapers, in conversations, perhaps – constitutes a micro-politics of visibility, while heritage and biopic elements threaten to erase queer visibility in favour of a looser lesbian and gay liberal aesthetic or in search of a wider but more traditionally cultured audience. Text and film cross-refer in the cases looked at in this chapter, constructing a community that is virtual – as audience – and specifically there, living queer Spanish lives.

NOTES

1. Hernández also suggested that the adverse trading conditions associated with Spain's growing economic instability amplified the already significant relative difficulties in finding commercially viable means of sustaining the supply of books for the lesbian market. Robbins, however, questions earlier statements in this vein (dating from 1999 and 2003) and interprets the problem, rather, as a misconception about LGBTQ consumers' book-shopping habits and as an underestimation of the effects and mechanisms of the global publishing industry (Robbins 2011: 155–6).
2. Work on the representation of lesbians on television is ongoing, as at April 2012, at the Universidad Complutense de Madrid by Beatriz González de Garay Domínguez under the supervision of Juan Carlos Alfeo Álvarez. See also Platero Méndez (2011).
3. For example, at <http://img.europapress.net/imagenes/cine/mini/mentiras200903_5. jpg> [last accessed 12 May 2012].
4. For example, the special issue of *Prólogo: Revista del lector*, 6 (February 1990), or the cover photograph of *El País*: Babelia (12 August 2000).

CONCLUSION

This book has set out to map a Spanish queer cinema made up of a network of images, moments and stories of emotional commitment, of community affiliation, and of political or artistic intent. These have been shown to be inflected by sexuality and by a fast-changing politics of gender in an unusual period in the history of Spain. Produced by the many connections and disconnections between the films, formats, writers, feelings and crises, queer as a concept attaching to Spanish cinema and to its ambient cultures has shifted scene by scene or from one film or sampling to another. I have researched some audiences through their reactions in print and hypothesised others, putting together possible or ideal viewing schedules and patterns of leisure consumption or of casual, domestic reconnection with images of LGBTQ life, just for comfort, entertainment or reassurance. The several modes of engagement available to the participant in, and recipient of, these queer Spanish images reconfigure imaginations whether through a resistant and politicised viewing or film-making strategy, by identification with fictional and non-fictional personalities, or by rethinking (or simply extending) some older forms of identity- and rights-based lesbian and gay political stories.

There are some startling contrasts in this set of films. The phenomenally popular two-minute *El mueble de las fotos* (The Photo Cabinet) (Giovanni Maccelli, 2009) with its many prizes (MECD 2009), offers a piquant contrast – in about two minutes – to the more sprawling comedies or romances or to the biopic and heritage elements in Spanish queer cinema. The artifice and dubious audience targeting of the staged encounter of two strangers in Medem's *Habitación en Roma* can be countered by the ephemeral and precarious intimacy of two mismatched women in *Acción reacción* (Action/Reaction) (David Illundain, 2008), a film that I missed until finalizing these pages. Here, across the class and generation gap, the two strangers dance and sleep among the washing on a terrace, in images of tender solidarity and fear in their shared indignation at *machista* fecklessness and cruelty. The fleeting issues and emotions are enhanced by the vivid and careful work of established cinematographer Paco Femenía. Again, because of the vicissitudes of this kind of project

Chus Gutiérrez's *Me gustaría estar enamorada – a veces me siento muy sola* (I'd Like to Be in Love: Sometimes I Feel Very Lonely) (2009) came to my attention as a late-arriving echo of some of the avant-garde civic spirit of *Spinnin'* (see Chapter 1). Made for the September 2009 Noche en Blanco (White Night/ All Night) community street festival in Madrid it is half documentary and half experimental in building a montage of late teenage lives, propelled by erotic attractions and changes of mind, but also by joyful solidarity and the hilarity of friendship on the streets or on the night bus home. The complex flows of being lesbian, becoming lesbian, caring (and the community caring for you) or loving are captured as amusingly and arrestingly here as in many a longer comedy piece with apparently lesbian content. The ongoing accumulation of films long and short about formalising relationships later in life – 'marriage' films, but also images of alternative continuous commitment – continued to populate the Spanish LGBT film festival programmes (dwindling though they were under economic and culturally reactionary pressures) as this book was completed in the spring of 2012. Through sheer repetition, that story – so old-style lesbian and gay, as the radical critics were reminding us in Chapter 1 – changes, putting torsion on the LGBT soubriquets and queering even the clichés of conformity (such as those we saw in Chapter 2). The urgency of organised resistance and of indignation in the face of austerity – in its symbolic as well as its socio-economic senses – places a yet more queer frame around these fictionalised or real-life stories on screen in Spain.

Some films never arrived on time, or I never managed to travel to them in time, or their scant archived copies had gone irredeemably astray just before the project began. *The Lesbian Movie* (Blanca H. Salazar, 2010 – by the director of *Bañofobia*), the films of Jorge Torregrossa and *King* (Iris Segundo, 2008) are among many circulating, perhaps, or waiting to be seen beyond the span of the writing of these pages. Spanish Queer Cinema is also made up of these gaps and uncertainties, of audiences never yet constituted, images recorded but waiting for further registration by being watched (perhaps again) or remembered by enough queer folk to spark a dialogue. However, it is mainly a substantial and collective process of identifications of many sorts – not all of them classic cinematic identifications – and a multifarious set of images, plots, performances and events. These resituate LGBT culture in Spain in the mind's eye of all who do and do not recognise themselves as simply bisexual, say, or as captured faithfully in the term trans, from one time to another, or as lesbian for a hundred minutes or gay for three, or over longer timespans, as they incorporate their viewing into their queer lives.

FILMOGRAPHY

Note. The films and other video productions listed here are those of primary reference only (other titles mentioned briefly in the text may be found in the index). The country of production is Spain unless otherwise indicated. English translations are given in the text.

Feature-Length Films

20 centímetros, film, directed by Ramón Salazar. Aligator Producciones, Divine Productions, Estudios Picasso, 2005.

80 egunean, film, directed by Jon Garaño and José María Goenaga. Irusoin, Moriarti Produkzioak, 2010.

A mi madre le gustan las mujeres, film, directed by Inés París and Daniela Fejerman. Fernando Colomo Producciones, 2002.

Amic/Amat, film, directed by Ventura Pons. Els films de la Rambla, Generalitat de Catalunya, 1998.

Amor, curiosidad, prozak y dudas, film, directed by Miguel Santesmases. Mate Producciones, 2001.

Ander, film, directed by Roberto Castón. Berdindu, Euskal Irrati Telebisa, 2009.

Arrebato, film, directed by Iván Zulueta. Nicolás Astarriaga, 1979.

Ataque verbal, film, directed by Miguel Albaladejo. Freedonia Producciones, Icónica SA, 2000.

Barcelona, un mapa, film, directed by Ventura Pons. Els films de la Rambla, 2008.

Cachorro, film, directed by Miguel Albaladejo. Hispanocine Producciones Cinematográficas, Star Line TV Productions, 2004.

Carícies, film, directed by Ventura Pons. Els films de la Rambla, TVE, 1998.

Carne de neón, film, directed by Paco Cabezas. Agencia Freak, 2010.

Chuecatown, film, directed by Juan Flahn. Canónigo Films, Filmax, 2006.

Clandestinos, film, directed by Antonio Hens. Darkwind Seven, David

Machado, Doce Gatos, El Reló, Galiardo Producciones, Junta de Andalucía, La Cruz de Piedra, Malas Compañías, Toma 27, 2007.

Días de voda, film, directed by Juan Pinzás. Atlántico Films, 2002.

El Calentito, film, directed by Chus Gutiérrez. Canal+ España, Estudios Picasso, Telespan 2000, 2005.

El Cónsul de Sodoma, film, directed by Sigfrid Monleón. Infoco, Radio Plus, Steinweg Emotion Pictures, Televisió de Catalunya, Trivisión, 2009

El Desenlace, film, directed by Juan Pinzás. Atlántico Films, 2005.

El dios de madera, film, directed by Vicente Molina Foix. Canal 9 Televisió Valenciana, DC Media, Institut Català de les Indústries Culturals, Institut Valenciá de Cinematografia, Metrojavier, Sagrera Audiovisual, TVE, 2010.

El mar, film, directed by Agustí Villaronga. Massa d'Or Produccions, 2000.

El sueño de Ibiza, film, directed by Igor Fioravanti. La Periférica Producciones, Maestranza Films, 2002.

Electroshock, film, directed by Juan-Carlos Claver. DACSA Productora, 2006.

Eloïse, film, directed by Jesús Garay. Els Quatre Gats Audiovisuals, Televisió de Catalunya, 2009.

En la ciudad, film, directed by Cesc Gay. Messidor Films, 2003.

Era outra vez, film, directed by Juan Pinzás. Atlántico Films, Televisión de Galicia, 2000.

Forasters, film, directed by Ventura Pons. Els films de la Rambla, Televisió de Catalunya, 2008.

Fuera de Carta, film, directed by Nacho Velilla. Antena 3 Televisión, Canguro Produzioni Internazionali Cinematografiche, Ensueño Films, 2008.

Habitación en Roma, film, directed by Julio Medem. Morena Films, Alicia Produce, Canal+ España, Instituto de Crédito Oficial, ICAA, Intervenciones Novo Film 2006, TVE, Wild Bunch, 2010.

I Love You Baby, film, directed by Alfonso Albacete and David Menkes. Alquimia Cinema, Twentieth Century Fox Film Corporation, 2001.

Kilómetro 0, film, directed by Yolanda García Serrano and Juan Luis Iborra. Cuarteto Producciones Cinematográficas, Media Park, Universal Pictures (Spain), 2000.

Krámpak, film, directed by Cesc Gay. Messidor Films, 2000.

La mala educación, film, directed by Pedro Almodóvar. El Deseo, Canal + España, TVE, 2004.

Little Ashes, film, directed by Paul Morrison. UK, Spain: APT Films, Aria Films, Factotum Barcelona, Met Film Production, Met Film, 2009.

Los dos lados de la cama, film, directed by Emilio Martínez Lázaro. Telespan 2000, Canal+ España, Estudios Picasso, Impala, Telecinco, 2005.

Los novios búlgaros, film, directed by Eloy de la Iglesia. Altube Filmeak, Conexión Sur, Creativos Asociados de Radio y Televisión, TVE, 2003.

Mentiras y gordas, film, directed by Alfonso Albacete and David Menkes. Agrupación de Cine 001, Castafiore Films, Tornasol Films, 2009.

Nacidas para sufrir, film, directed by Miguel Albaladejo. Tornasol Films, 2010.

Pa negre, film, directed by Agustí Villaronga. Massa d'Or Produccions, 2010.

Pourquoi pas moi?, film, directed by Stèphane Giusti. Spain, France, Switzerland: Alhena Films, Elzévir Films, Glozel-P. Goter, M6 Films, Maestranza Films, Sociedad General de Derechos Audiovisuales, 1999.

Reinas, film, directed by Manuel Gómez Pereira. Warner Bros. Pictures de España, 2005.

Sagitario, film, directed by Vicente Molina Foix. Fernando Colomo Producciones Cinematográficas, 2001.

Segunda piel, film, directed by Gerardo Vera. Antena 3 Televisión, Lolafilms, Vía Digital, 1999.

Sévigné (Júlia Berkowitz), film, directed by Marta Balletbò-Coll. Sherlock Films, 2004.

Spinnin', film, directed by Eusebio Pastrana. Big Bean & The Human Bean Band, Mundofree, 2007.

Todo me pasa a mí, film, directed by Miguel García Borda. Iris Star, 2001.

Todo sobre mi madre, film, directed by Pedro Almodóvar. Spain, France: El Deseo, Renn Productions, France 2 Cinéma, 1999.

Tú eliges, film, directed by Antonia San Juan. Trece Producciones, 2009.

Una palabra tuya, film, directed by Ángeles Gónzalez Sinde. Tesela Producciones Cinematográficas, 2008.

Documentaries

Campillo sí, quiero, film, directed by Andrés Rubio. Kokelandia, 2009.

El camino de Moisés, digital film hosted at <http://www.rtve.es/alacarta/>, directed by Cecilia Barriga. Producciones Orgánicas, 2004.

El muro rosa, film, directed by Enrique del Pozo and Julián Lara. Enrique del Pozo, 2010.

Guerriller@s, film, directed by Montse Pujantell. Montse Pujantell, 2010.

Homo Baby Boom: Famílies de lesbianes i gais, film, directed by Anna Boluda. Associació de Famílies Lesbianes i Gais, 2008.

Kenia y su familia, film, directed by Llorenç Soler. Canal+ España, Generalitat de Catalunya, Àrea de Televisió, 2005.

Las esquinas del arco iris, film, directed by Purificación Mora. Purificación Mora, 2006.

Tiras de mi piel, digital film hosted at <http://www.tirasdemipiel.blogspot. co.uk/> (Creative Commons licensed), directed by Ayoze Cabera and Enrique Poveda. FELGTB, COGAM and Ayoze Cabera, 2009.

Short Films

A cuestas con mis padres, film and hosted online by Notodo filmfest, directed by Vicente Bonet. The Social Dog, 2008.

A domicilio (o incluso también el amor), film, directed by Mariel Maciá. Enik Producciones, 2008.

A oscuras, film and Vimeo posting, directed by Eli Navarro. Producciones Puntos Suspensivos, 2009.

Acción Reacción, film, and Vimeo posting, directed by David Illundain. Tach Producciones, 2008.

Aliteración, film, directed by Roberto Menéndez. Hacheés Producciones, 2005.

Almas perdidas, film, directed by Julio de la Fuente. María Magdalena Llerandi Urrace, 2008.

Bañophobia, film, and Vimeo posting, directed by Blanca H. Salazar. Blankita Films, 2009.

Buenos días, film, directed by Laura A. Cancho. Producciones LaPasion, 2008.

Caníbales, film, directed by Juanma Carrillo. EmocionesProduce, 2009.

Cara o cruz, film, directed by Jacobo Echevarría. Escuela de Cinematografía y del Audiovisual de la Comunidad de Madrid, 2008.

Carne de neón, film and Vodpod posting, directed by Paco Cabezas. Agencia Freak, 2005.

Cerrojos, film and YouTube posting, directed by Carlos Ceacero. Carlos Ceacero and Pablo Sanz, 2004.

Dos maneras y media de morir, film and Vimeo posting, directed by Ruth Caudeli. Giovanna Martín, 2011.

El mueble de las fotos, film and archived by Notodofilmfest, directed by Giovanni Maccelli. Carlota Coronado, 2009.

El Rosario de la Aurora, film, directed by Iván Lara. Sandra Fernández and Iván Lara, 2007.

En malas compañías, film, directed by Antonio Hens. Antonio Hens Córdoba and Hasta en las Mejores Familias, 2000.

Esas nubes, film, directed by Álex Mene. Álex Mene, 2003.

Ester, film and Vimeo posting, directed by Maria Pavón and Rut Suso. Volandovengo, 2004.

Flores en el parque: o los primeros besos, film and YouTube posting, directed by Mariel Maciá. Enik Producciones, 2006.

Fuckbuddies, film and archived by Alacarta, Versión Española (TVE), directed by Juanma Carrillo. EmocionesProduce, 2011.

Gender Terrorists, film and YouTube posting, directed by Anty Productions. Anty Productions, 2008.

Happy Day in Barcelona, film, directed by Johann Pérez Viera. Johann Pérez Viera and ESCAC, Barcelona, 2009.

Homo Baby Boom: Famílies de lesbianes i gais, film, directed by Anna Boluda. Associació de famílies lesbianes i gais, 2008.

Imagina, film and YouTube posting, directed by Sagrario Villalba. Sagrario Villalba and Carmen Illán, 2005.

Implicación, film and YouTube posting, directed by Julian Quintanilla. El Hijo La Chary, 2004.

Invulnerable, film, directed by Álvaro Pastor and Antonio Naharro. Álvaro Pastor Gaspar, 2005.

K, film, directed by Juan Simons. Troinc Films, 2005.

Lala, film, directed by Esteban Crespo, Menos Veinte Producciones, Producciones Africanauan SL, 2009.

Las esquinas del arco iris, film, directed by Purificación Mora. Purificación Mora, 2006.

Lesbos Invaders From Outer Space, film, directed by Victor Conde. Lolita Peliculitas, 2008.

Lo que nunca te dije, film and Vimeo posting, directed by Carlos Gómez Baker. Mira, Mira, Mira, 2010.

Los requisitos de Nati, film and YouTube posting, directed by Roberto Castón. Ilusión Óptica, 2007.

Luz, film and Vimeo posting, directed by Pablo Aragüés. Fernando Lueches, David Sancho and Pablo Aragüés, 2011.

Mariquita con perro, film and YouTube posting, directed by Vicente Villanueva. Vicente Villanueva, 2007.

Me gustaria estar enamorada – a veces me siento muy sola, film and Vimeo posting, directed by Chus Gutiérrez. Pizca Gutiérrez, 2010.

Mon amour A, film, directed by Nicolás Álvarez. Nicolás Álvarez, 2005.

Muro, film and Vodpod posting, directed by Juanma Carrillo. EmocionesProduce, 2011.

Naranjas, film and Vimeo posting, directed by Eli Navarro. Producciones Puntos Suspensivos, 2010.

Pablo ¿has puesto la lavadora?, film, directed by Javier Haba. Javier Haba, 2005.

Pasajero, film and Vodpod posting, directed by Miguel Gabaldón Orcoyen. Escuela de Cinematografía y del Audiovisual de la Comunidad de Madrid, 2009.

Pasión por el futból, film and Vimeo and YouTube postings, directed by Maria Pavón and Rut Suso. Volandovengo, 2007.

Perfect Day, film, directed by Juanma Carrillo and Félix Fernández. EmocionesProduce, 2009.

Petunias, film and YouTube posting, directed by César Vallejo. Ana Martín Sevilla, 2005.

Ricardo: Piezas descatalogadas, film and Vimeo posting, directed by Herman@s Rico. Imago Producciones, 2005.

Sígueme, film, directed by Alejandro Durán. Das Tier, 2011.

Sirenito, film and YouTube posting, directed by María Crespo. Proyecta Films, 2004.

Sombras en el viento, film, directed by Julia Guillén Creagh. Atraco Perfecto Producciones Audiovisuales, 2009.

Terapia de choque, film and Vimeo posting, directed by Salva Cortés. Black Diamond, 2010.

¡¡¡Todas!!!, film and Vimeo posting, directed by Jose Martret. Jose Martret Homar, 2003.

The Lesbian Movie, film, directed by Blanca H. Salazar. Ole Ole Equipo Producciones, 2010.

Turistas, film and Orange Videos posting, directed by Isabel Coll and Marcos de Miguel. Marcos de Miguel, 2008.

Vestido nuevo, film, directed by Sergi Pérez. Sergi Pérez and Laia Nuñez, 2007.

Voces, film, directed by Eduardo Fembuena. Fundación First Team, 2010.

Yo sólo miro, film, directed by Gorka Cornejo. Common Films, 2008.

OTHER VIDEO PRODUCTIONS

Alguien se despierta en mi cama, videoart by Rut Suso, posted on Vimeo. Voandovengo, 2011.

Chica busca chica, online series, directed by Sonia Sebastián. Sin talenton, 2007–8; subsequently on DVD release distributed by Suevia Films, 2009.

Dreams Are the Matter We Are Made Of, videoart by J. F. Blanco, posted on Vimeo. [no producer], 2007.

Gayxample, online series, directed by Giuseppe Storelli, hosted on Vimeo and <http://gayxampleseries.blogspot.co.uk/>, part series. Spain [production company unknown], 2011.

La escalera, videoart by Rut Suso, hosted on Vimeo. Volandovengo, 2011.

Les étoiles, videoart by Rut Suso, hosted on Vimeo. Volandovengo, 2011.

Lo que surja, online series, directed by Jose Luis Lázaro. Singermorning, 2006–9; first season subsequently on DVD release distributed by Pride Films, 2007.

Orgullo nacional, music video directed by Rut Suso and María Pavón. Volando Vengo, 2010.

Une sensation de vide, videoart by Juanma Carrillo at <http://juanmacarrillo.com>. EmocionesProduce, 2011.

REFERENCES

7pk2 (2009) 'Chicos de cine ... criados en 625 líneas', in *7Pekados*, no date <http://www.7pekados.com/index.php?option=com_contentandview=articleandid=5> [last accessed 12 May 2012].

'A queer one/Julie Jordan' [pseudonym of Alberto Mira] (2006) 'Cinefilia gay', in *Miradas insumisas*, 30 September <http://www.lizhamilton.blogspot.com/2006/09/cinefilia-gay.html> [last accessed 12 May 2012].

abcguionistas (2008) 'Lesbianas pero "sexys", una moda de los guiones televisivos', in *abcguionistas.com (El Portal del Guión)*, 26 June, section Archivo: Noticias <http://www.abcguionistas.com/noticias/guion/lesbianas-pero-sexys-una-moda-de-los-guiones-televisivos.html> [last accessed 12 May 2012].

Academia de Cine (2010) Biographical note on 'Rosa María Sardà (Actriz)', in *academiadecine.com (Academia de las Artes y las Ciencias Cinematográficas de España)*, no date, section Premios: Medalla de Oro <http://www.academiadecine.com/premios/ganador.php?id_s=2andid_ss=30andid_ganador=57> [last accessed 12 May 2012].

Agencia EFE (2005) 'La Federación Estatal de Homosexuales llama a la ciudadanía a manifestarse por la igualdad de derechos el Día del Orgullo Gay', in *20minutos.es*, 18 June, section Nacional <http://www.20minutos.es/noticia/32514/0/dia/orgullo/gay/> [last accessed 12 April 2012].

Agencia EFE (2010) 'Dios de Madera, homosexualidad e inmigración, por Molina Foix', reproduced in *CineLGBT.com*, 13 June, section Noticias <http://www.cinelgbt.com/noticias/dios-de-madera-homosexualidad-e-inmigracion-por-molina-foix> [last accessed 12 May 2011].

Agencia EFE (2011) '"El cine trata con banalidad a los gays": Agustín Almodóvar y Esther García reciben el premio honorífico de Zinegoak', in *noticiasdegipuzkoa.com*, 23 January <http://www.noticiasdegipuzkoa.com/2011/01/23/ocio-y-cultura/cultura/el-cine-trata-con-banalidad-a-los-gays> [last accessed 12 May 2011].

Aguado, Txetxu (2009) 'Pedro Almodóvar, la Movida y la Transición: memoria, espectáculo y antifranquismo', *Letras peninsulares*, 22.1, 23–44.

Albaladejo, Miguel (2011) 'Nacidas para sufrir: Notas del director', in *LaHiguera.net*, no date, section Cinemanía [2009] <http://www.lahiguera. net/cinemania/pelicula/4361/comentario.php> [last accessed 12 May 2012].

Alfeo Álvarez, Juan Carlos (1999) 'La representación de la cuestión gay en el cine español', *Cuadernos de la Academia*, 5, 287–304.

Alfeo Álvarez, Juan Carlos (2001) 'El enigma de la culpa: la homosexualidad y el cine español', *Journal of Contemporary Iberian Studies*, 13.3, 136–47.

Alfeo Álvarez, Juan Carlos (2003) *El personaje homosexual masculino como protagonista en la cinematografía española*, PhD thesis [1997], on CD-ROM. Madrid: Universidad Complutense, Biblioteca Complutense.

Alfeo Álvarez, Juan Carlos, Beatriz González de Garay Domínguez and María Jesús Rosado Millán (2011) 'Adolescencia e identidades LGBT en el cine español: Evolución, personajes y significados', *Icono14*, online 9.3, 5–57, via <http://www.icono14.net/Archivos> [last accessed 21 May 2021].

Aliaga, Juan Vicente (2007) 'No hay igualdad sin diversidad', in Juan A. Herrero Brasas (ed.), *Primera Plana: ética y activismo – La construcción de una cultura queer en España*. Barcelona and Madrid: Egales, pp. 292–30.

Allinson, Mark (2001) *A Spanish Labyrinth: The Films of Pedro Almodovar*. London: I. B. Tauris. [Spanish translation *Un laberinto español. Las películas de Pedro Almodóvar*. Madrid: Ocho y medio, 2003.]

ALMA (2008) 'Ley de cine', in *abcguionistas.com*, no date [July] <http://www. abcguionistas.com/noticias/guion/boletin-informativo-de-alma.html> [last accessed 12 May 2012].

Alonso, Ismael (2001) 'Sagitario: Crítica', in *La Butaca.net: Especial IV Festival de Málaga*, no date <http://www.labutaca.net/malaga/sagitario1. htm> [last accessed 12 May 2012].

Ander (2009) Press pack for the 59th Berlinale, in *Eikencluster.com*, no date <http://www.eikencluster.com/uploads/file/Albisteak09/Ander_prentsa_txo stena.pdf> [last accessed 12 May 2012].

Antena3 (2011a) 'Yon González, un irresistible y rebelde galán que vuelve dispuesto a conquistarnos', *antena3.com*, 24 October, section Celebrities <http://www.antena3.com/celebrities/famosos-espanoles/yon-gonzalez-irre sistible-galan-que-vuelve-dispuesto-conquistarnos_2011100500016.html> [last accessed 12 May 2012].

Antena3 (2011b) 'La boda del año: La boda más esperada', *antena3.com*, no date, section Series: *Los Hombres de Paco* <http://www.antena3.com/series/ los-hombres-de-paco/eres-fan/Especiales/La%20Boda%20del%20año/boda -mas-esperada_2010053000032.html> [last accessed 12 May 2012].

Arce, José (2010) 'Habitación en Roma: Amor y presunción en la ciudad eterna', in *LaButaca.net (Revista de cine)*, 6 May <http://opinion.labutaca. net/2010/05/06/habitacion-en-roma-amor-y-presuncion-en-la-ciudad-eterna/> [last accessed 12 May 2012].

Argote, Rosabel (2003) 'La mujer inmigrante en el cine español del inaugurado siglo XXI', *Feminismo/s: revista del Centro de Estudios sobre la Mujer de la Universidad de Alicante*, 2, 121–38.

Armenteros, Carlos (2000) *El Lago*. Madrid: Odisea.

Armenteros, Carlos (2006) *Las aves del caos*. Madrid: Nuevosescritores.

'avendetta' (2010) Comment in response to 'Habitación en Roma, Medem demuestra su decadencia', posted by Alberto Abuín, in *Blog de Cine.com*, 11 May at 21:26 <http://www.blogdecine.com/cine-espanol/habitacion-en-roma-medem-demuestra-su-decadencia> [last accessed 12 May 2012].

Ayala, Miguel F. (2008) 'Pepón Nieto: "Conecto con Canarias porque soy malagueño y ser del sur nos une mucho"', in *laprovincia.es: diario de Las Palmas*, 15 January, section Entrevista <http://www.laprovincia.es/secciones/noticia.jsp?pRef=1667_31_124960__Entrevista-PEPON-NIETO-Conecto-Canarias-porque-mucho> [last accessed 12 May 2012].

Bad Object Choices (1991) *How Do I Look? Queer Film and Video*. Seattle, WA: Bay Press.

Ballesteros, Isolina (2001) *Cine (ins)urgente. Textos fílmicos y contextos culturales de la España postfranquista*. Madrid: Editorial Fundamentos.

Barker, Martin (2011) 'The pleasures of watching an "off-beat" film: the case of *Being John Malkovich*', *Scope*, 11 <http://www.scope.nottingham.ac.uk/article.php?issue=11andid=1020> [last accessed 12 May 2012].

Barón, Miguel, David Pallol and Pablo Pelado (eds) (1999) 'Almodóvar de la A a la Z', *Zero*, 7, 56–74.

Barriuso, Olatz (2011) 'Denuncian a dos excargos de Madrazo por desviar fondos públicos para una película', *elcorreo.com* [*El Correo*], 30 March <http://www.elcorreo.com/alava/v/20110330/politica/denuncian-excargos-madrazo-desviar-20110330.html> [last accessed 12 May 2012].

Barros, Anibal (2009) Comment in 'Blog de Vicente Molina Foix', in *El Boomeran(g).com*, 24 September at 13:48, <http://www.elboomeran.com/blog-post/79/7690/vicente-molina-foix/diario-de-rodaje-4-valencias-uno/#comentarios> [last accessed 12 May 2012].

Batlle Caminal, Jordi (2010) '*El cónsul de Sodoma*' [review], in *Fotogramas*, no date, section Crítica <http://www.fotogramas.es/Peliculas/El-Consul-de-Sodoma/Critica> [last accessed 12 May 2012].

Becker, Edith, Michelle Citron, Julia Lesage and B. Ruby Rich (1981) 'Introduction', *Jump Cut*, 24–5 (Special Issue 'Lesbians and Film'), 17–21; published online (2005) in *LesbiansandFilm.com*, no date <http://www.ejumpcut.org/archive/onlinessays/JC24-25folder/LesbiansAndFilm.html> [last accessed 12 May 2012].

'Begoña' (2009) Comment in 'Blog de Vicente Molina Foix', in *El Boomeran(g).com*, 24 September at 16:02 <http://www.elboomeran.com/blog-post/79/7690/vicente-molina-foix/diario-de-rodaje-4-valencias-uno/#comentarios> [last accessed 12 May 2012].

Beirne, Rebecca (2006) 'Fashioning *The L Word*', *Nebula*, 3.4, 1–37.

Belinchón, Gregorio (2010) 'Sexo libre en el País Vasco', in *El País.com*, 20

May, section Cultura <http://www.elpais.com/articulo/cultura/Sexo/libre/ Pais/Vasco/elpepucul/20100520elpepucul_11/Tes> [last accessed 12 May 2012].

Bell, David and Gill Valentine (1995) *Mapping Desires: Geographies of Sexualities*. London and New York: Routledge.

Bergman, David (2003) *The Violet Hour: The Violet Quill and the Making of Gay Culture*. New York: Columbia University Press.

Bersani, Leo and Ulysse Dutoit (2009) 'Almodóvar's girls', in Brad Epps and Despina Kakoudaki (eds), *All About* Almodóvar: *A Passion for Cinema*. Minneapolis and London: University of Minnesota Press, pp. 241–66.

Bingham, Dennis (2010) *Whose Lives Are They Anyway? The Biopic as Contemporary Film Genre*. New Brunswick, NJ: Rutgers University Press.

Bourdieu, Pierre (1990) 'The social definition of photography', in Pierre Bourdieu, Luc Boltanski, Robert Castel, Jean-Claude Chamboredon and Dominique Schnapper, *Photography: A Middle-Brow Art*, trans. Shaun Whiteside. Cambridge: Polity Press, pp. 73–98.

Brito, Sara (2010) 'La homosexualidad se cuenta en vasco', in *Público.es*, 21 May <http://www.publico.es/culturas/314471/la-homosexualidad-se-cuenta-en-vasco> [last accessed 12 May 2012].

Cairns, Lucille (2006) *Sapphism on Screen: Lesbian Desire in French Cinema*. Edinburgh: Edinburgh University Press.

Calvo Borobiá, Kerman (2005) *Ciudadanía y minorías sexuales: la regulación del matrimonio homosexual en España*. Madrid: Fundación Alternativas.

Camí-Vela, María Antonia (2005) *Mujeres detrás de la cámara: Entrevistas con cineastas españolas 1990–2004*. Madrid: Ocho y Medio.

Campo Vidal, Anabel (2004a) '*Carícies. 1997*', in *Ventura Pons.cat: La mirada libre*. Madrid: Fundación Autor <http://www.venturapons.cat/Mirada%20 Libre/11miradalibre.pdf> [last accessed 5 May 2012].

Campo Vidal, Anabel (2004b) '*Amic/Amat 1998*', in *Ventura Pons.cat: La mirada libre*. Madrid: Fundación Autor <http://www.venturapons.cat/ Mirada%20Libre/12miradalibre.pdf> [last accessed 12 May 2012].

Carrascosa, Sejo (2005) 'Qué es Queer?', in David Córdoba, Javier Sáez and Paco Vidarte (eds) (2011) *Teoría Queer: Políticas bolleras, maricas, trans, mestizas*. Barcelona and Madrid: Egales, pp. 179–80.

Carrillo, Juanma (2011) Website portfolio, no date [2010–12 ongoing] <http:// juanmacarrillo.com/> [last accessed 12 May 2012]

Casanova, Álec (2007) 'La transexualidad en espera: Motivación para el activismo', in Juan A. Herrero Brasas (ed.), *Primera Plana: ética y activismo – La construcción de una cultura queer en España*. Barcelona and Madrid: Egales, pp. 331–45.

Casañas, Jesús (2010) '*Habitación en Roma* (2010)', in *HoyCinema.com*, 6 May <http://www.hoycinema.com/criticas/Habitacion-Roma-2010/1988. htm> [last accessed 12 May 2012].

Cascales, Agustín G. (2010a) 'Ellos [*sic*] forman el alma de *Nacidas para sufrir*' interview with Petra Martínez and Adriana Ozores, in *shangay.com*, 17 February <http://www.shangay.com/nota/13719/ellos-forman-el-alma-de-"nacidas-para-sufrir"> [last accessed 12 May 2012].

Cascales, Agustín G. (2010b) 'Yon González' interview with photographs by Jesús Alonso, *Shangay Style*, 8, 1 and 13–16.

Castrejón, María (2008) *Que me Estoy Muriendo de Agua: Guía de narrativa lésbica española*. Barcelona and Madrid: Egales.

Chicabuscachica (2011) Publicity website for ¿Quién entiende ... a las mujeres? film project <http://chicabuscachica.tumblr.com/> [last accessed 12 May 2012].

chueca.com (2001) '*I Love You Baby*' [review note], in *chueca.com*, 30 October, section Cine <http://www.chueca.com/cine/i-love-you-baby.html> [last accessed 12 May 2012].

Ciáurriz, Alberto (2002) [1999] *El gran salto*. Madrid: Odisea.

Ciáurriz, Alberto (2006) *La terraza de enfrente*. Madrid: Odisea.

CIMA (2011) 'Proyectos' collected links, no date [2011–12] <http://www.cim amujerescineastas.es/htm/proyectos/estudios/estudios.php> [last accessed 28 August 2011].

COGAM (2010) 'El corto *Tiras de mi piel* ya está liberado en internet', Safer Sex and HIV posting, in *Cogam.es*, 24 June <http://www.cogam.es/ secciones/prevencion-y-vih/i/1062242/113/el-corto-tiras-de-mi-piel-ya-esta-liberado-en-internet> [last accessed 12 May 2012].

Colectivo Q8 (2008) *Queeruption 8 Karcalona* infozine <http://www.qzap.org /v5/gallery/main.php?g2_view=core.DownloadItem&g2_itemId=313> [last accessed 21 May 2012]

Collins, Jacky (2007) 'Challenging the rhetorical oxymoron: lesbian motherhood in contemporary European cinema', *Studies in European Cinema*, 4.2, 149–59.

Collins, Jacky (2009) 'Con voz propia y sin complejos: el desarrollo de la identidad lesbiana en la obra de Libertad Morán', in Elina Norandi (ed.), *Ellas y nosotras: Estudios lesbianos sobre literatura escrita en castellano*. Barcelona and Madrid: Egales, pp. 151–66.

Collins, Jacky (2011) '"Sisters are doing it for themselves": lesbian identities in contemporary Spanish literature', in Nancy Vosburg and Jacky Collins (eds) *Lesbian Realities/Lesbian Fictions in Contemporary Spain*. Lewisburg, PA: Bucknell University Press, pp. 175–92.

Córdoba, David, Javier Sáez and Paco Vidarte (eds) (2005) *Teoría Queer: Políticas bolleras, maricas, trans, mestizas*. Barcelona and Madrid: Egales.

'Crasamet' (2009) Comment no. 6 in response to Raúl Madrid (2009) 'Pedro Almodóvar, pedagogo de la realidad LGTB', in *DosManzanas.com*, 28 April at 15:58 <http://www.dosmanzanas.com/2009/04/pedro-almodovar-pedagogo-de-la-realidad-lgtb.html> [last accessed 12 May 2012].

Cristianos gays (2010) 'El cónsul de Sodoma' review, in CristianosGays.com, 25 January <http://www.cristianosgays.com/2010/01/25/el-consul-de-sodoma/> [last accessed 12 May 2012].

'D. M.' (2009) 'Dalmau, Miguel Ángel Fernandez y Joaquín Gómez escribieron la biopic sobre Gil de Biedma', in abcguionistas.com, 11 February <http://www.abcguionistas.com/noticias/guion/dalmau-miguel-angel-fernandez-y-joaquin-gomis-escribieron-la-biopic-sobre-gil-de-biedma.html> [last accessed 12 May 2012].

D'Lugo, Marvin (2006) Pedro Almodóvar. Urbana: University of Illinois Press.

D'Lugo, Marvin (2009) 'Postnostalgia in Bad Education: written on the body of Sara Montiel', in Brad Epps and Despina Kakoudaki (eds), All About Almodóvar: A Passion for Cinema. Minneapolis and London: University of Minnesota Press, pp. 357–85.

Dalmau, Miguel (2004) Jaime Gil de Biedma: Retrato de un poeta. Barcelona: Circe.

Davis, Glyn (2006) 'Taming Oscar Wilde: queerness, heritage and stardom', in Robin Griffiths (ed.), British Queer Cinema. London and New York: Routledge, pp. 195–206.

De Lauretis, Teresa (2007) 'Guerrilla in the midst: women's cinema in the '80s', in Jackie Stacey and Sarah Street (eds), Queer Screen: A Screen Reader. London and New York: Routledge, pp. 21–40.

De Zero a 100 (2003) 'Cine' [report on 7th LesGaiCineMad festival 2002], Zero, 58, 118.

del Amo, Álvaro (2002) 'Journal: Madrid', Film Comment, 38.6, 12–13.

'Despotorramiento feroz' (2009) Comment no. 6 in response to 'Flick' (2009) 'Una película retrata la tumultuosa relación homosexual entre Lorca y Dalí', in DosManzanas.com, 17 March at 19:27 <http://www.dosmanzanas.com/2009/03/una-pelicula-retrata-la-tumultuosa-relacion-homosexual-entre-lorca-y-dali.html#comments> [last accessed 12 May 2012].

Doane, Mary Anne (1992) 'Film and the masquerade: theorizing female spectatorship', in Screen [collective] (ed.), The Sexual Subject: A Screen Reader in Sexuality. London and New York: Routledge, pp. 227–43.

DosManzanas (2006) 'Reinas', review note in DosManzanas.com, 7 November, section Archivo <http://archivo.dosmanzanas.com/index.php?cat=4andpaged=24> [last accessed 12 May 2012].

DosManzanas (2009) 'El LesGaiCineMad distinguirá a Ventura Pons con un premio honorífico', press release of LesGaiCineMad festival, in DosManzanas.com, 22 September <http://www.dosmanzanas.com/2009/09/el-lesgaicinemad-distinguira-a-ventura-pons-con-un-premio-honorifico.html> [last accessed 12 May 2012].

Doty, Alexander (1993) Making Things Perfectly Queer: Interpreting Mass Culture. Minneapolis: University of Minnesota Press.

Drake, Philip (2003) '"Mortgaged to music": new retro movies in 1990s

Hollywood cinema', in Paul Grainge (ed.), *Memory and Popular Film*. Manchester and New York: Manchester University Press, pp. 183–201.

Dyer, Richard (1990) *Now You See It: Studies on Lesbian and Gay Film*. London and New York: Routledge.

'eduardo' (2010) Comment in response to elputojacktwist, 'Algunas peliculillas', in *DosManzanas.com*, 8 October at 8:18, section Desayuno en Urano <http://www.dosmanzanas.com/2010/10/algunas-peliculillas-i.html> [last accessed 12 May 2012].

El Castigador (2011) 'Entrevista a Eduardo Mendicutti: "Si el PP se volviera loco y se pusiera a prohibirlo todo, con cultura se puede hacer frente"', in *ambienteg.com*, 10 June <http://www.ambienteg.com/literatura/entrevista-a-eduardo-mendicutti-si-el-pp-se-volviera-loco-y-se-pusiera-a-prohibirlo-todo-con-cultura-se-puede-hacer-frente> [last accessed 12 May 2012].

El Internado (2008) Club de Fans de Yon Gonzalez user group, in *El Internado* <http://elinternado-talk.foroactivo.com/t84-club-de-fans-de-yon-gonzalez> [last accessed 12 May 2012].

Ellis, Robert Richmond (1997) *The Hispanic Homograph: Gay Self-representation in Contemporary Spanish Autobiography*. Urbana and Chicago: Illinois University Press.

Ellis, Robert Richmond (2010) 'Spanish constitutional democracy and cinematic representations of queer sexuality, or, saving the family: *Los novios búlgaros*, *Reinas*, and *Fuera de carta*', *Revista Canadiense de Estudios Hispánicos*, 34.1, 67–80.

EnikPro (2010) Facebook page for *Flores en el parque* <http://www.facebook.com/pages/Flores-en-el-Parque-Flowers-at-the-Park-by-Mariel-Macia/145550822138963> [last accessed 12 May 2012].

Epps, Brad and Despina Kakoudaki (eds) (2009) *All About Almodóvar: A Passion for Cinema*. Minneapolis and London: University of Minnesota Press.

'Esme Baltasar' (2011) Facebook comment on EnikPro (2010) Facebook page for *Flores en el parque*, 22 January at 22:29 <http://www.facebook.com/pages/Flores-en-el-Parque-Flowers-at-the-Park-by-Mariel-Macia/145550822138963> [last accessed 12 May 2012].

'Espectador contrariado' (2009) Comment in 'Blog de Vicente Molina Foix', in *ElBoomeran(g).com*, 23 September at 16:12 <http://www.elboomeran.com/blog-post/79/7690/vicente-molina-foix/diario-de-rodaje-4-valencias-uno/#comentarios> [last accessed 12 May 2012].

Esteban, Ángel L. (1999a) 'Barcelona por todo equipaje: Entrevista con Ventura Pons', *Zero*, 5: 96–7.

Esteban, Ángel L. (1999b) 'Homosexualidad', in Miguel Barón, David Pallol and Pablo Pelado (eds) (1999) 'Almodóvar de la A a la Z', *Zero*, 7, 64.

Esteban, Ángel L. (1999c) 'Dispuestos a chupar cámara', *Zero*, 12, 66–77.

Etxebarria, Lucía (2011a) 'The End' <http://www.adn.es/blog/lucia_etxebarria/> [last accessed 9 August 2011, now expired].

Etxebarria, Lucía (2011b) 'Hasta setiembre', in Lucía Etxebarria (2011a), 18 July <http://www.adn.es/blog/lucia_etxebarria/> [last accessed 9 August 2011, now expired]; cached as Facebook entry 'El jueves con suerte me voy a Donostia' <http://webcache.googleusercontent.com/search?q=cache:TfDZ9F9JMLgJ:www.facebook.com/note.php%3Fnote_id%3D10150264856764643> [last accessed 19 May 2012].

Europa Press (2009) 'El "amor latente" de *Nacidas para sufrir* abre la Mostra', in *elmundo.es*, 16 October <http://www.elmundo.es/elmundo/2009/10/16/valencia/1255698382.html> [last accessed 12 May 2012].

EurOut (2010) 'Interview: lesbian filmmaker Mariel Maciá', in *EurOut.com: The Magazine*, 4, 23–7 <http://issuu.com/sandrashowtime/docs/eurout_magazine_4> [last accessed 12 May 2012].

Evans, Caroline and Lorraine Gamman (2004) [1995] 'Reviewing queer viewing', in Harry Benshoff and Sean Griffin (eds), *Queer Cinema: The Film Reader*. London and New York: Routledge, pp. 209–24; reprinted, abridged, in Paul Burston and Colin Richardson (eds) (1995) *A Queer Romance: Lesbians, Gay Men and Popular Culture*. London and New York: Routledge, pp. 13–56.

Evans, Peter W. (2002) 'Victoria Abril: the sex which is not one', in Jo Labanyi (ed.), *Constructing Identity in Contemporary Spain: Theoretical Debates and Cultural Practices*. New York: Oxford University Press, pp. 128–37.

'Ex-usuaria' (2009) Comment on Fichas: *The L-Word*, in *lesbianlips.es*, 13 April at 22:06 <http://www.lesbianlips.es/fichas/the-l-word/233/P-2/#load_comments> [last accessed 5 May 2012].

'Ex-usuaria' (2010) Comment on Fichas: *80 Egunean*, in *lesbianlips.es*, 30 May at 16:53 <http://www.lesbianlips.es/fichas/80-egunean/2441/P-1/#load_comments> [last accessed 5 May 2012].

'fanhunter4ever' (2009) Comment in 'Blog de Vicente Molina Foix', in *El Boomeran(g).com*, 23 September at 20:32 <http://www.elboomeran.com/blog-post/79/7690/vicente-molina-foix/diario-de-rodaje-4-valencias-uno/#comentarios> [last accessed 12 May 2012].

Faulkner, Sally (2004) *Literary Adaptations in Spanish Cinema*. London: Tamesis.

Feenstra, Pietsie (2006) *Les nouvelles figures mythiques du cinéma espagnol. À corps perdu*. Paris: Harmattan.

Fernàndez, Josep-Anton (2000a) *Another Country: Sexuality and National Identity in Catalan Gay Fiction*. Leeds: Maney Publishing.

Fernàndez, Josep-Anton (ed.) (2000b) *El gai saber: introducció als estudis gais i lèsbics*. Barcelona: Llibres de l'índex.

Fernàndez, Josep-Anton (2000c) 'Introducció', in Josep-Anton Fernàndez (ed.), *El gai saber: introducció als estudis gais i lèsbics*. Barcelona: Llibres de l'índex, pp. 11–29.

Fernàndez, Josep-Anton (2000d) 'L'esdevenir-lesbiana de Catalunya: *Costa Brava* de Marta Balletbò-Coll', in Josep-Anton Fernàndez (ed.), *El gai saber: introducció als estudis gais i lèsbics*. Barcelona: Llibres de l'índex, pp. 393–412.

Fernàndez, Josep-Anton (2008) 'Immortal/undead: the body and the transmission of tradition in *Amic/Amat* (Ventura Pons, 1998)', in Joan Ramon Resina (ed.), *Burning Darkness: A Half Century of Spanish Cinema*. New York: SUNY Press, pp. 211–33.

Fernández, Lara (2010) 'Las subvenciones al "cine basura": un millón de euros para *Mentiras y gordas*', in *Vanitatis.com*, 31 December <http://www.vanitatis.com/noticias/subvenciones-sinde-cine-ministerio-cultura-mentiras-gordas-20101230-12342.html> [last accessed 12 May 2012].

Fernández, Lola (2009) 'Robert Pattinson', in *shangay.com*, 8 October <http://www.shangay.com/nota/9196/robert-pattinson; illustration at http://www.shangay.com/36-amp-out> [last accessed 11 May 2011].

Fernández, Miguel (2003) *Yestergay*. Madrid: Odisea.

Fish, Stanley (1980) *Is There a Text in This Class? The Authority of Interpretive Communities*. Cambridge, MA: Harvard University Press.

'Flick' (2009) 'Una película retrata la tumultuosa relación homosexual entre Lorca y Dalí', in *DosManzanas.com*, 17 March <http://www.dosmanzanas.com/2009/03/una-pelicula-retrata-la-tumultuosa-relacion-homosexual-entre-lorca-y-dali.html#comments> [last accessed 12 May 2012].

'Flick' (2010) 'La última cinta de Julio Medem, *Habitación en Roma*, una historia de amor entre dos mujeres', in *DosManzanas.com*, 5 May <http://www.dosmanzanas.com/2010/05/la-ultima-cinta-de-julio-medem-habitacion-en-roma-una-historia-de-amor-entre-dos-mujeres.html> [last accessed 12 May 2012].

'Flick' (2011) 'Presidenta del PP catalán: "no es cuestión solo de cambiar el nombre, es cuestión de que no todos los efectos civiles son los mismos"', in *DosManzanas.com*, 7 November–<http://www.dosmanzanas.com/2011/11/presidenta-del-pp-catalan-no-es-cuestion-solo-de-cambiar-el-nombre-es-cuestion-de-que-no-todos-los-efectos-civiles-son-los-mismos.html> [last accessed 12 May 2012].

Focoforo (2009) 'Pelotazo de Menkes y Albacete', in *elfocoforo: Cine y popcorn*, no date <http://focoblog.com/focoforo/topic.php?id=1766> [last accessed 9 June 2011; now expired].

Foster, David William (2003) *Queer Issues in Contemporary Latin American Cinema*. Austin: University of Texas Press.

Fotogramas (2009) 'Mentiras y gordas arrasa en la taquilla', in *Fotogramas.es*, 30 March <http://www.fotogramas.es/Noticias/Mentiras-y-gordas-arrasa-en-la-taquilla> [last accessed 12 May 2012].

Fouz-Hernández, Santiago (2004) 'Identity without limits. Queer debates and representation in contemporary Spain', *Journal of Iberian and Latin American Studies*, 10.1, 63–82.

Fouz-Hernández, Santiago (2009) 'Caresses: the male body in the films of Ventura Pons', in Santiago Fouz-Hernández (ed.) *Mysterious Skin:*

Male Bodies in Contemporary Cinema. London: I. B. Tauris, pp. 143–57.

Fouz-Hernández, Santiago (2010) 'Assimilation and its discontents: representations of gay men in Spanish cinema of the 2000s', *Revista Canadiense de Estudios Hispánicos*, 35.1, 81–104.

Fouz-Hernández, Santiago (2011) 'Queer in Spain: identity without limits', in Lisa Downing and Robert Gillet (eds), *Queer in Europe*. Aldershot: Ashgate, pp. 189–202.

Fouz-Hernández, Santiago and Alfredo Martínez-Expósito (2007) *Live Flesh: The Male Body in Contemporary Spanish Cinema*. London: I. B. Tauris.

Fouz-Hernández, Santiago and Chris Perriam (2007) 'El deseo sin ley: la representación de "la homosexualidad" en el cine español de los años noventa', in Félix Rodríguez González (ed.), *Perspectivas gays*, vol. 1 of Félix Rodríguez González and Angie Simonis (eds), *Cultura, homosexualidad y homofobia*. Barcelona: Laertes, pp. 61–79; original English-language version in David Alderson and Linda R. Anderson (eds) (2000) *Territories of Desire in Queer Culture: Refiguring Contemporary Boundaries*. Manchester: Manchester University Press.

Fritz, Ben (2010) 'In Spain, Internet piracy is part of the culture', *Los Angeles Times*, 30 March <http://articles.latimes.com/2010/mar/30/business/la-fi-ct-spain30-2010mar30> [last accessed 12 May 2012]

Fuentes, Pablo (2007) 'La transformación de las culturas homosexuales en la España del siglo XX', in Juan A. Herrero Brasas (ed.), *Primera Plana: ética y activismo – La construcción de una cultura queer en España*. Barcelona and Madrid: Egales, pp. 368–92.

Gallardo, Víctor Miguel (2010) 'Las columnas de opinión', *Lecturalia* blog (Mundo editorial, Noticias, prensa) <http://www.lecturalia.com/blog/2010/10/16/las-columnas-de-opinion/> [last accessed 12 May 2012].

Gara (2007) 'Claver recuerda en *Electroshock* una escalofriante historia de amor verídica', in *gara.net*, 25 January <http://www.gara.net/idatzia/20070125/art198523.php> [last accessed 12 May 2012].

Garaño, Jon and Jose Mari Goenaga (2012) '80 egunean: Memoria de dirección', in *LaHiguera.net*, no date <http://www.lahiguera.net/cinemania/pelicula/5045/comentario.php> [last accessed 12 May 2012].

García Rodríguez, Javier (2008) *El celuloide rosa*. Barcelona: Ediciones La tempestad.

García Serrano, Yolanda (2007) *Amor de hombre*. Madrid: Olalla Ediciones.

Garlinger, Patrick Paul (2005) *Confessions of the Letter Closet: Epistolary Fiction and Queer Desire in Modern Spain*. Minneapolis: University of Minnesota Press.

GayValencia (2010) 'Valencia, capital mundial del cine gay y lésbico', in *GayValencia.org*, section Cultura, 9 September <http://www.gayvalencia.org/cultura/festival-de-la-luna.php> [last accessed 12 May 2012].

Generelo, Jesús (2004) 'Ganando territorios (televisivos)', *Zero*, 60, 26–7.

George, David (2002) 'Del escenario a la pantalla: Sergi Belbel y Ventura Pons', *Anales de la Literatura Española Contemporánea*, 27.1, 89–102.

'George/tres tristes tigres' (2010) Comment in response to Vicente Molina Foix (2010) 'La película de Gil de Biedma', in *ElBoomeran(g).com*, 28 January at 20:49 <http://www.elboomeran.com/blog-post/79/8440/vicente-molina-foix/la-pelicula-de-gil-de-biedma/> [last accessed 12 May 2012].

Gibbs, Liz (ed.) (1994) *Daring to Dissent: Lesbian Culture from Margin to Mainstream*. London: Cassell.

Gil de Biedma, Jaime (1974) *Diario de un artista seriamente enfermo*. Barcelona: Lumen.

Gimeno, Beatriz (2007a) 'La doble discriminación de las lesbianas', in Angie Simonis (ed.), *Amazonia: retos de visibilidad lesbiana*, vol. 2 of Félix Rodríguez González and Angie Simonis (eds) *Cultura, homosexualidad y homofobia*. Barcelona: Laertes, pp. 19–26.

Gimeno, Beatriz (2007b) 'Matrimonio civil en España: Historia de una lucha', in Juan A. Herrero Brasas (ed.), *Primera Plana: ética y activismo – La construcción de una cultura queer en España*. Barcelona and Madrid: Egales, pp. 33–40.

Gimeno, Beatriz (2008) *Sexo*. Barcelona and Madrid: Egales.

Giraldo, Pablo (2009) 'Mario Casas nos cuenta *Mentiras y gordas*', in *Shangay.com*, 31 March <http://www.shangay.com/node/7774> [last accessed 12 May 2012].

Giraldo, Pablo (2011a) 'Juanma Carrillo is on Fire', in *Shangay.com*, 21 June <http://www.shangay.com/nota/25950/juanma-carrillo-fire> [last accessed 12 May 2012].

Giraldo, Pablo (2011b) 'Cumbre de actores', in *Shangay.com*, 3 August <http://www.shangay.com/nota/26292/cumbre-de-actores> [last accessed 12 May 2012].

Gómez, Iratxe (2006) 'Eusebio Poncela, actor: "Soy el primer actor que ha hecho de homosexual normal y corriente"', *ElCorreoDigital* (Cultura), 24 January <http://www.elcorreo.com/alava/pg060124/prensa/noticias/Cultura_VIZ/200601/24/VIZ-CUL-004.html> [last accessed 12 May 2012].

González, Clarisa (2011) 'Visibilidad y diversidad lésbica en el cine español: cuatro películas de la última década', *Icono*, online, 9.3, 221–55 <http://www.icono14.net/Archivos> [last accessed 21 May 2021].

'Graciela' (2010) Comment on 'Flick', 'La última cinta de Julio Medem, *Habitación en Roma*, una historia de amor entre dos mujeres' in *DosManzanas.com*, 6 May at 12:25 <http://www.dosmanzanas.com/2010/05/la-ultima-cinta-de-julio-medem-habitacion-en-roma-una-historia-de-amor-entre-dos-mujeres.html> [last accessed 18 December 2011].

Gras-Velázquez, Adrián (2011) 'Boystown: representations of queer space in recent Spanish cinema', *Spaces and Flows: An International Journal of Urban and Extraurban Studies*, 1.1, 97–108.

Griffiths, Robin (ed.) (2006a) *British Queer Cinema*. London and New York: Routledge.

Griffiths, Robin (2006b) 'Introduction: Queer Britannia – a century of *sin*ema', in Robin Griffiths (ed.), *British Queer Cinema*. London and New York: Routledge, pp. 1–20.

Griffiths, Robin (2008) *Queer Cinema in Europe*. Bristol: Intellect.

Grupo de Trabajo Queer (ed.) (2005) *El eje del mal es heterosexual: Figuraciones, movimientos y práctica feministas queer*. Madrid: Traficantes de Sueños.

Guasch, Óscar (2007) 'No és aixó, companys, no és aixó', in Juan A. Herrero Brasas (ed.), *Primera Plana: ética y activismo – La construcción de una cultura queer en España*. Barcelona and Madrid: Egales, pp. 357–65.

Guasch, Óscar and Olga Viñuales (2003) 'Introducción: Sociedad, sexualidad y teoría social: la sexualidad en perspectiva sociológica', in Óscar Guasch and Olga Viñuales (eds), *Sexualidades: Diversidad y control social*. Barcelona: Edicions Bellaterra, pp. 9–18.

Gutiérrez-Albill, Julian Daniel (2008) *Queering Buñuel: Sexual Dissidence and Psychoanalysis in His Mexican and Spanish Cinema*. London: I. B. Tauris.

Guzner, Susana (2004) *Punto y aparte*. Barcelona and Madrid: Egales.

Hamer, Diane and Belinda Budge (eds) (1994) *The Good, the Bad and the Gorgeous: Popular Culture's Romance with Lesbianism*. London: HarperCollins.

Hanson, Ellis (ed.) (1999a) *Out Takes: Essays on Queer Theory and Film*, Durham, NC: Duke University Press.

Hanson, Ellis (1999b) 'Introduction: out takes', in Ellis Hanson (ed.), *Out Takes: Essays on Queer Theory and Film*. Durham, NC: Duke University Press, pp. 1–19.

Harbord, Janet (2002) *Film Cultures: Production, Distribution and Consumption*. London: Sage.

Hayward, Susan (1998) '"Hardly grazing", Josiane Balasko's *Gazon maudit* (1995): the mise-en-textes and mise-en-scène of Sexuality/ies', in Owen Heathcote, Alex Hughes and James S. Williams (eds), *Gay Signatures: Gay and Lesbian Theory, Fiction and Film in France, 1945–1995*. Oxford: Berg, pp. 131–49.

Hedgecoe, Guy (2011) 'In Madrid, noted bookseller pushes LGBT visibility', in *GlobalPost.com*, 27 October, section Regions (Europe) <http://www.globalpost.com/dispatch/news/regions/europe/spain/111026/noted-bookseller-pushes-LGBT-visibility> [last accessed 12 May 2012].

Hellekson, Karen and Kristina Busse (2006) *Fan Fiction and Fan Communities in the Age of the Internet: New Essays*. Jefferson: McFarland.

Henderson, Lisa (2008) 'Simple pleasure: lesbian community and *Go Fish*', in Suzanne Ferriss and Mallory Young (eds), *Chick Flicks: Contemporary Women at the Movies*. London and New York: Routledge, pp. 132–57.

Hennessy, Rosemary (2000) *Profit and Pleasure: Sexual Identities in Late Capitalism*. London and New York: Routledge.

Hernández, Carmen G. (2007) 'El armario de nuevo: la invisibilidad de las activistas lesbianas en la construcción histórica del movimiento LGTB español', in Angie Simonis (ed.), *Amazonia: retos de visibilidad lesbiana*, vol. 2 of Félix Rodríguez González and Angie Simonis (eds), *Cultura, homosexualidad y homofobia*. Barcelona: Laertes, pp. 55–84.

Hernández, Mili (2007) 'Así lo he vivido', in Juan A. Herrero Brasas (ed.), *Primera Plana: ética y activismo – La construcción de una cultura queer en España*. Barcelona and Madrid: Egales, pp. 209–13.

Hernández, Óscar (2005) *El viaje de Marcos*. Madrid: Odisea.

Herrero Brasas, Juan A. (2001) *La sociedad gay: una invisible minoría*. Madrid: Foca.

Herrero Brasas, Juan A. (ed.) (2007) *Primera Plana: ética y activismo – La construcción de una cultura queer en España*. Barcelona and Madrid: Egales.

Hidalgo, Carmen (2011) '"Mi mayor orgullo es haberle cambiado la vida a muchos gays y lesbianas": Entrevista a Mil Hernández', in *elmundo. es*, 1 June, section Cultura <http://www.elmundo.es/elmundo/2011/06/30/cultura/1309445352.html> [last accessed 12 May 2012].

Hills, Matt (2002) *Fan Cultures*. London and New York: Routledge.

HoyCinema (2006) 'Molina Foix: la temática gay hoy es natural, pero el inicio fue heroico', in *HoyCinema.com*, 23 January <http://www.hoycinema.com/actualidad/noticias/PVASCO-CINE-Molina-Foix-tematica-gay-hoy-natural-pero-inicio-fue-heroico.htm> [last accessed 15 July 2011; now expired].

Humble, Nicola (2001) *The Feminine Middlebrow Novel: Class, Domesticity and Bohemianism*. Oxford: Oxford University Press.

InCinema (2011) 'Mariel Maciá: "Ser mujer, directora y guionista es un privilegio, una responsabilidad y una lucha constante"' interview, in *InCinema. com (Cine desde dentro)*, 3 April <http://revistaincinema.wordpress.com/2011/04/03/mariel-macia-"ser-mujer-directora-y-guionista-es-un-privilegio-una-responsabilidad-y-una-lucha-constante"/> [last accessed 12 May 2012].

'iure' (2009) Comment no. 5 in response to Raúl Madrid, 'Pedro Almodóvar, pedagogo de la realidad LGTB', in *DosManzanas.com*, 28 April at 17:05 <http://www.dosmanzanas.com/2009/04/pedro-almodovar-pedagogo-de-la-realidad-lgtb.html> [last accessed 12 May 2012].

Izquierdo, Gonzalo (2010) 'Luis Antonio de Villena: "Para Gil de Biedma, ligar era un ritual casi cotidiano"', in *Terra Noticias.es*, 20 January <http://noticias.terra.es/2010/genteycultura/0120/actualidad/entrevista-luis-antonio-de-villena-homosexualidad-era-uno-pivotes-vida-jaime-gil-de-biedma.aspx> [last accessed 12 May 2012].

J. O. (2011) '*I Love You Baby*', *Bloggermania.com*, no date [2001?], section Críticas <http://www.bloggermania.com/i/i-love-you-baby.html> [last accessed 12 May 2012].

Jackson, Claire and Peter Tapp (1997) *The Bent Lens: A World Guide to Gay and Lesbian Film*. St Kilda, Vic.: Australian Catalogue Company.

Jennings, Ros (2006) '*Beautiful Thing*: British queer cinema, positive unoriginality and the everyday', in Robin Griffiths (ed.), *British Queer Cinema*. London and New York: Routledge, pp. 183–94.

Jerez-Farrán, Carlos and Samuel Amago (eds) (2010) *Unearthing Franco's Legacy: Mass Graves and the Recovery of Historical Memory in Spain*. Notre Dame, IN: University of Notre Dame Press.

Jiménez, Jose Manuel (HL) (2009) '*Mentiras y gordas* (2009)' review-comment, in *tublogdecine.es* (TBDC), 1 April–<http://www.tublogdecine.es/criticas/mentiras-y-gordas-2009> [last accessed 12 May 2012].

Jiménez Ariza, Pedro (2003) *La noche en que me enamoré de River Phoenix*. Barcelona and Madrid: Egales.

Joreen, Saskia (2010) News post 'Movies of Interest at This Year's Berlinale', in *EurOut.org (European Lesbian News)*, 12 February <http://eurout.org/2010/02/11/movies-interest-years-berlinale?page=0,1> [last accessed 12 May 2012].

Joric, Carlos (2007) Review comment on *Chuecatown*, in *chueca.com*, 3 July <http://www.chueca.com/fotos/chuecatown/nuestra-critica.html> [last accessed 12 May 2012].

Josephson, Jyl (2005) 'Citizenship, same-sex marriage, and feminist critiques of marriage', *Perspectives on Politics*, 3, 269–84.

'Juan' (2010) Comment in response to 'Matrimonio lésbico en *Nacidas para sufrir*', in *estanochegay.com*, 11 March <http://www.estanochegay.com/2010/02/matrimonio-de-lesbianas-de-conveniencia-en-nacidas-para-sufrir/> [last accessed 12 May 2012].

'KAT' (2011) 'Revista revela con fotos lesbianismo de famosa actriz española Elena Ayaya', 25 August at 09:40 <http://guialesbicaperu.blogspot.co.uk/2011/08/revista-revela-con-fotos-lesbianismo-de.html> [last accessed 19 May 2012].

Klemm, Michael D. (2009) Review of *Chef's Special* (*Fuera de carta*) in 'October Grab Bag', *CinemaQueer.com*, no date [October] <http://www.cinemaqueer.com/review%20pages%203/chefsspecial.html> [last accessed 12 May 2012].

La Acera de Enfrente (2010) 'El quiosco de Terenci', in *LaAceradeEnfrente.es*, 15 November <http://www.laaceradeenfrente.es/blog/tag/jaime-gil-de-biedma/> [last accessed 12 May 2012].

La Higuera (2011) '*Spinnin*': comentario' <http://www.lahiguera.net/cinemania/pelicula/4372/comentario.php> [last accessed 12 May 2012].

Labanyi, Jo and Tatjana Pavlović (eds) (2012) *A Companion to Spanish Cinema*. Hoboken, NJ: John Wiley & Sons.

Lacan, Jacques (1979) *The Four Fundamental Concepts of Psychoanalysis*, ed. Jacques-Alain Miller, trans. Alan Sheridan. London: Penguin.

Lázaro, Margarita (2008) 'Ponga una lesbiana en su serie', in *soitu.es*, 25 June at 20:34 <http://www.soitu.es/soitu/2008/06/25/actualidad/1214405830_758408.html> [last accessed 15 December 2011].

lesbiana.es (2011) '*Habitación en Roma*' thread (May 2010-April 2011) in *lesbiana.es* <http://www.lesbiana.es/phpBB303/viewtopic.php?f=13and t=2069andstart=10> [last accessed 12 May 2012].

lesbianlips (2009) Review note and comments on *A mi madre le gustan las mujeres*, in *lesbianlips.es*, 15 November 2004 – 29 April 2009 <http://www.lesbianlips.es/fichas/a-mi-madre-le-gustan-las-mujeres/62/P-6/#load_comments> [last accessed 12 May 2012].

LesPlanet (2011) 'Las películas CENSURADAS en el Festival de Cine de Chicago', in *LesPlanet.co.uk*, 11 April <http://lesplanetagain.blogspot.co.uk/2011/04/las-peliculas-censuradas-en-el-festival.html> [last accessed 12 May 2012].

Librería Cómplices (2011) <http://libreriacomplices.blogspot.com/> [last accessed 12 May 2012].

Lim, Dennis (2000) 'In the heat of the moment', *Village Voice*, 1 February <http://www.villagevoice.com/2000-02-01/film/in-the-heat-of-the-moment/1/> [last accessed 6 July 2012].

Linares, Jota (2010) 'Juanma Carrillo, de profesión pornógrafo visual', in *ElCeluloideOculto.com*, 9 September <http://elceluloideoculto.blogspot.com/2010/09/juanma-carrillo-de-profesion-pornografo.html?zx=247543290e7d5377> [last accessed 12 May 2012].

Lindo, Elvira (2008) 'Antes de Chueca', in *elviralindo.com: Don de Gentes*, 13 September <http://www.elviralindo.com/blog/don-de-gentes/antes-de-chueca/#more-87> [last accessed 12 May 2012].

Lindo, Elvira (2010a) 'Los necios', *El País.com*, 24 March <http://www.elpais.com/articulo/ultima/necios/elpepiult/20100324elpepiult_1/Tes> [last accessed 12 May 2012].

Lindo, Elvira (2010b) 'Matrimonio', *El País.com*, 3 November, section Archivo <http://www.elpais.com/articulo/ultima/Matrimonio/elpepuopi/20101103elpepiult_1/Tes> [last accessed 12 May 2012].

Llamas, Ricardo (1998) *Teoría torcida: Prejuicios y discursos en torno a 'la homosexualidad'*. Madrid: Siglo XXI.

Llopis, María (2010) *El postporno era eso*. Madrid: Melusina.

'lol' (2009) Comment no. 5 in response to Raúl Madrid, 'Pedro Almodóvar, pedagogo de la realidad LGTB', in *DosManzanas.com*, 28 April at 14:41 <http://www.dosmanzanas.com/2009/04/pedro-almodovar-pedagogo-de-la-realidad-lgtb.html> [last accessed 12 May 2012]

López García, Isabelle (2008) 'El cuerpo "sextual" errante como lugar de resistencia en *Loco Afán. Crónicas de sidario*, del escritor chileno Pedro Lemebel', in Beatriz Ferrús and Núria Calafell (eds), *Escribir con el cuerpo*. Barcelona: UOC, pp. 101–10.

López Manjón, Pedro (2011) 'Los rostros (conocidos) del sida', in *rtve.es*

(Radio Televisión Española), 2 June <http://www.rtve.es/noticias/20110602/rostros-mas-famosos-del-sida/436520.shtml> [last accessed 12 May 2012].

López Penedo, Susana (2008) *El laberinto queer: la identidad en tiempos de neoliberalismo*. Barcelona and Madrid: Egales.

Maciá, Mariel (2010) 'LesGaiCineMad', in Eduardo Cardoso (ed. and co-ord.), *El cortometraje español en 100 nombres: Guía para entender el mundo del cortometraje*. Madrid: Eduardo Cardoso Aymerich. <http://www.elcortometrajen100nombres.com> [last accessed 12 May 2012].

MacKinnon, Kenneth (2006) 'Intermingling under controlled conditions: the queerness of *Prick up Your Ears*', in Robin Griffiths (ed.), *British Queer Cinema*. London and New York: Routledge, pp. 121–56.

Maddison, Stephen (2000) 'All about women: Pedro Almodóvar and the heterosocial dynamic', *Textual Practice*, 14.2, 265–84.

Madrid, Raúl (2009) 'Pedro Almodóvar, pedagogo de la realidad LGTB', in *DosManzanas.com*, 28 April <http://www.dosmanzanas.com/2009/04/pedro-almodovar-pedagogo-de-la-realidad-lgtb.html> [last accessed 12 May 2012].

'Maria Oliva' (2011) Facebook comment on EnikPro (2010) Facebook page for *Flores en el parque*, 6 June at 04:54 <http://www.facebook.com/pages/Flores-en-el-Parque-Flowers-at-the-Park-by-Mariel-Macia/145550822138963> [last accessed 12 May 2012].

Marín-Dòmine, Marta (2006) 'Sueños y pesadillas: efectos subjetivos de la Guerra Civil española a través de cierta mirada cinematográfica', *Amnis*, 6: Special Issue on 'La guerre et ses victimes' <http://amnis.revues.org/888> [last accessed 12 May 2012].

maríocasasfans (2012) Fan website <http://mariocasasfans.creatuforo.com/index.php> [last accessed 12 May 2012].

MarioCasasWeb (2011a) Noticias, in *MarioCasasWeb.com* <http://www.mariocasasweb.com/web/index.php/noticias.html> [last accessed 12 May 2012].

MarioCasasWeb (2011b) 'Foro, Premios Shangay 2009', in *MarioCasasWeb.com* <http://www.mariocasasweb.com/foro/viewtopic.php?f=13andt=61> [last accessed 12 May 2012].

'marotorod' (2009) Comment no.13 in thread 'No solo los internautas nos metemos con González Sinde', in *menéame.net*, 14 April at 14:19 <http://www.meneame.net/story/no-solo-internautas-nos-metemos-gonzalez-sinde> [last accessed 12 May 2012].

Martí-Olivella, Jaume (2000) 'Ventura Pons o la teatralizació de la impostura', in Josep-Anton Fernàndez (ed.), *El gai saber: introducció als estudis gais i lèsbics*. Barcelona: Llibres de l'índex, pp. 373–92.

Martin-Márquez, Susan (1999) *Feminist Discourse and Spanish Cinema. Sight Unseen*. Oxford: Oxford University Press.

Martínez, Isabel C. (2011) 'El Gobierno contrató a Aukeratu al mes de asumir Gonzalo su dirección', *El País.com*, 31 March, section País Vasco

<http://www.elpais.com/articulo/pais/vasco/Gobierno/contrato/Aukeratu/mes/asumir/Gonzalo/direccion/elpepuespvas/20110331elpvas_7/Tes> [last accessed 12 May 2012].

Martínez March, Manuel (2001) '*I Love You Baby*: Crítica', in *LaButaca. net: estrenos*, 26 October – 1 November <http://www.labutaca.net/films/5/iloveyoubaby1.htm> [last accessed 12 May 2012].

Martínez Pulet, José Manuel (2005) 'La construcción de una sujetividad perveersa: El SM como metáfora política y sexual', in David Córdoba, Javier Sáez and Paco Vidarte (eds), *Teoría Queer: Políticas bolleras, maricas, trans, mestizas*. Barcelona and Madrid: Egales, pp. 213–28.

Martínez-Expósito, Alfredo (1998) *Los escribas furiosos: configuraciones homoeróticas en la narrativa española*. New Orleans: University Press of the South.

Martínez-Expósito, Alfredo (2004) *Escrituras torcidas: Ensayos de crítica 'Queer'*. Barcelona: Laertes.

Martínez-Expósito, Alfredo (2006) 'Signification et fonction du lesbianisme dans *Les Soldats de Salamine* (2003) de David Trueba', *Inverses*, 6, 45–62.

Martínez March, Manuel (2001), '*I Love You Baby*: Crítica' in *LaButaca.net: estrenos*, 26 October–1 November <http:www.labutaca.net/films/5/iloveyoubaby1.htm> [last accessed 12 May 2012].

'marylyz' (2009) Comment on Fichas: The L-Word, in *lesbianlips.es*, 5 October at 21:04 <http://www.lesbianlips.es/fichas/the-l-word/233/P-2/#load_comments> [last accessed 12 May 2012].

MECD [Ministerio de Educación, Cultura y Deportes] (2009) 'El mueble de las fotos', entry in *Catálogo [Anuario] Cinespañola 2010*, online <http://catalogocine.mcu.es/comun/bases/cine/Anuarios/2009/P188909.pdf> [last accessed 24 May 2012].

MECD [Ministerio de Educación, Cultura y Deportes] (2012) *Base de datos de películas calificadas*, online database <http://www.mcu.es/cine/CE/BBDDPeliculas/BBDDPeliculas_Index.html> [last accessed 12 May 2012].

Medhurst, Andy (2009) 'Heart of farce: Almodóvar's comic complexities', in Brad Epps and Despina Kakoudaki (eds), *All About Almodóvar: A Passion for Cinema*. Minneapolis and London: University of Minnesota Press, pp. 118–39.

Melero, Alejandro (2010) *Placeres ocultos: Gays y lesbianas en el cine español de la transición*. Madrid: Notorious Ediciones.

Melero, Luis (2001) *El espejo líquido*. Madrid: Odisea.

Menchén, Pedro (1999) *Una playa muy lejana*. Barcelona: Los libros de la frontera.

Mendicutti, Eduardo (1991) *El palomo cojo*. Barcelona: Tusquets.

Mendicutti, Eduardo (1998) *Los novios búlgaros*, 3rd edn. Barcelona: Tusquets.

Mendicutti, Eduardo (2005) *California*. Barcelona: Tusquets.

Mira, Alberto (ed.) (1999) *Para entendernos. Diccionario de cultura homo-sexual, gay y lésbica*. Barcelona: Ediciones de la Tempestad.

Mira, Alberto (2004) *De Sodoma a Chueca: Una historia cultural de la homo-sexualidad en España en el siglo XX*. Barcelona and Madrid: Egales.

Mira, Alberto (2008) *Miradas insumisas: Gays y lesbianas en el cine*. Barcelona and Madrid: Egales.

Mira, Alberto and Fefa Vila (1999) 'Activismo en España', in Alberto Mira (ed.), *Para entendernos. Diccionario de cultura homosexual, gay y lésbica*. Barcelona: Ediciones de la Tempestad, p. 45.

Moi, Toril (1985) *Sexual/Textual Politics: Feminist Literary Theory*. London: Methuen.

Molina Foix, Vicente (1998) 'La teoría marica', *El País.com*, 23 June, section Cultura <http://www.elpais.com/articulo/cultura/DOMINGO/_PLACIDO_/OPERA/teoria/marica/elpepicul/19980623elpepicul_5/Tes> [last accessed 12 May 2012].

Molina Foix, Vicente (2003) 'El "caso Wanninkhof": lo oculto', *El País.com*, 10 October, section Opinión <http://www.elpais.com/articulo/opinion/caso/Wanninkhof/oculto/elpepiopi/20031010elpepiopi_12/Tes> [last accessed 12 May 2012].

Molina Foix, Vicente (2006) 'Mis bodas gays', *El País.com*, 24 June, section Opinión <http://www.elpais.com/articulo/opinion/bodas/gays/elpporopi/20060624elpepiopi_5/Tes> [last accessed 12 May 2012].

Molina Foix, Vicente (2007) 'El espejo del cine gay', *Tiempo*, 24–30 June <http://www.tiempodehoy.com/opinion/vicente-molina-foix/el-espejo-del-cine-gay> [last accessed 9 April 2012; now expired].

Molina Foix, Vicente (2009a) 'Cine o literatura', in *ElBoomeran(g).com*, 7 October <http://www.elboomeran.com/blog-post/79/7576/vicente-molina-foix/cine-o-literatura/> [last accessed 12 May 2012].

Molina Foix, Vicente (2009b) 'Diario de rodaje. 1 Piezas sueltas', in *ElBoomeran(g).com*, 14 November <http://www.elboomeran.com/blog-post/79/7648/vicente-molina-foix/diario-de-rodaje-1-piezas-sueltas/> [last accessed 12 May].

Molina Foix, Vicente (2009c) 'El otro Alas', in *ElBoomeran(g).com*, 26 November <http://www.elboomeran.com/blog-post/79/8072/vicente-molina-foix/el-otro-alas/> [last accessed 12 May 2012].

Molina Foix, Vicente (2010a) 'La película de Gil de Biedma', in *ElBoomeran(g).com*, 28 January <http://www.elboomeran.com/blog-post/79/8440/vicente-molina-foix/la-pelicula-de-gil-de-biedma/> [last accessed 12 May 2012].

Molina Foix, Vicente (2010b) 'Pospo', in *ElBoomeran(g).com*, 19 April <http://www.elboomeran.com/blog-post/79/8841/vicente-molina-foix/postpo/> [last accessed 12 May 2012].

Molina Foix, Vicente (2010c) 'Los jueves, cine', in *ElBoomeran(g).com*, 31 May <http://www.elboomeran.com/blog-post/79/9080/vicente-molina-foix/los-jueves-cine/> [last accessed 12 May 2012].

Monleón, Sigrid (2010) 'Gil de Biedma ante su película', *El Mundo*, 24 January, section Cultura, p. 51.

Moore, Andrew (2006) 'Neil Jordan's *The Crying Game*', in Robin Griffiths (ed.), *British Queer Cinema*. London and New York: Routledge, pp. 153–69.

Morán, Libertad (2006) *Mujeres estupendas*. Madrid: Odisea.

Morán, Libertad (2007) *Una noche más*. Madrid: Odisea.

Morgado, Nuria (2005) 'Entrevista: Una conversación con Elvira Lindo', *Arizona Journal of Hispanic Cultural Studies*, 9, 99–110.

Morte, Andrés (2004) *Tierra caliente*. Barcelona: Laertes.

Mucientes, Esther (2008) 'Indignación entre colectivos gays por las palabras de la Reina sobre homosexuales', in *ElMundo.es*, 30 October <http://www.elmundo.es/elmundo/2008/10/30/espana/1225351675.html> [last accessed 12 May 2012].

Müller, Enrique (2009) 'La española *Ander* presenta una historia sobre el mundo gay rural', in *ideal.es*, 2 December <http://www.ideal.es/granada/20090212/cultura/espanola-ander-presenta-historia-20090212.html> [last accessed 12 May 2012].

Nabal, Eduardo (2005) 'La hora de los malditos. Hacia una genealogía imposible de algo llamado New Queer Cinema', in David Córdoba, Javier Sáez and Paco Vidarte (eds), *Teoría Queer: Políticas bolleras, maricas, trans, mestizas*. Barcelona and Madrid: Egales, pp. 229–38.

'Nacho' (2008) Comment on *Una palabra tuya*, in *AmbienteG.com*, 11 September at 23:22, section Cine <http://www.ambienteg.com/cine/una-palabra-tuya> [last accessed 12 May 2012].

'Nazareno' (2009) Comment no. 2 in response to Raúl Madrid, 'Pedro Almodóvar, pedagogo de la realidad LGTB', in *DosManzanas.com*, 28 April at 10:39 <http://www.dosmanzanas.com/2009/04/pedro-almodovar-pedagogo-de-la-realidad-lgtb.html> [last accessed 12 May 2012].

Norandi, Elina (ed.) (2009a) *Ellas y nosotras: Estudios lesbianos sobre literatura escrita en castellano*. Barcelona and Madrid: Egales.

Norandi, Elina (2009b) 'Feminismo, genealogía y cancelación del patriarcado en las novelas de Isabel Franc-Lola Van Guardia', in Elina Norandi (ed.), *Ellas y nosotras: Estudios lesbianos sobre literatura escrita en castellano*. Barcelona and Madrid: Egales, pp. 115–31.

O'Sullivan, Sue (1994) 'Girls who kiss girls, and who cares?', in Diane Hamer and Belinda Budge (eds), *The Good, the Bad and the Gorgeous: Popular Culture's Romance with Lesbianism*. London: HarperCollins, pp. 78–95.

ohmygodmagazine (2010) 'Nacha la Macha entrevista a Concha Velasco', in *YouTube.com*, 20 December <http://www.youtube.com/watch?v=eaB0hcDZOyc> [last accessed 12 May 2012].

Orgullo Indignado (2011) 'Orgullo Indignado Transmaribolleras en lucha', in *orgulloindignado.com*, no date [June] <http://orgulloindignado.blogspot.com/2011/06/comenzamos.html> [last accessed 12 May 2012].

Ortiz, Tomás (2003) *Seguiré aquí cuando despiertes*. Madrid: Odisea.

Osborne, Raquel (2008) 'Entre el rosa y el violeta. Lesbianismo, feminismo y movimiento gay: relato de unos amores difíciles', in Raquel Platero Méndez (ed.), *Lesbianas. Discursos y representaciones*. Santa Cruz de Tenerife: Melusina, 85–105.

Palencia, Leandro (2005) 'Diamantes en la mina', *Zero*, 76, 54–8.

Palencia, Leandro (2011) *El cine queer en 33 películas*. Madrid: Editorial Popular.

Paternotte, David (2008) 'Les lieux d'activisme : le "mariage gai" en Belgique, en France et en Espagne', *Canadian Journal of Political Science / Revue canadienne de science politique*, 41.4, 935–52.

Pavlović, Tatjana (2003) *Despotic Bodies and Transgressive Bodies. Spanish Culture from Francisco Franco to Jesús Franco*. Albany, NY: SUNY Press.

Pelayo, Irene [Pelayo García, Irene] (2009) *Imagen fílmica de lesbianismo a través de los personajes protagonistas en el cine español*. PhD thesis, Universidad Complutense, Madrid.

Pérez Toledo, Roberto (2011) 'Corto en ruta: *Fuckbuddies,* de Juanma Carrillo', comment in *lavidaescorta.es* (via Fotogramas.es), 1 April <http://la-vida-es-corta.blogs.fotogramas.es/2011/04/01/corto-en-ruta-fuckbuddies-de-juanma-carrillo/> [last accessed 12 May 2012].

Pérez-Sánchez, Gema (2007) *Queer Transitions in Contemporary Spanish Culture*. New York: SUNY Press.

Perriam, Chris (2003a) *Stars and Masculinities in Spanish Cinema: From Banderas to Bardem*. Oxford: Oxford University Press.

Perriam, Chris (2003b) 'Heterosociality in *Segunda piel* (Gerardo Vera, 2000) and *Sobreviviré* (Alfonso Albacete and David Menkes, 1999): strong women or the same old story?', in Steven Marsh and Parvati Nair (eds), *Gender and Spanish Cinema*. Oxford: Berg, pp. 151–63.

Perriam, Chris (2007a) 'Victoria Abril in transnational context', *Hispanic Research Journal*, 8.1, 27–38.

Perriam, Chris (2007b) 'Sara Montiel: entre dos mitos', *Archivos de la filmoteca*, 54, 196–209.

Perriam, Chris (2011) 'Eduardo Noriega's transnational projections', in Lúcia Nagib, Chris Perriam and Rajinder Dudrah (eds), *Theorizing World Cinema*. London: I. B. Tauris, pp. 77–92.

Perriam, Chris (forthcoming) '*En la ciudad sin límites* (Antonio Hernández, España, 2002): dos o tres pasos hacia el pasado, y un paso hacia delante', in Manuel Palacio (ed.), *Memoria histórica en el cine de la Transición: represión interpretativa y violencia narrativa*. Madrid: Biblioteca Nueva.

Pertusa, Inmaculada and Nancy Vosburg (eds) (2009a) *Un deseo propio: Antología de escritoras españolas contemporáneas*. Barcelona: Bruguera.

Pertusa, Inmaculada and Nancy Vosburg (2009b) 'Un deseo propio: a Chloe le gusta Olivia', in Inmaculada Pertusa and Nancy Vosburg (eds), *Un deseo propio: Antología de escritoras españolas contemporáneas*. Barcelona: Bruguera, pp. 7–44.

Pertusa-Seva, Inmaculada (2011), 'Flavia Company: from lesbian passion to gender trouble', in Nancy Vosburg and Jacky Collins (eds), *Lesbian Realities/Lesbian Fictions in Contemporary Spain*. Lewisburg, PA: Bucknell University Press, pp. 236–67.

Pierrot (2010) *Un falo lo tiene cualquiera*. Barcelona: Morales i Torres.

Pineda, Empar (2007) 'Lesbiana, yo soy lesbiana, porque quiero y me da la gana', in Juan A. Herrero Brasas (ed.), *Primera Plana: ética y activismo – La construcción de una cultura queer en España*. Barcelona and Madrid: Egales, pp. 318–19.

Pineda, Empar (2008) 'Mi pequeña historia del lesbianismo organizado en el movimiento feminista de nuestro país', in Raquel Platero Méndez (ed.), *Lesbianas. Discursos y representaciones*. Santa Cruz de Tenerife: Melusina, pp. 31–55.

Pingree, Geoff (2004) 'Pedro Almodóvar and the New Politics of Spain', *Cineaste*, 30.1, 4–8.

Pita, Elena (2001) 'Conversaciones íntimas con Eusebio Poncela', in *El Mundo Magazine.es*, 24 June <http://www.elmundo.es/magazine/m91/textos/eusebio1.html> [last accessed 12 May 2012].

Platero, Lucas (2011) 'The narratives of transgender rights mobilisation in Spain', *Sexualities*, 14.5, 597–614.

Platero Méndez, Raquel (2005) '¿Invisibiliza el matrimonio homosexual a las lesbianas? Una crítica feminista sobre la construcción y representación del lesbianismo en el matrimonio homosexual', *Orientaciones: revista de homosexualidades*, 10, 103–22.

Platero Méndez, Raquel (2007a) 'Entre la invisibilidad y la igualdad formal: perspectivas feministas ante la representación del lesbianismo en el matrimonio homosexual', in Angie Simonis (ed.), *Amazonia: retos de visibilidad lesbiana*, vol. 2 of Félix Rodríguez González and Angie Simonis (eds), *Cultura, homosexualidad y homofobia*. Barcelona: Laertes, pp. 85–106; reprint, with minor revisions and updates, of Raquel Platero Méndez (2005) '¿Invisibiliza el matrimonio homosexual a las lesbianas? Una crítica feminista sobre la construcción y representación del lesbianismo en el matrimonio homosexual', *Orientaciones: revista de homosexualidades*, 10, 103–22.

Platero Méndez, Raquel (2007b) 'Love and the state: gay marriage in Spain: Spanish Law no. 13/2005, 1 July 2005, concerning, through a change in the Civil Code, the access of lesbians and gay men to the institution of marriage', *Feminist Legal Studies*, 15: 329–40.

Platero Méndez, Raquel (ed.) (2008) *Lesbianas. Discursos y representaciones*. Santa Cruz de Tenerife: Melusina.

Platero Méndez, Raquel (2011) 'Transitions and representations of lesbianism in the Spanish media', in Nancy Vosburg and Jacky Collins (eds), *Lesbian Realities/Lesbian Fictions in Contemporary Spain*, Lewisburg, PA: Bucknell University Press, pp. 60–103; English version of 'Las lesbianas en los medios de comunicación: madres, folclóricas y masculinas', in Raquel Platero

Méndez (ed.) (2008), *Lesbianas. Discursos y representaciones*. Santa Cruz de Tenerife: Melusina, pp. 307–38.

Pons, Ventura (2011) Biografía in *venturapons.cat (El Films de la Rambla)* <http://www.venturapons.cat/catala.html> [last accessed 12 May 2012].

Preciado, Beatriz (2005) 'Cuerpo y discurso en la obra de Judith Butler', in David Córdoba, Javier Sáez and Paco Vidarte (eds), *Teoría Queer: Políticas bolleras, maricas, trans, mestizas*, Barcelona and Madrid: Egales, pp. 111–32.

Preciado, Beatriz (2008) *Testo yonqui*. Madrid: Espasa Calpe.

Preciado, Beatriz (2011) *Manifiesto contrasexual*. Barcelona: Anagrama.

Prout, Ryan (2010) 'Speaking up / coming out: regions of authenticity in Juan Pinzás's gay Galician dogma trilogy', *Galicia*, 21, Issue B, 68–91.

Pujol Ozonas, Cristina (2011) *Fans, cinéfilos y cinéfagos: Una aproximación a las culturas y los gustos cinematográficos*. Barcelona: UOC.

Ramos, Alicia (1995) 'Eduardo Mendicutti: *Los novios búlgaros*' [review], *Hispania* 78.2, 314.

Rees-Roberts, Nick (2008) *French Queer Cinema*. Edinburgh: Edinburgh University Press.

Reger, Jo (1999) 'Bookstores', in *Encyclopedia of Lesbian and Gay Histories and Cultures*, vol. 1, ed. Bonnie Zimmerman. New York: Garland, pp. 125–6.

Rei, Álex (2005) *El diario de JL*. Madrid: Odisea.

Rei, Álex (2007) *Abriendo puertas*. Madrid: Odisea.

Resina, Joan Ramon and Ulrich Winter (eds) (2006) *Lugares de memoria de la Guerra Civil y el franquismo: Representaciones literarias y visuales*. Madrid and Frankfurt: Vervuert-Iberoamericana.

Retamar, Ángel (2000a) 'Ponerse a corto', *Zero*, 20, 66–8.

Retamar, Ángel (2000b) 'Cine-Barcelona Gay-Festival' [report on the 6th Mostra Internacional de Cinema Gai i Lésbic e Barcelona], *Zero*, 21, 86–9.

Rivadulla Corcón, X. H. (2010) 'I Encuentro de Guionistas', in *fagaweb. org (Foro de Asociaciones de Guionistas Audiovisuales (FAGA))*, no date [October] <http://www.fagaweb.org/?lg=3andid=4andnid=16> [last accessed 12 May 2012].

Robbins, Jill (2003) 'The (in)visible lesbian: the contradictory representations of female homosexuality in contemporary Spain', *Journal of Lesbian Studies*, 7.3, 107–31.

Robbins, Jill (2011) 'Lesbian literary identities in the Chueca book business', in Nancy Vosburg and Jacky Collins (eds), *Lesbian Realities/Lesbian Fictions in Contemporary Spain*. Lewisburg, PA: Bucknell University Press, pp. 149–72.

'robgordon' (2009) '¡Vuelve el destape!', in *Elséptimocielo.com*, no date [April] <http://e7cielo.blogspot.com/2009/04/vuelve-el-destape.html> [last accessed 12 May 2012].

Rodríguez González, Félix (ed.) (2007) *Perspectivas gays*, vol. 1 of Félix

Rodríguez González and Angie Simonis (eds), *Cultura, homosexualidad y homofobia*. Barcelona: Laertes.

'Rogue' (2010) '*80 Egunean*: Reseña Lesbicanaria', in *lesbicanarias.es*, 8 June <http://lesbicanarias.es/2010/06/08/80-egunean-resena-lesbicanaria/> [last accessed 12 May 2012].

Román, Ángel (2011) 'Anatomía de la emoción: La erotización de la mirada audiovisual en los contextos digitales en la obra de Juanma Carrillo', in *21 Le Mag (for your eyes only)*, no date [2010] <http://www.marianartes.com.ar/21%20Le%20Mag%202.pdf> [last accessed 12 May 2012].

Rubin, Joan Shelley (1992) *The Making of Middlebrow Culture*. Chapel Hill, NC and London: University of North Carolina Press.

Ruiz Mantilla, Jesús (2010) 'Controversia en Sodoma: Juan Marsé arremete contra la película sobre el poeta Gil de Biedma', *El País.com*, 8 January <http://www.elpais.com/articulo/cine/Controversia/Sodoma/elpepuculcin/20100108elpepicin_6/Tes> [last accessed 12 May 2012].

Russo, Vito (1987) [1981] *The Celluloid Closet*, 2nd revised edn. New York: Harper & Row.

Saenz, Noelia (2009) 'The absence of place in a borderless city: exploring the psychic and transnational spaces of En la ciudad sin limites', *Spectator – The University of Southern California Journal of Film and Television*, 29.1, 47–53 <http://cinema.usc.edu/archivedassets/096/15614.pdf> [last accessed 12 May 2012].

Sáez, Javier (2007) 'La destrucción de una cultura en España', in *Hartza.com*, no date <http://www.hartza.com/herrerobrasas.htm> [last accessed 12 May 2012].

Sáez, Javier and Sejo Carrascosa (2011) *Por el culo. Políticas anales*. Barcelona and Madrid: Egales.

Salanova, Marisol (2012) *Postpornografía*. Madrid: Pictografía.

Sánchez, Sergi (2007) 'Cansancio en la comedia española: llegan a la cartelera varios títulos que confirman el mal momento del género', *elcultural.es (El Mundo)*, 5 July, section Suplemento Cultural <http://www.elcultural.es/version_papel/CINE/20931/Cansancio_en_la_comedia_espanola> [last accessed 12 May 2012].

Sargeant, Amy (2002) 'The content and the form: invoking "pastness" in three recent retro films', in Claire Monk and Amy Sargeant (eds), *British Historical Cinema: The History, Heritage and Costume Film*. London and New York: Routledge, pp. 199–216.

Schehr, Lawrence R. (2005) 'Relire les homotextualités', in Lawrence R. Schehr (ed.), *Aimez-vous le queer?* Amsterdam and New York: Rodopi, pp. 5–11.

Screen [collective] (ed.) (1992) *The Sexual Subject: A Screen Reader in Sexuality*. London and New York: Routledge.

'sergiomora' (2010) Comment in response to '*Habitación en Roma*, Medem demuestra su decadencia', posted by Alberto Abuín, in *blogdecine.com*,

11 May at 17:02 <http://www.blogdecine.com/cine-espanol/habitacion-en-roma-medem-demuestra-su-decadencia> [last accessed 12 May 2012].

Shangay Express (2008) 'Concha Velasco, una actriz soberbia', in *shangay. com*, 27 February <http://www.shangay.com/nota/983/concha-velasco-una-actriz-soberbia> [last accessed 12 May 2012].

Shonfield, Katherine (2000) *Walls Have Feelings: Architecture, Film and the City*. London and New York: Routledge.

Simonis, Angie (ed.) (2007a) *Amazonia: retos de visibilidad lesbiana*, vol. 2 of Félix Rodríguez González and Angie Simonis (eds), *Cultura, homosexualidad y homofobia*. Barcelona: Laertes.

Simonis, Angie (2007b) 'Introducción: siempre nos quedará la ironía', in Angie Simonis (ed.), *Amazonia: retos de visibilidad lesbiana*, vol. 2 of Félix Rodríguez González and Angie Simonis (eds), *Cultura, homosexualidad y homofobia*. Barcelona: Laertes, pp. 9–18.

Smith, Paul Julian (1992) *Laws of Desire: Questions of Homosexuality in Spanish Writing and Film 1960–1990*. Oxford: Clarendon Press.

Smith, Paul Julian [1994] (2000a) *Desire Unlimited: The Cinema of Pedro Almodóvar*, 2nd edn. London: Verso

Smith, Paul Julian (2000b) 'Spanish quality TV? The periodistas notebook', *Journal of Spanish Cultural Studies*, 1.2, 173–91.

Smith, Paul Julian (2003) *Contemporary Spanish Culture: Television, Fashion, Art and Film*. London: Polity.

Smith, Paul Julian (2010a) 'When Spanish cultural studies met TV studies: travelling narratives and life strategies', *Journal of Spanish Cultural Studies*, 11.3–4, 305–14.

Smith, Paul Julian (2010b) 'Hispanic gay autobiography: from text to film', David Vilaseca Memorial Lecture given at Royal Holloway, University of London, 19 October; audio recording available at <http://backdoorbroadcasting.net/2010/10/paul-julian-smith-hispanic-gay-autobiography-from-text-to-film/> [last accessed 12 May 2012].

Smith, Paul Julian (2011) 'Spanish Spring', *Sight and Sound*, 21.7, 34–7.

'Sofia/Srta Russ' (2007) '*A mi madre le gustan las mujeres*' review comment no. 4, in *www.culturalesbiana.blogsome.com*, 22 June at 12:22 <http://culturalesbiana.blogsome.com/2005/11/11/a-mi-madre-le-gustan-las-mujeres/#comments> [last accessed 23 August 2011, now expired].

Soley-Beltran, Patricia (2010) *Transexualidad y la matriz heterosexual*. Barcelona: Bellaterra.

Soria, Alfonso (2009) '*El cónsul de Sodoma*' review note, in *www.chueca.com*, 23 December, section Cine <http://www.chueca.com/cine/consul-sodoma. html> [last accessed 12 May 2012].

Soto, Francisco (2002) 'García Lorca, Federico' encyclopedia entry, in *www. glbtq.com: An Encyclopedia of Gay, Lesbian, Bisexual, Transgender, and Queer Culture*, no date, section Literature <http://www.glbtq.com/literature/garcialorca_f.html> [last accessed 12 May 2012].

Spargo, Tamsin (1999) *Foucault and Queer Theory*. Cambridge: Icon Books.

Stacey, Jackie and Sarah Street (eds) (2007) *Queer Screen: A* Screen *Reader*. London and New York: Routledge.

Stevenson, Jack (2003) *Dogme Uncut: Lars von Trier, Thomas Vinterberg, and the Gang That Took on Hollywood*. Santa Monica, CA: Santa Monica Press.

Stone, Rob (2004) '¡Victoria? A modern Magdalene', in Steven Marsh and Parvati Nair (eds), *Gender and Spanish Cinema*. Oxford: Berg, pp. 165–82.

Straayer, Chris and Tom Waugh (eds) (2005) 'Queer film and video festival forum: take one: curators speak out', *GLQ: A Journal of Lesbian and Gay Studies*, 11.4, 579–603.

Straayer, Chris and Tom Waugh (eds) (2006) 'Queer film and video festival forum, take two: critics speak out', *GLQ: A Journal of Lesbian and Gay Studies*, 12.4, 599–625.

Suárez, Juan A. (2006) 'Surprise me', in Chris Straayer and Tom Waugh (eds), 'Queer film and video festival forum, take two: critics speak out', *GLQ: A Journal of Lesbian and Gay Studies*, 12.4, 600–2.

Subero, Gustavo (2006) 'The different caminos of Latino homosexuality in Francisco J. Lombardi's *No se lo digas a nadie*', *Studies in Hispanic Cinemas*, 2.3, 189–204.

Subero, Gustavo (forthcoming) *Queer Masculinities in Latin American Cinema: Male Bodies and Narrative Representations*. London: I. B. Tauris.

Sullivan, Nikki (2003) *A Critical Introduction to Queer Theory*. New York: New York University Press.

Suso, Rut (2011) Textual presentation, in *vimeo.com: rutsuso*, no date [November] <http://vimeo.com/user9176013> [last accessed 12 May 2012].

Suso, Rut and María Pavón (2009) Textual presentation, in *vimeo.com: rutsusomariapavon*, text, April/in process <http://vimeo.com/user1520100> [last accessed 12 May 2012].

'Tahamata' (2009) 'Mentiras y gordas de una Ministra de Cultura' comment, in *miguel-delamo.blogspot.co.uk*, 7 April at 06:13 <http://miguel-delamo.blogspot.com/2009/04/mentiras-y-gordas-de-una-ministra-de.html> [last accessed 12 May 2012].

Tasker, Yvonne (1994) 'Pussy Galore: lesbian images and lesbian desire in the popular cinema', in Diane Hamer and Belinda Budge (eds), *The Good, the Bad and the Gorgeous: Popular Culture's Romance with Lesbianism*. London: Pandora, pp. 172–83.

'terrorinword' (2011) '¿Guión? ¿Qué guión?' comment, in *ecartelera.com*, 25 June at 15:49, section Película: Crítica (Mentiras y gordas) <http://www.ecartelera.com/peliculas/3135/mentiras-y-gordas/critica/4839/> [last accessed 12 May 2012].

The Big Bean and The Human Bean Band (2011) 'Sobre la producción de *Spinnin*'', in La Higuera, '*Spinnin*': comentario' <http://www.lahiguera.net/cinemania/pelicula/4372/comentario.php> [last accessed 12 May 2012].

Tormo, Luis (2010) 'Preestreno de *El cónsul de Sodoma* de Sigfrid Monleón en los cines Babel de Valencia' review, in *Aquí un amigo – El blog de Encadena2*, 7 January at 20:43 <http://aquiunamigo-elblogdeencadenados.blogspot.com/2010/01/preestreno-de-el-consul-de-sodoma-de.html> [last accessed 12 May 2012].

Trans-Block (2011) 'Mi sexualidad es una creación artística', in *transblock.wordpress.com: Piratas del género*, 11 February <http://transblock.wordpress.com/2011/02/11/mi-sexualidad-es-una-creacion-artistica/> [last accessed 12 May 2012].

Triana Toribio, Núria (2011) '*Ficxixón* and *Seminci*: two Spanish film festivals at the end of the festivals era', *Journal of Spanish Cultural Studies*, 12.2, 217–36.

Tropiano, Stephen (1997) 'Out of the cinematic closet: homosexuality in the films of Eloy de la Iglesia', in Marsha Kinder (ed.), *Refiguring Spain: Cinema/Media/Representation*. Durham, NC and London: Duke University Press, pp. 157–77.

Trujillo Barbadillo, Gracia (2005) 'Desde los márgenes: Prácticas y representaciones de los grupos *queer* en el Estado Español', in Grupo de Trabajo Queer (ed.), *El eje del mal es heterosexual: Figuraciones, movimientos y prácticas feministas queer*. Madrid: Traficantes de Sueños, pp. 29–44.

Trujillo Barbadillo, Gracia (2008a) *Deseo y resistencia: Treinta años de movilización lesbiana en el Estado Español (1977–2007)*. Barcelona and Madrid: Egales.

Trujillo Barbadillo, Gracia (2008b) 'Sujetos y miradas inapropiables/adas: el discurso queer', in Raquel Platero Méndez (ed.), *Lesbianas. Discursos y representaciones*. Santa Cruz de Tenerife: Melusina, pp. 107–19.

Tsuchiya, Akiko (2002) 'The "new" female subject and the commodification of gender in the works of Lucia Etxebarria', *Romance Studies*, 20.1, 77–87.

Ugarte Pérez, Francisco Javier (2008) '¿De qué homosexualidad en el cine hablamos cuando se menciona la homosexualidad en el cine?', in *Lesgaicine (co-ord) Programme to 13th Festival Internacional de Cine Lésbico y Gai de Madrid*. Madrid: Fundación Triángulo, pp. 140–2.

Vall, Pere (2009) 'Mentiras y gordas', in *fotogramas.es*, no date, section Película: Crítica <http://www.fotogramas.es/Peliculas/Mentiras-y-gordas/Critica> [last accessed 12 May 2011].

Vázquez García, Francisco and Richard Cleminson (2011) *Los invisibles: Una historia de la homosexualidad masculina en España, 1850–1936*. Granada: Comares; revised translated version of '*Los invisibles': A History of Male Homosexuality in Spain, 1850–1939*. Cardiff: University of Wales Press, 2007.

Vélez-Pelligrini, Laurentini (2011) *Sujetos de contra-discurso: Una historia intelectual de la producción teórica gay, lesbiana y queer en España*. Barcelona: Bellaterra.

'Veruska Morales Roa' (2010) Facebook comment on EnikPro, Facebook page for *Flores en el parque*, 13 August at 12:02 <http://www.facebook.com/pages/Flores-en-el-Parque-Flowers-at-the-Park-by-Mariel-Macia/14555082 2138963> [last accessed 12 May 2012].

Vidarte, Paco (2007a) *Ética marica*. Barcelona and Madrid: Egales.

Vidarte, Paco (2007b) 'El internauta desnudo: la autoimagen pornográfica en el imaginario yoico', in *hartza.com*, no date <http://www.hartza.com/pacopornoweb.htm> [last accessed 12 May 2012].

Vila Nuñez, Fefa (2005) 'La fuga de las bestias', in David Córdoba, Javier Sáez and Paco Vidarte (eds), *Teoría Queer: Políticas bolleras, maricas, trans, mestizas*. Barcelona and Madrid: Egales, pp. 181–6.

Vilarós, Teresa (1998) *El mono del desencanto. Una crítica cultural de la transición española (1973–1993)*. Madrid: Siglo XXI.

Vilaseca, David (2003) *Hindsight and the Real: Subjectivity in Gay Hispanic Autobiography*. Bern: Peter Lang.

Vilaseca, David (2010) *Queer Events: Post-deconstructive Subjectivities in Spanish Writing and Film 1960s–1990s*. Liverpool: Liverpool University Press.

Villamil, Fernando (2004) *La transformación de la identidad gay en España*. Madrid: Universidad Complutense, Facultad de Ciencias Políticas y Sociología/Los Libros de la Catarata.

Villena, Luis Antonio de (2000) 'Gil de Biedma: Vocación de escándalo', *El Mundo*, 8 January, section Cultura, p. 49.

Villena, Luis Antonio de (2006) *Retrato (con flash) de Jaime Gil de Biedma*. Barcelona: Seix Barral.

Villora, Pedro Manuel (2000) 'Eusebio Poncela: "Mi profesión también son mis novios"', *Zero*, 14, 68–75.

Viñuales, Olga [1999] (2006) *Identidades lésbicas*, 2nd edn. Barcelona: Ediciones Bellaterra.

Visible Cinema (2011) 1 Muestra de Cine de Temática LGTB (A Coruña), in *www.festivalgayvisible.com: visible cinema*, April <http://www.festivalgayvisible.com/visiblecinema/cinema.html> [last accessed 12 May 2012].

Visible11 (2011) Programme for 7ª Edición Visible Madrid: Festival Internacional de Cultura LGTB de COGAM FELGTB, in *festivalgayvisible.com*, June–July <http://www.festivalgayvisible.com/revistaflash5/Default.html> [last accessed 12 May 2012].

'volandovengo' (2008) Vimeo textual presentation, in *vimeo.com: volandovengo*, December <http://vimeo.com/volandovengocom> [last accessed 12 May 2012].

Vosburg, Nancy (2011) '"All L breaks loose": Lola Van Guardia's lesbian trilogy', in Nancy Vosburg and Jacky Collins (eds), *Lesbian Realities/Lesbian Fictions in Contemporary Spain*. Lewisburg, PA: Bucknell University Press, pp. 193–210.

Vosburg, Nancy and Jacky Collins (eds) (2011a) *Lesbian Realities/Lesbian Fictions in Contemporary Spain*. Lewisburg, PA: Bucknell University Press.

Vosburg, Nancy and Jacky Collins (2011b) 'Introduction: lesbian identity in Spain', in Nancy Vosburg and Jacky Collins (eds), *Lesbian Realities/Lesbian Fictions in Contemporary Spain*. Lewisburg, PA: Bucknell University Press, pp. 9–27.

Waldron, Darren (2001) 'Fluidity of gender and sexuality in *Gazon maudit*', in Lucy Mazdon (ed.), *France on Film: Reflections on Popular French Cinema*. London: Wallflower Press, pp. 65–78.

Warner, Michael (1994) 'Introduction', in Michael Warner (ed.), *Fear of a Queer Planet: Queer Politics and Social Theory*. Minneapolis and London: University of Minnesota Press, pp. vii–xxxi.

Waugh, Thomas (2000) *The Fruit Machine: Twenty Years of Writings on Queer Cinema*. Durham, NC: Duke University Press.

Wilton, Tamsin (ed.) (1995) *Immortal, Invisible: Lesbians and the Moving Image*. London and New York: Routledge.

Yon González (2011) Facebook page for Yon González/El Internado, photo album <http://www.facebook.com/media/set/?set=a321309438494.149878 .321302133494andtype=3> [last accessed 5 May 2012].

Young, Claire F. L. and Susan B. Boyd (2007) 'Challenging heteronormativity? Reaction and resistance to the legal recognition of same-sex partnerships', in Dorothy E. Chunn, Susan B. Boyd and Hester Lessard (eds), *Reaction and Resistance: Feminism, Law, and Social Change*. Vancouver: University of British Columbia, pp. 262–90.

Zatlin, Phyllis (2007) 'From stage to screen: the adaptations of Ventura Pons', *Contemporary Theatre Review*, 17.3, 434–5.

Zerolo, Pedro (2007) 'Matrimonio y dignidad', in Juan A. Herrero Brasas (ed.), *Primera Plana: ética y activismo – La construcción de una cultura queer en España*. Barcelona and Madrid: Egales, pp. 52–62.

Zielinski, Ger (2011) *Furtive Glances: On the Cultural Politics of Lesbian and Gay Film Festivals*. Abstract of PhD thesis 'Furtive, Steady Glances: On the Cultural Politics of Lesbian and Gay Film Festivals', McGill University, Montreal, 2008 <http://media.mcgill.ca/en/node/918/print> [last accessed 12 May 2012].

INDEX

3 metros sobre el cielo (*Three Steps over Heaven*) (Fernando González Molina, 2011), 88

20 centímetros (*20 Centimetres*) (Ramón Salazar, 2005), 7, 15, 82, 90

80 egunean (*For 80 Days*) (Jon Garaño and José María Goenaga, 2010), 39, 61–2, 126

101 Reykjavik (Baltasar Kormakur, 2001), 68

A domicilio: o incluso también el amor (*At Home: or Love As Well*) (Mariel Maciá, 2007), 103–4

A los que gritan (*Sara's Shout*) (Juanan Martínez, 2010), 50, 119

A mi madre le gustan las mujeres (*My Mother Likes Women*) (Inés París and Daniela Fejerman, 2002), 15, 43, 65

A oscuras (*In The Dark*) (Eli Navarro, 2009), 40, 100

A un dios desconocido (*To An Unknown God*) (Jaime Chávarri, 1977), 51, 58

Abrazos rotos, Los (*Broken Embraces*) (Pedro Almodóvar, 2009), 87

Abril, Victoria, 38, 48, 64, 66–8

Acción reacción (*Action/Reaction*) (David Illundain, 2008), 148

activism, 37, 66, 101–4, 138
    queer, 13–14, 22

age difference, in same-sex relationships, 31, 70, 78–9, 81, 120, 136–7

Aguilera, Marián, 84

Aizpuru, Itziar, 61–2

Albacete, Alfonso *see Entre vivir y soñar; I Love You Baby; Más que amor frenesí; Mentiras y gordas; Sobreviviré; see also* David Menkes

Albalá, Javier, 46

Albaladejo, Heli, 134

Albaladejo, Miguel, 29, 35, 98–9, 134

Albert, Nao, 140

Alegre ma non troppo (Fernando Colomo, 1994), 15

Alguien se despierta en mi cama (*Someone Wakes Up In My Bed*) (Rut Suso, 2008), 106

Alice in Andrew's Land (Lauren Mackenzie, 2011), 119

Aliteración (*Alliteration*) (Roberto Menéndez, 2005), 19

Almas perdidas (*Lost Souls*) (Julio de la Fuente, 2008), 19, 58

Almejas y mejillones (*Mussels and Clams*) (Marcos Carnevale, 2000), 42, 86

Almodóvar, Agustín, 5

Almodóvar, Pedro, 10, 39, 48, 50–3, 66, 78, 79, 80–1, 90, 99, 140; *see also Átame; Entre tinieblas; Kika; La ley del deseo; La mala educación; Matador; Pepi, Luci, Bom y otras chicas del montón; ¿Qué he hecho yo para merecer esto!; Tacones lejanos; Todo sobre mi madre*

Alterio, Ernesto, 25

Alterio, Héctor, 66, 139

Alterio, Malena, 133

Álvarez, Emma, 100

Amantes (*Lovers*) (Vicente Aranda, 1989), 67

Amic/Amat (*Beloved, Friend*) (Ventura Pons, 1998), 14, 58, 75, 77, 78

Amor de hombre (*The Love of a Man*) (Yolanda García Serrano and Juan Luis Iborra, 1997), 45, 129–30

Anaya, Elena, 96–7

Andamio (*Scaffolding*) (Juanma Carrillo, 2012), 108

Ander (Roberto Castón, 2009), 14, 30, 39, 58

Año sin amor, Un (*A Year Without Love*) (Anahí Berneri, 2005), 54

Aquí no hay quien viva (*This Is No Place for Anyone to Live In*) (Antena 3), 71

Aragüés, Pablo *see Luz*

Aranda, Vicente, 65, 67

Argoitia, José Ramón, 61

Arias, Celia, 101
Arias, Imanol, 66
Aristarain, Adolfo *see Martín (Hache)*
Armas, Ana de, 87, 89
Armendáriz, Montzo *see Historias del Kronen*
Armenteros, Carlos, 109, 128–9
Arrebato (Rapture) (Iván Zulueta, 1980), 51, 66
Átame (Tie Me Up, Tie Me Down) (Pedro Almodóvar, 1990), 67
Ataque verbal (Verbal Attack) (Miguel Alabaladejo, 1999), 98–9, 134
Atxaga, Bernardo, 59
auteurism, 39, 66, 80, 85, 90, 95, 111, 114
Ayaso, Dunia *see Perdona, bonita, pero Lucas me quería a mí*
Azcona, Anna, 47

Balcón abierto, El (The Open Window) (Jaime Camino, 1984), 142
Balduz, Dafnis, 78
Balletbò-Coll, Marta
  actor, 47, 84
  director, 6, 38, 48, 90, 125
  see also Costa Brava (Family Album); *Gazon maudit*; *Sévigné (Júlia Berkowitz)*
Banderas, Antonio, 51–2, 66
Bañophobia (Fear of the Ladies) (Blanca H. Salazar, 2009), 41, 101
Barceló, Manel, 78
Barcelona
  activist groups, 8, 14, 93
  festivals, 2, 24, 82, 115–18
  Gayxample area, 126
  literary scene, 71, 143
  as setting, 33–4, 58, 75, 143–4
Barcelona, un mapa (Barcelona – A Map) (Ventura Pons, 2007), 58
Bardem, Carlos, 31
Bardem, Javier, 66, 67, 69
Bardem, Miguel *see Más que amor, frenesí*
Baroja, Pío, 59
Barriga, Cecilia, 6
Barros, Marra, 100
Basque cinema, 60–1
'bear' culture, 35, 72–3, 84
Beautiful Thing (Hettie Macdonald, 1996), 34, 49
Becerra, Paco, 83
Belén, Ana, 72
Belle époque (Fernando Trueba, 1993), 86
Beltrán, Javier, 141
Benzal, Saida, 110
Bergonzini, Bruno, 54
Berneri, Anahí *see Año sin amor, Un*
Bigas Luna, Juan José *see Jamón, Jamón*
biopics *see Little Ashes; El cónsul de Sodoma*
bisexuality 6, 70
Bize, Matías *see En la cama*

Blanco, J. F. *see Dreams Are the Matter We Are Made Of*
Blokes (Marialy Rivas, 2010), 117
Blum, Bettiana, 26
Bobo, Jacinto, 116
Bock, Maria *see Skallaman*
bookshops (LGBT), 12, 30, 92–5, 123–4, 133
Borau, José Luis *see Furtivos*
Bosé, Bimba, 143
Botto, Juan Diego, 131
Bradbury, Jason *see We Once Were Tide*
Breach of Etiquette (Mark Levine, 2010), 119
Brondo, Cristina, 45
Buena estrella, La (The Lucky Star) (Ricardo Franco, 1997), 131
Buenos días (Laura A. Cancho, 2008), 100
Buñuel, Luis, 9, 141, 142
  L'Age d'or, 111

Cabezas, Paco *see Carne de neón*
Cabrera, Ayo *see Tiras de mi piel*
Cachorro (Bear Cub) (Miguel Alabaladejo, 2004), 35, 85
Calentito, El (Chus Gutiérrez, 2005), 49, 120
Cambio de sexo (Sex Change) (Vicente Aranda, 1975), 65
Camino, Jaime *see Balcón abierto, El*
Camino de Moïses, El (Moses's Way) (Cecilia Barriga, 2004), 6
camp, 44, 51, 53, 72, 83, 84, 135–6
Campillo sí, quiero (Campillo, Yes; I Do) (Andrés Rubio, 2007), 27, 40
Campoy, Comba, 31
Cancho, Laura A., 6, 100
Caníbales (Cannibals) (Juanma Carrillo, 2009), 108, 129
Cantó, Toni, 81
Carícies (Caresses) (Ventura Pons, 1998), 45, 77, 78
Carne de neón (Red Light Fodder) (Paco Cabezas, 2005), 68
Carnevale, Marcos *see Almejas y mejillones*
Carrillo, Juanma, 14, 41, 90, 107–11
  EmocionesProduce, 101
  video artist, 19, 107, 110–11
  see also Caníbales; Fuckbuddies; Muro; Perfect Day
Casal Lambda, 93
Casamajor, Roger, 54
Casas, Mario, 64, 87
Castiñeiras, Monti, 31
Castón, Roberto, 14, 30, 39, 44, 58
Catalan cinema, 47, 66, 74–9, 116
Catalonia
  culture, 76, 78
  identity, 47
Caudeli, Ruth *see Dos maneras y media de morir*
Caza, La (The Hunt) (Carlos Saura, 1965), 109

Cervera, Mónica, 82
Chao, Ernesto, 31
Chaplin, Geraldine, 55
Charles, Leslie, 47
Chávarri, Jaime, 79; *see also A un dios desconocido*; *Las cosas del querer*; *Las cosas del querer II*
Chica, Pablo de la, 17–18
Chica busca chica (Girl Seeks Girl) (Terra [web] TV), 6, 65, 125
Chloe (Atom Egoyan, 2009), 95
Chueca *see* Madrid
Chuecatown (*Boystown*) (Juan Flahn, 2007), 35, 43, 65, 66, 71, 81–4
Ciáurriz, Alberto, 127–8
CIMA (Asociación de Mujeres Cineastas y de Medios Audiovisuales), 102
cinephilia, 89, 91, 94, 114
civil unions and partnerships, 1, 5, 21–2, 27, 134
Cixous, Hélène, 47
Clandestinos (*In Hiding*) (Antonio Hens, 2007), 49, 65
Claros motivos del deseo, Los (*The Clear Motives of Desire*) (Miguel Picazo, 1977), 48
Claver, Juan Carlos *see Electroshock*
clichés, 42, 44, 68, 70, 72–3, 117, 139
closetry, 31, 40, 43, 45, 58, 69, 78, 86, 90, 96, 98, 100–1, 109, 128
COGAM (Colectivo de Lesbianas, Gays, Transexuales y Bisexuales de Madrid), 28, 92, 119
Col.lectiu Gai de Barcelona, 93
Colomo, Fernando *see Alegre ma non troppo*
Coll, Isabel *see Turistas*
Collado, Adrià, 71
Collet, Jordi, 46
comedy, 24, 25, 26, 29, 45, 69, 71–3, 83–4, 85, 99, 126, 129–30, 136
and reactionary representations, 42–4
and LGBT visibility, 43
coming out, 39, 42, 48–50, 65, 71, 74, 80–1, 82, 85–6, 90, 119, 124, 141; *see also* identity
Conde, Dámaso, 68
Conde, Víctor *see Lesbos Invaders From Outer Space*
Cónsul de Sodoma, El (*The Consul of Sodom*) (Sigrid Monleón, 2009), 39, 69, 138, 142–3, 146
Cortés, Salva *see Terapia de choque*
Cosas del querer, Las (*The Things of Love*) (Jaime Chávarri, 1989), 15
Cosas del querer II, Las (*The Things of Love II*) (Jaime Chávarri, 1994), 43
Costa Brava (*Family Album*) (Marta Balletbò-Coll, 1994), 47
Crespo, Esteban *see Lala*
Crespo, María *see Sirenito*

Cría cuervos (*Raise Ravens*) (Carlos Saura, 1976), 59
cruising, 82, 108–9, 129, 142
Cruz, Penélope, 68
Crying Game, The (Neil Jordan, 1992), 10
Cuerpos deshonrados (Dishonoured Bodies) (Juanma Carrillo, 2010), 110

Desenlace, El (*The Ending*) (Juan Pinzás, 2005), 31
Días de voda (*Wedding Days*) (Juan Pinzás, 2002), 31, 69
Díaz Yanes, Agustín, 67–8
Díez, Diana, 102
Diocou, Madi, 140
Diputado, El (*The Deputy/The Congressman*) (Eloy de la Iglesia, 1978), 14
Dios de madera, El (*The Wooden God*) (Vicente Molina Foix, 2010), 6, 40, 85, 138–41
Doble fila (*Double Parking*) (Olaf González Scheeneweiss, 2011), 120
Dos lados de la cama, Los (*The Two Sides of the Bed*) (Emilio Martínez Lázaro, 2005), 24, 43, 45, 100
Dos maneras y media de morir (Two and a Half Ways to Die) (Ruth Caudeli, 2011), 117
drag *see* transvestite performance
Dreams Are the Matter We Are Made Of (J. F. Blanco, 2007), 19
Drowning by Numbers (Peter Greenaway, 1988), 33
Dueñas, Lola, 45

Egoyan, Atom *see Chloe*
Eguileor, Zorion, 61
El Deseo (production company), 5
Electroshock (Juan Carlos Claver, 2006), 38, 39, 56–8, 65
Elias, Carmen, 56–7
Eloïse (Jesús Garay, 2009), 6, 14, 39–40, 100
EmocionesProduce *see* Carrillo, Juanma
En construcción (*In Construction*) (José Luis Guerin, 2001), 108
En la cama (*In Bed*) (Matías Bize, 2005), 95
En la ciudad/A la ciutat (*In The City*) (Cesc Gay, 2003), 6, 45, 50, 101
En malas compañías (*Doors Cut Down*) (Antonio Hens, 2000), 50, 65, 81, 120
Enríquez, Daniel, 116
Entre tinieblas (*Dark Habits*) (Pedro Almodóvar, 1983), 38, 52
Entre vivir y soñar (*Searching for Love*) (Alfonso Albacete and David Menkes, 2004), 131
Era outra vez (*Once Upon Another Time*) (Juan Pinzás, 2000), 31

Escalera, La (The Stairwell) (Rut Suso, 2011), 104
Escobar, Luis *see Muy mujer*
Esperas (Long Waits) (Juanma Carrillo, 2011), 108–9
Esquinas del arco iris, Las (The Different Corners of the Rainbow) (Purificación Mora, 2006), 72
Esquivel Christian, 59
Esteban, Belén, 88
Ester (María Pavón and Rut Suso, 2004), 97–8, 104
Étoiles, Les (Rut Suso, 2011), 98, 107
Europride *see* Madrid
Etxeandia, Asier, 89
Etxebarria, Lucía, 85, 123, 130–1, 134

family
    alternative, 35, 68, 116–17
    normative, 23, 32, 63–4, 82, 128, 129, 134, 144
    patriarchal, 24, 74, 78
Fassbinder, Rainer Werner *see Querelle*
Federación Estatal de Lesbianas, Gays, Transexuales, y Bisexuales (FELGTB) (State Federation of Lesbians, Gays, Transexuals and Bisexuals), 21, 22, 72
Fejerman, Daniela, 6; *see also A mi madre le gustan las mujeres*
Femenía, Paco, 148
Fernán Gómez, Fernando, 54–6
Fernández, Félix *see Perfect Day*
Fernández, Miguel, 128
Fernández, Olav, 27, 33
Fernández, Ramón *see No desearás al vecino del quinto*
Fernández-Muro, Marta, 99
festivals, 2, 4, 8, 10, 15, 20, 46, 49, 65, 66, 79, 81, 90, 91, 93, 108, 112–21, 124
    A Coruña Visible, 112
    Annual Festival of New Spanish Cinema (USA, travelling), 61
    CineGaiLesAST (Asturias), 102, 115
    Entendiéndonos (Granada), 77
    FanCineGay (Extremadura), 77, 141
    Festival de Cine y Derechos Humanos (San Sebastián), 60
    Festival de Cultura LGTB Visible (Madrid), 137
    Festival Lésbico MíraLes (Madrid), 92
    Festival del Sol (Las Palmas de Gran Canaria), 82, 103
    FICLGB (Barcelona), 82, 115–18
    FIRE!! (Barcelona), 24, 107–8, 112, 113
    LesGaiCineMad (Madrid), 4, 69, 77, 82, 88, 101, 102, 103, 108, 112, 115, 118–21
    Málaga Film Festival, 66, 138
    Mimi (Barcelona/Sitges), 115

Mostra Lambda, 43: *see also* festivals: FIRE!!
Muestra de Cine Gay, Lésbico, Bisexual y Transexual (Fuerteventura), 115
Muestra de Cine Lésbico (Madrid), 103, 112
Notodofilmfest (web-based), 108
Noche en Blanco (Madrid), 149
Optica (multi-country), 110
Pequeño Certamen de Cine de Ambiente La Pecca (Seville), 115
programming, 9, 113
San Sebastián Film Festival, 61
Tokyo International Gay Film Festival, 40
Zinegoak (Bilbao), 61, 67, 72, 100, 107, 108, 112, 113, 138
Fioravanti, Igor *see Sueño de Ibiza, El*
Física o química (Physics or Chemistry) (Antena 3), 65, 89
Flahn, Juan *see Chuecatown*
Flores en el parque (o los primeros besos) (*Flowers in the Park, or Those First Kisses*) (Mariel Maciá, 2006), 102–3
Flores también producen espinas, Las (Flowers Also Yield Thorns) (Juanma Carrillo, 2007), 110
Fluid (Dara Sklar, 2011), 119
Food of Love (*Manjar de amor*) (Ventura Pons, 2002), 49, 74, 77
Forasters (*Strangers*) (Ventura Pons, 2008), 78
Forqué, Verónica, 26, 64, 85, 86–7
Frears, Stephen *see My Beautiful Launderette*
Franc, Isabel, 101
Franco, Ricardo *see* González-Sinde, Ángeles
Francoism
    annulment of civil marriages, 134
    legal and medical discourses on homosexuality, 41
    pseudo–clinical treatment of homosexuality, 57, 115
    political resistance to, 55
    propaganda, 29
    repression relating to homosexuality, 19, 58, 128, 137
Front d'Alliberament Gai de Catalunya (Gay Liberation Front of Catalonia), 93
Fuckbuddies (Juanma Carrillo, 2011), 16, 17
Fuembuena, Eduardo *see Voces*
Fuente, Julio de la *see Almas perdidas*
Fuentes, Carlos, 64, 73, 83
Fundación Triángulo, 4, 27
Fuera de carta (*Chef's Special*) (Nacho G. Velilla, 2008), 53
Furtivos (*Poachers*) (José Luis Borau, 1975), 59

Gabaldón Orcoyen, Miguel *see Pasajero*
Galicia, culture, 31–2
Gamarra, Inma, 100

Garaño, Jon *see 80 egunean*
Garay, Jesús *see Eloïse*
García, Esther, 5
García Bernal, Gael, 52–3
García Borda, Miguel *see Todo me pasa a mí*
García Lorca, Federico, 93, 137, 141–2
    Casa de Bernarda Alba, La (*The House of Bernardo Alba*), 59
García Pérez, José Luis, 35
García Serrano, Yolanda *see Amor de hombre*
Gazon maudit (*French Twist*) (Marta Balletbò-Coll, 1995), 47, 67–8
Gay, Cesc *see En la ciudad*; *Krámpack*
gay fiction, 126–9
Gender Identity Law *see* Ley de Identidad de Género
Gil de Biedma, Jaime, 69–71, 109, 118, 143–6
Gimeno, Beatriz, 21–2, 94
Giner, Silvia, 84
Goenaga, José María *see 80 egunean*
Gómez, Juan, 110
Gómez, Elena, 100
Gómez, Tania, 117
Gómez Baker, Carlos *see Lo que nunca te dije*
Gómez Pereira, Manuel, 25, 87, 130
González, Yon, 87–9
González Molina, Fernando *see 3 metros sobre el cielo*
González Scheeneweiss, Olaf *see Doble fila*
González-Sinde, Ángeles
    Minister of Culture, 2, 134
    President of Academia de las Artes y las Ciencias Cinematográficas de España, 131
    screenwriter, 131, 152
    see also Una palabra tuya
Guerin, José Luis *see En construcción*
Guerriller@s (Montse Pujantell, 2010), 6–7, 114
Guillén Creach, Julia *see Sombras en el viento*
Gurruchaga, Javier, 31
Gutiérrez, Chus
    director, 6, 89, 102: *see also El calentito*; *Me gusta estar enamorada – a veces me siento muy sola*
    Vice-Chair of CIMA, 102
Guznar, Susana, 125

Haba, Manuel *see Pablo ¿has puesto la lavadora?*
Habitación en Roma/Room in Rome (Julio Medem, 2010), 6, 95–7, 148
Happy Day in Barcelona (Johann Pérez Viera, 2009), 33–4
Hendler, Daniel, 26
Hens, Antonio, 41, 90, 115; *see also Clandestinos*; *En malas compañías*

Herederos (The Inheritors) (TVE), 89
Hernández, Mili, 58, 92, 100, 124
Hernández, Óscar, 128
heteronormativity, 3, 19, 29, 55–6, 61, 70
    anti-, 11, 68, 145
HIV/AIDS, 4, 14, 27, 35, 136
    as documentary subject, 19–20
Historias del Kronen (*Stories of the Kronen*) (Montzo Armendáriz, 1995), 69, 87
Homar, Lluís, 26
Hombres de Paco, Los (Paco's Men) (Antena 3), 84, 87, 89
Homo Baby Boom: Famílies de lesbianes i gais (Homo Baby Boom: Lesbian and Gay Families) (Anna Boluda, 2009), 114–15
homophobia, 5, 6, 19, 21, 23, 30, 55–6, 69, 78, 86, 128, 142
    internalised, 54–5
homosociality, 25, 29–30, 83–4, 89, 133
Hospital Central (Central Hospital) (Tele5), 101
Hotel y domicilio (*In Calls and Out*) (Ernesto del Río, 1995), 86, 89

I Love You Baby (David Menkes and Alfonso Albacete, 2001), 85–7, 131
Iborra, Juan Luis *see Amor de hombre*
identification, 34, 64, 69, 73, 81, 97, 103, 121, 123, 125, 148
identity, 42, 44, 49, 50, 51, 128, 145, 148
    in *Alguien se despierta en mi cama*, 106
    in *Ataque verbal*, 99
    and coming out, 141
    gay, 31: in *Chuecatown*, 71; in work of Ventura Pons, 74
    lesbian, 45: in *101 Reykjavik*, 68
    in *La mala educación*, 52–3
    and marriage, 22
    in *Muy mujer*, 120
    national, 32, 47
    transgender, 31
Iglesias, Maxi, 89
Iglesia, Eloy de la, 40, 51, 79; *see also A un dios desconocido*; *El diputado*; *Los novios búlgaros*
Illundain, David *see Acción reacción*
integration, 41–6, 52, 62, 93, 102, 103, 125
Internado, El (The Boarding School) (Antena 3), 87, 88, 89
Invulnerable (Álvaro Pastor and Antonio Naharro, 2005), 4
Isbert, Bego, 100

Jaenada, Óscar, 68
Jamón, jamón (Juan José Bigas Luna, 1992), 69
Jaque a la dama (*Queen in Check*) (Francisco Rodríguez, 1978), 72
Jiménez, Lucía, 25, 100

Jiménez, Miguel Ángel, 18
Jiménez, Raúl, 26
Jiménez Ariza, Pedro, 79, 127
Jordan, Neil see Crying Game, The
Jové, Duna, 87

K (Juan Simons, 2005), 18
Kika (Pedro Almodóvar, 1993), 52, 67, 87
King (Iris Segundo, 2008), 149
Kormakur, Baltasar see 101 Reykjavik
Krámpack (Nico and Dani) (Cesc Gay,
    2000), 6, 39, 49
Kristeva, Julia, 107
Kroley, Zoraida, 32

La Lupe, 120, 121
Lala (Esteban Crespo, 2009), 128
Lancho, Guadalupe, 110
Lane, Becky see Pokerface
Lara, Julián see El Muro rosa
Latre, Georgina, 117
León, Paco, 25
León de Aranoa, Fernando see Princesas
lesbian chic, 100–1
lesbian feminism, 7, 11–12, 22
lesbian fiction, 124–6
Lesbos Invaders From Outer Space
    (Víctor Conde, 2008), 38
lesbophobia, 14, 22, 27, 40, 50, 56–7, 119
    and narrative mechanisms, 118
Levine, Mark see Breach of Etiquette
Ley del deseo, La (Law of Desire) (Pedro
    Almodóvar, 1986), 14, 51, 65–6, 79
Ley de Identidad de Género (Gender Identity
    Law), 1–2
Lindo, Elvira, 133–4
Little Ashes (Sense límits or Sin límites)
    (Paul Morrison, 2008), 141–2
Lizarribar, Aitor, 17–18
Llach, Lluís, 19
Lo que nunca te dije (What I Never Told
    You) (Carlos Gómez Baker, 2010), 49
Lombardi, Francisco see No se lo digas a
    nadie
Luis, Maribel, 7
Luz (Pablo Aragüés, 2011), 44, 117, 120–1
L-Word, The (Showtime), 100

Maccelli, Giovanni see Mueble de las fotos,
    El
Macdonald, Hettie see Beautiful Thing
Maciá, Mariel, 114
    cultural activist, 102
    director, 6, 16, 66, 90, 102: see also A
        domicilio; Flores en el parque
    film marketing, 66
    producer, 16: Enikpro, 101
    scriptwriter, 102–3
    theatre director see 'Monólogos de bollería
        fina'

Mackenzie, Lauren see Alice in Andrew's Land
McNulty, Matthew, 141–2
Madrid
    Chueca, 3–4, 35, 44, 73, 84, 92, 124, 126,
        134, 138: as setting see Chuecatown
    Europride, 71
    festivals, 2, 4, 69, 82, 103, 112, 113, 114,
        118–21, 137
    movida, 51
    Orgullo (Pride), 87, 102
    production companies, 104
    as setting, 17–18, 27–8, 35, 67, 71–3, 85,
        109, 128, 136, 141–2, 149
    theatre venues, 102
Magill, Santiago, 86
mainstream fiction, 135–8
Mala educación, La (Bad Education) (Pedro
    Almodóvar, 2004), 52, 79, 81, 129
Mar, El (The Sea) (Agustí Villaronga, 2000),
    39, 53–5
Mariquita con perro (Queen with Dog)
    (Vicente Villanueva, 2007), 44, 126
marriage, 19, 24–7, 29–32
    feminist critique of, 23–4
    same-sex, 1, 5, 21–4: and the Church, 29;
        as documentary subject, 28–9; and the
        law, 21–2
Márquez, Áurea, 101
Martín (Hache) (Adolfo Aristarain, 1997),
    45, 67
Marsé, Juan, 146
Martínez, Juanan see A los que gritan
Martínez, Petra, 29, 58
Martínez Lázaro, Emilio see Dos lados de la
    cama, Los
Martret, José see ¡¡Todas!!
Más que amor frenesí (More Than Love,
    Frenzy) (Alfonso Albacete, David
    Menkes and Miguel Bardem, 1995), 43,
    45–6
masculinity, 59, 68–9, 79, 89, 105, 131, 142
Matador (Pedro Almodóvar, 1986), 66
Maura, Carmen, 26, 51
Mayoral, Marina, 125–6
Me gustaría estar enamorada – a veces me
    siento muy sola (I'd Like to Be in Love:
    Sometimes I Feel Very Lonely) (Chus
    Gutiérrez, 2009), 149
Medem, Julio see Habitación en Roma;
    Vacas
Melero, Luis, 127
Melero, May, 116
Menchén, Pedro, 127
Mendicutti, Eduardo, 58, 79, 92, 135–7
Menéndez, Roberto see Aliteración
Menkes, David, 90; see also Albacete,
    Alfonso
Mentiras y gordas (Sex, Party and Lies)
    (David Menkes and Alfonso Albacete,
    2009), 6, 49, 65, 87–90, 94, 110, 131–3

Merlo, Luis, 71
middlebrow fictions, 124–9
Miguel, Marcos de *see Turistas*
modes of representation, 34, 40–2, 45–6, 48
Molina, Angela, 67, 139
Molina Foix, Vicente
    director, 141: *see also El dios de madera; Sagitario*
    writer 94, 123, 135, 137–9
Mollà, Jordi, 48, 64, 67, 69–71, 84
Monleón, Sigrid *see El cónsul de Sodoma*
'Monólogos de bollería fina', 102
Montalá, Irene, 76, 79
Montiel, Sara, 9, 53
Morán, Libertad, 124
Morrison, Paul *see Little Ashes*
Mueble de las fotos, El (*The Photo Cabinet*) (Giovanni Maccelli, 2009), 148
Muerte de Mikel, La (*The Death of Mikel*) (Imanol Uribe, 1984), 58
Muro (*Wall*) (Juanma Carrillo, 2011), 108
Muro rosa, El (*The Pink Wall*) (Enrique del Pozo and Julián Lara, 2011), 58, 114, 137
Muy mujer (*So Womanly*) (Luis Escobar, 2011), 119–120
My Beautiful Launderette (Stephen Frears, 1986), 16

Nacidas para sufrir (*Born to Suffer*) (Miguel Albaladejo, 2009), 29, 126
Nadie hablará de nosotras cuando hayamos muertos (*No-One Will Speak of Us Once We're Dead*) (Agustín Díaz Yanes, 1995), 67–8
Naharro, Antonio *see Invulnerable*
Naranjas (*Oranges, or Couples*) (Eli Navarro, 2009), 100
Navarro, Eli, 40, 100
Nabatian, Kaveh *see Vapor*
Nieto, Pepón, 64, 84, 136
No desearás al vecino del quinto (*Thou Shalt Not Covet Thy Fifth-Floor Neighbour*) (Ramón Fernández, 1970), 42
No se lo digas a nadie (*Don't Tell Anyone*) (Francisco Lombardi, 1998), 86
Noriega, Eduardo, 66
normalisation, 26, 34, 35, 44, 46, 124, 125, 131
    in *Chuecatown*, 72, 73
    in *El cónsul de Sodoma*, 143
    in *El dios de madera*, 139–40
    in *Habitación en Roma*, 95–6
    in *Segunda piel*, 69
    in *Turistas*, 101
    in *Una palabra tuya*, 133
    in Ventura Pons films, 77
    in *Voces*, 121
Novios búlgaros, Los (novel), 135–7

Novios búlgaros, Los (*Bulgarian Lovers*) (film) (Eloy de la Iglesia, 2003), 6, 39, 43, 84, 135–7, 140

Ocaña, retrat intermitent (*Ocaña, An Intermittent Portrait*) (Ventura Pons, 1978), 51, 83
opinion pieces
    in newspapers, 134, 135, 138
    online, 114, 131, 138–9
Orgullo (Pride) *see* Madrid
Oteagi, Pedro, 60
Ouaarab, Soufianne, 140
outing, 96, 116
Ozores, Adriana, 29–30

Pablo ¿has puesto la lavadora? (*Pablo: Have You Put The Washing On?*) (Manuel Haba, 2005), 18
Padre nuestro (*Our Father*) (Francisco Regueiro, 1984), 68
Pagoaga, Mariasun, 61–2
Pajarico (*Little Bird*) (Carlos Saura, 1998), 48
Paredes, Marisa, 26, 81, 140
parenting
    lesbian, 27, 34, 68, 74, 97
    same-sex, 22, 139
París, Inés *see* Fejerman, Daniela
Pàrt, Arvo, 109
Pasajero (Passing Through) (Miguel Gabaldón Orcoyen, 2009), 17–18
Pasión por el fútbol (A Passion for Football) (Maria Pavón and Rut Suso, 2007), 104–5
Pastor, Álvaro *see Invulnerable*
Pastor, Gonzalo, 117
Pastrana, Alejandra P., 32
Pastrana, Eusebio *see Spinnin'*
Paton, Belén, 104
Pattinson, Robert, 141–2
Pavón, María
    director, 6, 90, 104–5: *see also Ester; Pasión por el fútbol*
    producer, 103–4, 107
    see also Suso, Rut
Pedreño, Esperanza, 133
Peña, Candela, 81
Pepi, Luci, Bom, y otras chicas del montón (*Pepi, Luci, Bom and Other Girls Like Mom*) (Pedro Almodóvar, 1980), 83
Perdona, bonita, pero Lucas me quería a mí (Excuse Me Darling, But Lucas Was in Love With Me!) (Dunia Ayaso and Félix Sabroso, 1997), 43, 69–70, 84–85
Pérez, Sergi *see Vestido nuevo*
Pérez Viera, Johann see *Happy Day in Barcelona*
Perfect Day (Juanma Carrillo and Félix Fernández, 2010), 109, 110

Periodistas (Journalists) (Tele5), 84
Petunias (César Vallejo, 2005), 88
Picazo, Miguel *see Claros motivos del deseo, Los*
Pinzás, Juan, 31; *see also Días de voda; Era outra vez; El desenlace*
Pokerface (Becky Lane, 2011), 119
politics
    cultural, 114
    gay, 22, 24
    gender, 129, 148
    identity, 13, 22, 34, 46, 67
    lesbian feminist, 22, 62, 68
    lesbian and gay, 5, 23, 83
    post-identity, 1, 13
    queer, 12, 13, 24, 62, 71, 80, 104
    sexual, 4, 11, 19, 27, 40–1, 51, 75, 77, 83, 145
Polvorosa, Ana María, 64, 87–8
Poncela, Eusebio, 48, 51–2, 64–7, 69, 139
Pons, Ventura, 10, 48–51, 58, 66, 73–9, 95; *see also Amic/Amat; Barcelona un mapa; Carícies; Food of Love; Ocaña, retrat intermitent*
¿Por qué lo llaman amor cuando quieren decir sexo? (*Why Do They Call It Love When They Mean Sex?*) (Manuel Gómez Pereira, 1993), 87
post-porn, 4
Pou, Josep Maria, 47, 78–9
Poveda, Enrique *see Tiras de mi piel*
Pozo, Enrique del *see El Muro rosa*
Princesas (*Princesses*) (Fernando León de Aranoa, 2005), 85
Protegidos, Los (The Protected Ones) (Antena 3), 89
publishers (LGBT), 12, 92–3, 124–5
Pujantell, Montse *see Guerriller@s*
Puyol, Pablo, 64–5, 73, 81–3

¿Qué he hecho yo para merecer esto! (*What Have I Done To Deserve This?*) (Pedro Almodóvar, 1984), 87
queer
    as aesthetic, 6, 15, 34, 77, 101, 104, 133
    as term 1, 3–5, 9–15
    see also politics
queer theory, 5, 11–12, 22,80, 93, 124, 138
Querelle (Rainer Werner Fassbinder, 1982), 54, 70, 109
Quiroga, Álex, 18

Reinas (*Queens*) (Manuel Gómez Pereira, 2005), 25, 35, 43, 86, 130
Requisitos de Nati, Los (*Nati's Requirements*) (Roberto Castón, 2007), 44
Revueltas, Paco, 60
Reyes, Isaac de los, 70, 143
Ricardo: Piezas descatalogadas (*Ricardo: Discontinued Items*) (Herman@s Rico, 2005), 83
Rico, Herman@s *see Ricardo: Piezas descatalogadas*
Río, Ernesto del *see Hotel y domicilio*
Rivas, Marialy *see Blokes*
Rivera, Mamen, 60
Rodríguez, Francisco *see Jaque a la dama*
Rodríguez, Israel, 65, 81
Ruano, Carlos *see Turno de noche*
Rubio, Andrés *see Campillo sí, quiero*
Rueda, Victor, 31
Ruiz, Agustín, 32
rural settings, 28–31, 58–62, 101, 126

Saavedra, Pilar, 32
Sabroso, Félix *see Ayaso, Dunia*
Sáez, Javier, 13, 93–4
Sagitario (*Sagittarius*) (Vicente Molina Foix, 2001), 66–7, 139
Salazar, Blanca, H., 6, 125; *see also Bañophobia; The Lesbian Movie*
Salazar, Ramón *see 20 centímetros*
Sampietro, Mercedes, 25
San Juan, Antonia, 58, 65, 81
Sánchez, Isabel, 102
Sánchez, Laura, 84
Sánchez, Susi, 56–7
Sánchez, Verónica, 25, 100
Sanz, Jorge, 42, 64, 66, 85–6
Sardà, Rosa Maria, 64, 66, 72–6, 87
Saura, Carlos *see La caza; Cría cuervos; Pajarico*
Sbaraglia, Leonardo, 55
Scanda, Tiaré, 85
screenwriters, 129–31, 133–4
Sebastián, Sonia *see Chica busca chica*
Segunda piel (*Second Skin*) (Gerardo Vera, 2001), 6, 45, 67, 69, 70, 131
Segundo, Iris *see King*
Serna, Assumpta, 117, 121
Serrano, Julieta, 57
Serrau, Coline *see Trois hommes et un couffin*
Sévigné (*Júlia Berkowitz*) (Marta Balletbò-Coll, 2004), 46–7, 84
short films
    in festivals, 116–21
    and political commitment, 15, 19–20
    as queer, 16–20, 108–11
Si te dicen que caí (*If They Say I Fell*) (Vicente Aranda, 1989), 67
Sígueme (*Follow Me*) (Alejandro Durán, 2011), 116–7
Silva, Hugo, 26, 87, 89
Simons, Juan *see K*
Sin noticias de Dios (*Don't Tempt Me*) (Agustín Díaz Yanes, 1995), 68
Sirenito (Little Boy Mermaid) (María Crespo, 2004), 20

Skallaman (Maria Bock, 2011), 118
Sklar, Dara *see Fluid*
SMS: Sin miedo a soñar (Not Afraid of
   Dreaming, TxT) (La Sexta), 87, 88
Sobreviviré (*I Will Survive*) (Alfonso Albacete
   and David Menkes, 1999), 71
Sombras en el viento (*Shadows in the Wind*)
   (Julia Guillén Creach, 2009), 42
Spinnin' (Eusebio Pastrana, 2007), 27, 32–4,
   39, 100, 149
stereotypes, 41–4, 48, 52, 68, 69, 73–4, 79,
   105, 113, 117, 121, 130, 136
Sueño de Ibiza, El (*Ibiza Dream*) (Igor
   Fioravanti, 2002), 14, 50, 71
Suso, Rut
   director, 41: *see also Ester; Pasión por el
      fútbol*
   producer, 103–4, 107: VolandoVengo,
      104
   video artist, 19, 105–7
   see also Pavón, María

Tacones lejanos (*High Heels*) (Pedro
   Almodóvar, 1991), 67
Terapia de choque (*Shock Therapy*)
   (Salva Cortés, 2010), 44
Tiras de mi piel (*You Tug At My Skin*)
   (Ayo Cabrera and Enrique Poveda,
   2009), 19, 21
¡¡Todas!! (*All!*) (José Martret, 2007), 7, 115
Todo me pasa a mí (*Everything Happens To
   Me*) (Miguel García Borda, 2001), 38,
   45, 50
Todo sobre mi madre (*All About My Mother*)
   (Pedro Almodóvar, 1999), 33, 52, 66,
   81, 129, 141
Toledo, Guillermo, 7, 25
Torre, Antonio de la, 133
Torregrossa, Jorge, 149
Touceda, Carolina, 27
Tous, Alejandro, 27, 33
transgender 9, 31, 68, 81, 90–1, 119, 129
   as documentary subject, 6–7
transition to democracy (Spain), 37–42, 51,
   135
transphobia, 6, 115
transsexuality, 6, 53, 82, 125
   as documentary subject, 6–7, 115–16
transvestite performance, 52, 53, 72, 89, 117,
   120
Tras el cristal (*In A Glass Cage*) (Agustí
   Villaronga, 1986), 15, 51
Trois hommes et un couffin (*Three Men and
   a Cradle*) (Coine Serreau, 1985), 35
Trueba, Fernando *see Belle époque*
Tú eliges (*You Choose*) (Antonia San Juan,
   2009), 58
Turistas (*Tourists*) (Marcos de Miguel and
   Isabel Coll, 2008), 101

Turno de noche (*Night Shift*) (Carlos Ruano,
   2011), 119–20

Ugalde, Unax, 26
Una palabra tuya (*One Word from You*)
   (Ángeles González-Sinde, 2008),
   133
under-representation
   lesbian filmmakers, 103
   women filmmakers, 103
Une Sensation de vide (Juanma Carrillo,
   2011), 110, 111
Uribe, Imanol *see La Muerte de Mikel*

Vacas (*Cows*) (Julio Medem, 1992),
   59
Vallejo, César *see Petunias*
Valdivia, Arantxa, 27
Valverde, Maria, 88
Van Guardia, Lola, *pseudonym of* Franc,
   Isabel
Vapor (Kaveh Nabatian, 2010), 117
Velasco, Concha, 65, 72–3
Velilla, Nacho G. *see Fuera de carta*
Vera, Gerardo, 6, 45, 67, 90
Vestido nuevo (A New Dress)
   (Sergi Pérez, 2007), 20
Vic, Mónica, 103–4
Vico, Patricia, 101
videoart, 98, 101, 104, 106–8, 109–11; *see
   also* Carrillo, Juanma; Suso, Rut
Villanueva, Vicente *see Mariquita con perro*
Villaronga, Agustí, 90, 94, 146; *see also El
   mar; Tras el cristal*
Villena, Luis Antonio de, 94, 135,
   146
visibility
   gay, 56
   and HIV/AIDS, 20
   lesbian, 6, 14, 34, 45–8, 96–7, 126
   LGBT, 3, 41, 43, 46, 52, 71, 88, 92–3,
      146–7
   politics of, 100, 133, 137, 146–7
   and social issues, 20
Voces (*Voices*) (Eduardo Fuembuena, 2010),
   120–1
VolandoVengo *see* Pavón, María; Suso,
   Rut
Vradiy, Marina, 103–4

We Once Were Tide (Jason Bradbury, 2011),
   118

Yarovenko, Natasha, 96–7
Yo sólo miro (I Only Watch) (Gorka Cornejo,
   2008), 40

Zerolo, Pedro, 21
Zulueta, Iván *see Arrebato*